IDLE THOUGHTS ON JEROME K JEROME

A 150th Anniversary Celebration

p. 171

Dedication

This volume is dedicated to Tony Gray, Hon. Sec. of the Jerome K Jerome Society. Without his immense contribution editing the Society's newsletter *Idle Thoughts* this book would not have been possible.

It is impossible to enjoy idling thoroughly unless one has plenty of work to do.

'On Being Idle' from *The Idle Thoughts of an Idle Fellow* (1886)

I did not know I was a humorist. I have never been sure about it. In the middle ages, I should probably have gone about preaching and got myself burned or hanged.

My Life and Times (1926)

IDLE THOUGHTS ON JEROME K JEROME
A 150th Anniversary Celebration

Edited by
Jeremy Nicholas

with a foreword by
Gyles Brandreth

© The Jerome K Jerome Society / Toynbee Editorial Services Ltd

First published 2009

Published by
The Jerome K Jerome Society
Editorial Office
Unit 24
The Bardfield Centre
Great Bardfield
Essex CM7 4SL, UK
www.jeromekjerome.com

British Library Cataloguing in Publication Data

A catalogue record for this book is available from the British Library

ISBN 978-0-9562212-0-9

Designed and project managed by Toynbee Editorial Services Ltd

Typeset in Optima and Garamond by
Bookcraft Publishing Services (I) Pvt Ltd, Chennai, India
Cover design by Bookcraft Ltd
Cover image Courtesy of Wallsall Local History Centre

Printed in Wiltshire, England by
CPI Antony Rowe

CONTENTS

FOREWORD

by Gyles Brandreth

Patron of the Jerome K Jerome Society

Jerome K Jerome shares his 150th anniversary with Arthur Conan Doyle. He was born on 2 May 1859, just twenty days earlier than his friend. What an extraordinary generation of writers Jerome belonged to – Conan Doyle himself, Oscar Wilde, Bram Stoker, Robert Louis Stevenson et al: writers who managed to cast a spell that has not yet been broken.

But the spell most of these writers cast is a shadowy one. They speak to us by night in the dark. JKJ's spell is full of sunshine. That is the essential Jeromian flavour. He had his serious side (less successful, critics will tell you) and one that has not stayed the course, yet his autobiographical novel *Paul Kelver* is a fine achievement; *The Passing of the Third Floor Back* was among the most successful stage plays of its era. But it is Jerome's inimitable light touch as a (very English) humorist that endures. *The Idle Thoughts of an Idle Fellow*, *The Diary of a Pilgrimage* (the first half, at least), *The Second Thoughts of an Idle Fellow*, *Three Men on the Bummel* (most of it), *Ideal Ideas in 1905*, and his forgotten novel *They and I* are representative. His autobiography *My Life and Times* is sparkling, eclectic, anecdotal and often very funny. Above all towers his masterpiece, *Three Men in a Boat*. Whether or not he liked the fact, this was Jerome's finest hour.

In this book, itself celebrating its 120th birthday this year, Jerome didn't create a myth like Dracula or the portrait in the attic. He created a world. And what a world! J M Barrie created Wonderland, but it is a fantasy where frightening elements are always lurking. Kenneth Grahame created a cosy world, but it is essentially fantastical, full of talking animals...

The genius of Jerome K Jerome is to have created a world that is magical and at the same time *real*. In this he is unique for it is a world we know we could step into. Holmes is superhuman, Toad is a toad, Peter Pan is a myth, Dracula terrifies us, Dr Jekyll and Mr. Hyde remind us of our darker selves... But *Three Men in a Boat* brings us sunshine and laughter in a world we know. JKJ brings us ourselves as we would like to be. It's Greyfriars for grown-ups, Milton's *Paradise Regained* in prose and with laughs, a classic that gives delight and hurts not. Enjoy! Celebrate! And in the pages that follow discover how much more there was to Jerome than you ever realised.

Yours affectionately

Jerome K. Jerome

INTRODUCTION

When the Jerome K Jerome Society was founded in 1985, there could be only one possible title for its newsletter: *Idle Thoughts*. The first edition appeared in February 1986 – 12 pages produced on something called a typewriter, photocopied (which did nothing for the photographs that illustrated the text), put in between cardboard covers and stapled. The cover, however, was graced with a drawing by Posy Simmons no less. Since then, *Idle Thoughts* has appeared more or less twice a year, depending on the whim or workload of the Hon. Sec. Edition no. 30 (Summer 2008) boasted 59 pages, many crisply-produced colour photographs, and a now familiar mix of news, reviews, the trivial, the scholarly, and reports on all things Jeromian.

When considering the best ways in which to celebrate the sesquicentenary of Jerome's birth, I suggested the publication by the Society of a 'best of' volume culled from the past pages of *Idle Thoughts*. The idea was taken up eagerly by the Chairman and seized on with as much alacrity as the Hon. Sec. can muster. It was agreed that the Chairman would submit her choice from the early years, the President would tackle the middle period, and the Hon. Sec. the later editions. The guiding principle would be to select pieces that threw a new light on some aspect of Jerome's life and work, seasoned with a sprinkling of other miscellaneous contributions and some of Jerome's lesser known writings that had been reproduced in the pages of *Idle Thoughts* over the years. All these would be ordered to follow, roughly, the chronology of Jerome's life. I undertook the task of making the final selection and editing the result. I hope you enjoy it – and that it will add to your knowledge and appreciation of one of England's most enduring and endearing authors.

Jeremy Nicholas
President, Jerome K Jerome Society
2 May 2009

ACKNOWLEDGEMENTS

There are many people to thank for the appearance of this miscellany, not least the many contributors to *Idle Thoughts* over the past 23 years. It is, however, the Society's Hon. Sec. Tony Gray to whom the biggest thanks are owed. It is his assiduous efforts in editing (all but the earliest) *Idle Thoughts* – collating and ordering the material, arranging its production and distribution – to say nothing of his own inimitable contributions to each issue, that have made it the success it is. It is a mystery how he manages to do this while working at least several hours each week, maintaining a heretical devotion to the works of James Joyce and Samuel Beckett, and following the hopeless cause of his local football club, simultaneously ensuring that all the finest hostelries in the West Midlands are kept in healthy profit.

The Jerome K Jerome Society would like to thank sincerely the following for permission to reproduce their contributions:

Tony Benson, The *Birmingham Post*, the late R R Bolland and Oast Books (publishers), Gyles Brandreth, Ian Chapman, Peter Christie, Sarah Elsom, Roy Farrow, the late David Fink, Dan Glaister and *The Idler*, Tony Gray, the late Hubert Gregg, Peter C Hall, Rachel Hertz (Harry Ransom Humanities Research Center) for Jerome's letter in 'Jerome the party politician', Ivor Hussey, the late Harold King, the late Celia Lamont-Jones OBE, Robert G Logan, Robert McCrum and *The Observer*, Dr Paul McDonald, Bill Newsom, Derek O'Connor, Pitman (M Wright, JP), Andrew P Read, Frank Rodgers, Peter Shaw, William Simcock, Christine Stockwell, *The Times*, Ruth Vyse (Walsall Local History Centre), Alan R Whitby, Maurice W White, Dr Jonathan Wild and Palgrave Macmillan (publishers), Dr Aubrey Wilson, Peter Wilson, Dr Richard G Wilson FRCP DCH, Ian Wood.

We have attempted to contact all copyright holders for their permission to have their writing reproduced. If we have failed to reach you, please accept our apologies. We will undertake to rectify any omission in future printings. To those whose work appears in these pages, we raise our collective hats. To those whose writing has not been included, we can only apologise and hope that they will understand that the constraints of space and the limited scope of the book are the only reasons for their exclusion.

A huge debt of gratitude is due to Jeremy Toynbee of Toynbee Editorial Services Ltd, Great Bardfield. His advice, expertise and generous collaboration have been fundamental in getting this volume into print. Thanks are also due to Sue Wain of Fraser Wood, Walsall; Philip Porter (publisher / member) of Porter Press, Knighton-on-Teme; Sarah Elsom, chairman of the Jerome K Jerome Society and erstwhile Keeper of Local History, Walsall; David Wingate of Finchingfield; Andrew Steven of SKA Ltd; Wendy Scott and Huw Alexander of SAGE Publications; and Alison Waggitt of the Society of Indexers for her great kindness in supplying the superb index.

A NOTE ON THE TEXT

Any potential inconsistency of spellings, presentation and biography arises from the fact that the material has been collected from many authors, sources and different time periods. In the main, the original texts have been preserved as originally published in *Idle Thoughts*.

1

THE JEROME K JEROME BIRTHPLACE MUSEUM

by Sarah Elsom

In 2008, after just twenty four years, the Jerome K Jerome Birthplace Museum in Bradford Street, Walsall, closed its doors to visitors for the last time. First opened in 1984, it was unfortunately destined to have a short life and latterly, because of manning problems, was only able to attract small handfuls of visitors. Had it not existed, however, today's thriving Jerome K Jerome Society would never have come into being.

The inspiration for starting a museum in Jerome's birthplace came from local architect and entrepreneur, Gordon Foster. He decided to buy and renovate the building, known as Belsize House after Jerome's last abode in London. In its heyday it had been an elegant, early 19th Century end-of-terrace stuccoed town house, situated close to the town's race-course on the road leading out to Wednesbury. However, by the 1980s when Foster bought it, it had become a sorry dilapidated sight and the area round about it had moved decidedly down market. Because of its location, he was able to apply for money through the Council and planned to restore it as office accommodation. The total cost of the project was to be £130,000, with the Department of the Environment putting up 75% of the funding and the Council 25%. A condition of the DoE grant, however, was that a museum element should be included as a memorial to, arguably, the town's most famous son.

To design and fit out the proposed Museum, Gordon Foster was offered the expertise of the Borough's Library and Museum Service and a rather bemused Keeper of Local History. I was ordered to research and write the storyline for the Museum. For one who at that stage had not even read *Three Men in a Boat* it was a daunting prospect. Of course, once the Curator (aka Keeper) ceased to be an ignoramus about Jerome and had laughed myself silly in railway carriages while reading *Three Men and other works*, the job became a great deal easier, as well as being tremendous fun. The Museum Service also called upon the Art Department of West Midlands College to provide design and graphics expertise. David Lewis, the Departmental head, and his colleague John Woodman came up with a lively magazine format for the graphic style, based on Jerome's own *To-Day* magazine. Their interpretation panels stood the test of time, still reading well over twenty years later.

Where were the objects going to come from and what was going to go on show? After all, Jerome as we know, had left the town when he was two years old, only returning as an old man in 1927 to be honoured with the Freedom of the Borough. However, as a result of a JKJ Centenary Exhibition being staged by the Public Library in 1959, Jerome's daughter Rowena had presented the town with a large collection of memorabilia relating to her father. There existed a rich collection of letters, photographs, first editions and other papers, supplemented by a few actual personal belongings; his Freedom Scroll in its Walsall-made exquisitely tooled leather case, his cigarette case, part of his French World War One ambulance driver's uniform, a little inlaid table and ... his desk.

This collection was not enough to fill the two rooms earmarked for the Museum, so it was decided that the front room should be used to re-create a 1850s parlour, typical of that of a middle-class household similar to the Jeromes'. I was allowed to go on a spending spree with £4,000 to purchase all the necessary furniture and fittings, while a further sum of £5,000 was to be spent on the exhibition room itself as well as the necessary security systems.

As the project progressed and contacts were made with people who remembered Jerome, further objects and snippets of information relating to Jerome materialised. I remember a journey to Marlow to interview eighty year old Daisy May Walker. Her father, Mr. Ted Hammond, had been the Jeromes' chauffeur for thirteen years before the First World War and she herself was brought up by Mrs. Jerome until the age of seven, living as one of the family. Speaking to someone who had actually known Jerome himself was an extraordinary privilege. A meeting with Reg Bolland, author of *Victorians on the Thames* and a devotee of Jerome, procured a generous donation of JKJ's own ruler and a couple of his pens. This took place in a shady corner of the Embankment Gardens in London and was redolent of a scene from a John Le Carré story!

Efforts to trace members of Jerome's family proved far from easy. His only child, Rowena, had never married and on her death the residue of her estate had passed to a relative of her long-time companion, Maisie Frith. So it was that I found myself having tea with Celia Lamont-Jones, inheritor of the family possessions, whose pleasant apartment near Brighton was filled with Jerome's furniture. Tea was taken from Jerome's own tea service and a whole trunk full of letters, papers and priceless family photographs were pored over. Many of these items were copied for the new displays.

Of course the centrepiece of the Museum should have been Jerome's desk, given to Walsall in 1959 by Rowena and residing in a corner of the Mayor's Parlour in the Town Hall. Jerome mentions this desk in *My Life and Times*, recording that he bought it with the first five pound note that he ever earned for a piece of writing. It was with disbelief that we all heard that the Council would not allow the desk to be moved to the new museum. The outcry over this overshadowed all other publicity for the grand opening of the Museum, and even made the national press. A former Mayor was quoted as saying

'Guests (to the Parlour) are always fascinated by it and it is staying here where it belongs'. Even now the Desk is always toasted when members of the Jerome K Jerome Society are gathered together, rather as the Jacobites always toasted 'the King over the water'.

Running and maintaining the Museum, once open, was always going to present difficulties. Fortunately, in its early years, the tenant of the other half of the ground floor was a little shop specialising in buttons and other sewing necessities. Pauline Walker, its owner who traded as 'The Button Lady', would open the Museum for visitors and sell post-cards and books. The Council was prepared to pay an annual grant towards running costs and provide professional expertise when necessary. However, since the Museum was not located in a public building, it did not become an integral part of the Museum Service and alternative ways of managing it had to be found.

Some creative thinking among interested parties led to the formation of a Jerome K Jerome Museum Trust and the foundation of a Society, the subscriptions to which would provide income for the Museum.

The scepticism as to whether this Society would flourish was matched only by the negativity with which the opening of the Museum was met by the inhabitants of Jerome's native town. One famous remark by a passer-by interviewed for the radio on the day the Museum opened bears repetition: 'Three Men in a Boat? Isn't that a pub on the Beechdale Estate?' A writer to the *Express and Star* at the time opined 'To spend £9,000 on his [JKJ's] memory is a shameful waste of taxpayers' money.'

Jerome K Jerome's birthplace, Walsall

Jerome outside his house at Gould's Grove in the late 1890s

The Jerome K Jerome Society begged to differ. Now, as we know, it has a world-wide membership. The Society's dismay at the Walsall Metropolitan Borough Council's withdrawal of its grant to the Birthplace Museum in 2007, effectively forcing its closure, was changed to delight in 2008. In the space of six months, the new owners of the building, Edmunds and Co., a firm of solicitors, made a magnificent job of restoring and upgrading Belsize House. Once more, Jerome's birthplace is looking worthy of its name. Edmunds and Co. are prepared to allow public access for Jeromians and anyone interested in JKJ. They have installed in their waiting room the fine copy we have of the de Lazlo portrait of Jerome, and there is a Jerome display in the reception area. The firm is keen to continue the Jerome connection, including links with the Jerome K Jerome Society. In September 2008, a blue Heritage plaque was fixed on the building.

So the legacy of this fascinating little Museum lives on in the Society's aims to promote the works of Jerome and to remember him through its many activities, both eccentric and scholarly. The Jerome collection itself is still cared for by the Council, with the books and archives being available for consultation at the Walsall Local History Centre. An hour or longer spent with this material for company will give the reader a vivid impression of Jerome, both man and writer.

2
JEROME – A POTTED BIOGRAPHY

by Jeremy Nicholas

Jerome was still a struggling unknown when he confided to his friend George Wingrave that he had four ambitions in life:

To edit a successful journal.
To write a successful play.
To write a successful book.
To become a Member of Parliament.

Only the last eluded him. Not a bad achievement, especially when you consider Jerome's background, one that did not exactly augur success, certainly not in a theatrical or literary career, let alone as the author of a comic masterpiece that has become among the most enduring and endearing books in the English language.

As a minister and part-time farmer in Appledore, Devon, Jerome Senior was comfortably off and well-respected. It was after some unsuccessful speculative mining on his land that things began to go wrong. When he moved to Walsall, Staffordshire, in 1854 and became first a partner in an iron works and then ventured into coal mining, things went horribly wrong.

Jerome Klapka Jerome was born into this unorthodox, highly-religious family on 2 May 1859. He had three exotically-named older siblings: his two sisters Paulina Deodata and Blandina Dominica, and a brother, Milton Melancthon, who was born in 1855 and died of the croup aged six.

Jerome Jerome père boasted the unusual middle name of Clapp. To his congregation in Devon he was known as Parson Clapp. When he left with his family to move to the Midlands, he dropped Clapp and began calling himself Rev. Jerome. All biographical references to JKJ reiterate the story that his unusual middle name of Klapka, a near-homonym of his father's, was adopted en homage to General George Klapka, the young hero of the 1849 Hungarian War of Independence who had left his country for Britain and was commissioned to write his autobiography. Needing somewhere quiet, he had accepted the invitation of Rev. Jerome to stay and subsequently became a family friend. This story, however, is almost certainly a fabrication.

Jerome's birth certificate gives his Christian names as 'Jerome Clapp'; and it has now been established that when JKJ's mother died on 20 July 1875, the death certificate notes 'J C Jerome, son, present at the death'. In other words, JKJ was christened with the same name that his father had adopted (to avoid confusion between the two Jerome Jeromes, JKJ was known in the family as 'Luther'). It seems that he changed his name from Jerome Clapp Jerome to Jerome Klapka Jerome only when he needed a pen-name. The first mention of the General Klapka story appears to be in a letter to *The Times,* published shortly after Jerome's death (and reproduced elsewhere in this volume), by a Professor Michal M Bálint in Budapest.

The year of JKJ's birth saw the family plunge from tottering financial stability to total ruin. Jerome Senior's coal-mining venture, into which he pumped the remainder of his wife's estate, proved a disaster. He was forced to sell up and move the family to Stourbridge. Now desperate for money he went alone to London and bought a failed ironmongery business in Lime-house. He lived in Poplar for two years before sending for his family to join him. It was here, in London's East End, that JKJ spent his childhood – in abject poverty.

Just before his tenth birthday he gained admission to the Philological School in Lisson Grove, remaining there from New Year 1869 to July 1873. Jerome's father died on 3 June 1871, just after JKJ's 12th birthday.

At the age of fourteen JKJ left school to begin a succession of jobs, first as a clerk on the London and North Western Railway at Euston. He began work here on 12 January 1874, a fact noted in his mother's diary. As we have seen, his mother passed away some eighteen months later. By now his sisters had left home and Jerome, at sixteen, was completely alone. But Blandina had fired her young brother with a fascination for the theatre. He became involved with a stage company and eventually chucked the railway in favour of 'the life whose glorious uncertainty almost rivals that of the turf'. Jerome made his professional debut at the age of eighteen under the name of Harold Crichton, touring the country with a succession of third-rate outfits.

Three years' hard labour on the road left him demoralised and disillu-sioned. By the time he was in his mid-twenties, he was at the bottom of the social pile, penniless and living in dosshouses. He drifted into journalism, spending all his spare time writing short stories, essays and satires ... and getting rejected. Next he tried school-mastering in Clapham, then worked in turn for an illiterate north London builder, as a buyer and packer for some commission agents, for a firm of parliamentary agents and ended up as a solicitor's clerk, with vague thoughts of training for the law. Nothing gelled.

Then, inspired by one of Longfellow's poems from *By the Fireside* (with the curious title of 'Gaspar Becerra'), Jerome had the idea of writing about his experiences as an actor. The result was *On the Stage – and Off, The Brief Career of a Would-Be Actor.* After several publications had supplied him with the familiar rejection slips, a new magazine came up trumps: *The Play,* edited by a retired actor, Aylmer Gowing. In 1885 the work was published in book form. It remains one of the most detailed, absorbing (and under-rated) portraits of late-Victorian theatre life. It is also very funny.

A collection of humorous essays followed, *The Idle Thoughts of an Idle Fellow* (1886). Two years later he married Georgina Elizabeth Henrietta Stanley Marris, known by her pet name of Ettie. When Jerome first met her, she was married to a Mr. Marris with a five-year old daughter, also christened Georgina but known as Elsie. Ettie filed for divorce, it became absolute on 12 June 1888 and Jerome and she were married nine days later.

Jerome never referred to Ettie's first marriage. Her background is something of a mystery: nothing is known of her parents with their unusual surname, Nesza, but Ettie is listed in the 1861 census as the niece of the highly-respected Scottish opera singer, John Templeton (1802–86) and his Irish wife Letitia. Names are a peculiar source of fascination in Jerome's life. Apart from the change of his father's and his own baptismal names, his step-daughter Elsie eventually married a Thomas Riggs-Miller whose original name was Ryan: he was obliged to change it in order to receive an inheritance. Furthermore, what is little known about Ettie is that she was, in fact, a relation of JKJ. Jerome's father had two older siblings, Sarah and William. Both of them married into the Shorland family in the 1820s. Sarah Clapp's sixth child, Robert Shorland, became Paulina Deodata Clapp's husband (i.e. she married her cousin); their son, Frank Shorland, became a celebrated record-breaking cyclist in the 1890s. William Clapp's fourth child, Marianna, married Joseph Marris, the father of Ettie's first husband. In other words, JKJ married his second cousin's ex-wife.

They were both twenty-nine years old at the time. The honeymoon was spent on the Thames and Jerome began writing Three Men in a Boat on his return.

The book appeared in 1889 and made him rich and famous. In one leap he was made for life, part of the literary establishment, sitting above the salt with a loosely-knit circle of friends who included Eden Phillpotts, J M Barrie, Rider Haggard, H G Wells, Conan Doyle, W W Jacobs, Hall Caine, Thomas Hardy, Israel Zangwill and Rudyard Kipling.

The Diary of a Pilgrimage (a trip to Oberammergau to see the Passion Play) followed Boat, then collections of short stories and essays at the rate of nearly one a year until Three Men on the Bummel (1900) in which George, Harris and J made their second and final appearance together. Only a dozen or so titles were published after that, the most distinguished of which is his autobiographical novel Paul Kelver (1902), widely-praised at the time and, indeed, considered by some critics worthy to be put alongside Dickens.

Three Men In A Boat so overwhelms the mention of Jerome's name that his other achievements remain quite obscured. There was Jerome the dramatist: between his first book and his most famous, he had four plays produced in London and wrote a further fifteen, many of them achieving respectable runs in London and America. By far the most celebrated and successful of these was The Passing of the Third Floor Back (1908), in which a charismatic Christ-like stranger visits a run-down boarding house and transforms the lives of its inhabitants. The first production starred the greatest Hamlet of his day, Sir Johnston Forbes-Robertson. It was a huge hit and, though its maudlin sentiment renders it unperformable today, it continued to be revived well into the 1960s.

There was Jerome the editor and prolific columnist: he was preferred to Kipling as the chief of a new monthly magazine called *The Idler*, founded in 1892. The following year JKJ founded the weekly *To-Day* which survived till 1905. Both of these he edited until 1898 when the enormous costs incurred after losing a libel case (his opponent was awarded a farthing damages) necessitated selling his interests in both publications.

Jerome was much in demand as a lecturer, an occupation which complimented his love of travel, and we find him quite at home in Russia, America and especially Germany. His own daughter Rowena was born in 1898 (like her father, she too was to have a brief stage career) and in 1900 he moved the whole family to Dresden for two years. The First World War came as a terrible blow to him. At the age of 57, rejected by his own country for active service, he enlisted in the French army as a front line ambulance driver. When he returned home, his secretary wrote, 'the old Jerome had gone. In his place was a stranger. He was a broken man'. Another black event was the death of his stepdaughter Elsie in 1921 at the early age of thirty-eight. She, his beloved Ettie and Rowena receive barely a mention in his autobiography. That part of his life he preferred to keep private. *My Life and Times* (1926), though frustratingly short on domestic details and with no attempt at chronology, is among Jerome's most vital and entertaining books, his personality imprinted on every page.

He and Ettie were on a motoring tour returning to London from Devon via (in typical Three Men fashion) Cheltenham and Northampton when Jerome suffered a paralytic stroke and a cerebral haemorrhage. He lingered on in the Northampton General Hospital for two weeks, unable to move or speak, before dying on 14 June 1927.

His wife outlived him by eleven years. Rowena, who never married, died in 1966, the last surviving member of that branch of the Jerome family. JKJ, Ettie, Elsie and Jerome's sister Blandina lie side by side in the beautiful churchyard of Ewelme, Oxfordshire, not far from the River Thames.

3
APPLEDORE, WALSALL AND POPLAR

THE REVEREND JEROME CLAPP IN APPLEDORE 1840–1855
by Peter Christie

One of the most popular English fictional works is *Three Men in a Boat*. First published in 1889 it went through many editions and is still in print today. Its author was Jerome K Jerome whose father was Jerome Clapp Jerome or, as he was more commonly known, Jerome Clapp. It is not generally realised that Jerome senior had close links with Devon, having spent some 15 years in Appledore. This article will examine his life here in the county which is both fairly typical for a nineteenth-century nonconformist minister – and yet rather more colourful than most. It will also explore certain aspects of Appledore's past – a settlement which still awaits a definitive history. The whole is based on evidence from newspapers, books, court cases and oral tradition which is presented chronologically.

Jerome senior was born in London in 1807 and though there was a claim that he attended the Merchant Taylor School this is almost certainly incorrect. [1] Another possibly incorrect claim is that he began training as an architect before leaving 'still in his teens' to enter the non-conformist ministry. He attended the Rothwell Nonconformist Academy in Northamptonshire and, although possibly never becoming fully ordained, became minister at the Independent Chapel in Marlborough, Wiltshire, around the age of 21. From here he moved to Cirencester and then to Dursley. In August 1840 the Independent congregation in Appledore invited him to become their minister. [2] This group was established around 1662 and latterly worshipped in a chapel that had been enlarged in 1816 to hold some 570 people.

In the Census of June 1841 Clapp appears listed first in a household occupying a house on Marine Parade, Appledore. [3] This would appear to be the prominent corner house that still stands today at the junction of the Quay and Marine Parade in the village. Four other people are listed: Ann Morgan aged 70 and of 'Independent Means', Henry Hellier, aged 25, a printer, George Hitchins a 25 year old schoolmaster, and Ann Bowden a 21 year old servant. Clapp's age is given as 33.

A few weeks later the North Devon Congregational Association meeting at Barnstaple 'Resolved that Rev.Mr.Clapp of Appledore be received as a Member of this Association.' [4] It was at the same meeting that the first local evidence of Clapp's radical view on life became apparent. The minutes record 'That Mr. Clapp having expressed his determination to attend the approaching Manchester meeting on the Corn Laws It is resolved that Mr.Clapp be appointed as a deputie from the N.D.Association and that after the Appledore people have contributed their part the ministers of the association agree to raise the residue of the Expence.'

The *Report of the Conference of Ministers of all denominations on the Corn Laws* contains the proceedings of the Manchester meeting when 645 ministers spent four days in August 1841 protesting against the Corn Laws. [5] This was a politically sensitive subject though Clapp, as a dissenter, would naturally have opposed these laws which maintained artificially high bread prices to the detriment of the poor. At this meeting there were two sessions a day, each lasting 4–5 hours, with a wide array of speakers including Richard Cobden MP Clapp is recorded as seconding a resolution against the Corn Laws which he saw as 'a great national offence against that Being by whom kings reign, and princes decree justice'. He backed this up by declaring 'Let us … speak again for God on behalf of the poor' – stirring words from a young preacher indeed.

In June of the following year the *North Devon Journal* carried a small announcement that the Rev. Jerome Clapp of the Independent congregation at Appledore had married a Miss Margaret Jones of Bideford at the Independent chapel in the latter place. [6] His new wife, whose name is variously spelt as Margarette or Marguerite, was the 23 year old Swansea-born daughter of a draper. She is said to have brought a 'modest' fortune to her new husband. [7]

According to his son's autobiography Clapp 'farmed land at Appledore'. [8] No record of his purchasing land is extant but in 1854 a court case (referred to later) states he was the owner of the 'Berners' estate of 20 acres. Under the name 'Burners' this was for sale in January 1850 which was presumably when Clapp acquired it. [9] His son, however, says Clapp brought his mother home to a farm 'after their honeymoon' so Clapp senior must have purchased a property around 1842. The only other landholding his name is connected with as owner is Milton Farm. This was sold by Clapp in July 1855 and is described then as 'consisting of 50 acres of very superior Arable, Meadow and Pasture Land … in the highest state of Cultivation, worthy of being styled a Model Farm.' [10] Accommodation consisted of 'a newly built Farm House' with two labourers' cottages. Interestingly the property included a 'Tower' and a 'Quarry'. The former was Chanter's Folly built by a rich local shipowner Thomas Chanter in 1841 as a lookout. The latter still exists today just behind the large modern shipbuilding yard in Appledore. Its origin is described later. This mix of ministry and agriculture does not appear to have been that unusual as most dissenting clergy had to find a second income to subsidise their preaching activities – though few perhaps were farmers on quite Clapp's scale.

One other land holding is accredited to Clapp. In 1857 the Knapp estate was sold and Clapp was listed as tenant of two fields Windmill Field and East Hill which were adjacent to Bloody Corner, the traditional spot at which a marauding Viking was killed. [11] Jerome junior in his autobiography claims, with tongue firmly in cheek, that this Viking, whom he calls Clapa, was the 'Founder of our House'. [12] The Viking is usually referred to as Hubba and his presumed tomb was excavated in September 1841 by an unnamed antiquarian but nothing much of interest was found. [13]

The newly married young minister, not content with farming and preaching, had within weeks of his arrival in North Devon become the Secretary of, and Editor for, The Congregational Tract Society which was established to 'diffuse extremely cheap treatises and tracts on Protestant Dissent'. [14] At the August 1841 meeting of the North Devon Congregational Association it was noted 'That the Ministers of this association cordially approve of the principles and plans of the Congregational Tract Society, become Member of its corresponding committee and recommend the circulation of its Cheap publications.' [15] Three different titles from a series of at least 20 have survived among the archives of what is now the Appledore United Reform Church. [16] Number 19 carried the legend 'Printed by the Society at their Depository, Appledore, Devon.' and was sold at 3/6 (17p) per 100. A list of officers is given which includes Clapp as 'Secretary and Editor'. The treasurer was James Haycroft of Bideford who was helped by a six man Publication Committee and a six man General Committee. One assumes that the printer Henry Hellier listed as living in Clapp's house in the 1841 Census was employed in producing these tracts. Where the printing press came from is a puzzle as at this date in North Devon such machines were very rare. The Society does not seem to have made much headway amongst the numerous sects of early Victorian Britain or even within Devon.

Clapp's address on Number 19 in the series is given as Odun House, Appledore which places its publication as somewhere around December 1847 as, in that month, the *North Devon Journal* notes the birth of a daughter to the Clapps and gives their address as the imposing Odun House. [17] This building was one of the grander houses in the village having eight bedrooms, and again indicates Clapp's wealth. It still exists today and now houses the Appledore Maritime Museum. Whether the house was rented or purchased is not clear but on Clapp's removal in 1856 the house and three adjoining cottages were put up for sale so perhaps his wife's money had been used to buy the freehold. [18]

Clapp was not content to just publicise his views in the form of pamphlets. He had 'a natural and forceful flair for public speaking' – a flair often reported on in the *North Devon Journal* which itself was run by a Methodist family and thus presumably was sympathetic to dissenters in general. [19] Further evidence of Clapp's politics came in May 1843 when he spoke at a public meeting in Barnstaple Guildhall called to promote the repeal of the

Corn Laws. [20] He moved the vote of thanks to the representatives of the National Anti-Corn Law League 'for their exertions to procure a repeal of the corn laws'. His speech was fairly outspoken – as when he said of the League, 'They had looked upon the distresses of the country – they beheld its energies crippled, its commercial and manufacturing interests depressed, and its mechanics and their families huddled together in hovels unfit for human habitation – unemployed and starving: and for their fraternal regard they deserved our honour, that they came forth to the help of the poor – to the help of the poor against the oppressor.'

He then widened the discussion by going on to attack two 'solutions' to the problem of unemployment that some had advocated – machine breaking or emigration. He himself was strongly in favour of mechanisation, indeed he said 'Let machinery be multiplied' as this could only generate extra wealth for all. As to emigration he had, on the previous Sunday, preached to about 400 on the deck of an emigrant ship about to cross the Atlantic from Appledore. The tears he had seen shed by these poor people forced to leave the country of their birth through sheer poverty only made him more determined to see the Corn Laws abolished and food made cheaper. He sat down, as the report notes, to 'loud and long continued cheers'. A month later Clapp addressed a meeting in Bideford's Wesleyan chapel protesting about the clauses in a Factory Bill that dealt with the compulsory education of young workers and the perceived bias in the bill towards Church of England teachings. [21]

In August 1843 Clapp's 14 year old nephew Arthur Shorland of London 'here on a visit to his grandmother' was staying with his uncle when he decided to go swimming in the Torridge. Sadly he drowned and Clapp 'who was much affected' officiated at the burial which, poignantly, was the first interment at the cemetery newly opened by the Appledore Independents – though where this was is uncertain. [22]

Occasional references over the next few months show Clapp preaching in Appledore or addressing public meetings. In February 1844, for example, Clapp chaired a meeting in Bideford where two ministers from Edinburgh and London came to appeal for funds for building 'new churches for the Free Church Secession in Scotland'. [23] Clapp's speech was described as 'excellent' and presumably this helped raise the sum of £6 collected from his listeners.

A more unusual meeting was held in March 1844 which was a display of the then popular subject of 'Mesmerism'. [24] Presented by a Mr. Davey at the rather odd venue of the Appledore Bethel it doesn't seem to have made much impression on the hard-headed seamen of the village. Davey made various excuses for this failure and Clapp invited him 'to attend at his library the following morning, where he should find a candid audience without heat, or noise, or cold, or laughter'. Davey did attend and tried to 'mesmerise' three boys but again failed and Clapp apparently became so worried at this 'system which had driven some into a madhouse and others into a grave' that he gave a lecture in his chapel denouncing the whole thing. This included 'some striking facts which had come under his own observation when studying anatomy in London' which suggests another strand to Clapp's life.

To drive the point home, Clapp held a public meeting in Appledore a few days later to discuss the following strongly worded resolution 'That this meeting, after giving the subject the closest attention, avow their belief that the principles of mesmerism are utterly false, and the practice of it both physically and morally dangerous, and that all the results of mesmeric manipulation may be easily accounted for on physical grounds alone.' Davey wrote to the *Journal* defending himself and attacking Clapp accusing him amongst other things of 'barefaced duplicity'. [25] This sparked a flurry of letters both for and against both mesmerism and Clapp with the minister being charged with 'sarcastic irony' and of having hired the 'Cryer' of Appledore to spread falsehoods about Davey. [26] Davey, however, came off worst in these exchanges and no further references to mesmerism in Appledore have been found.

In April 1844 the North Devon Congregational Association meeting at Chulmleigh appointed Clapp 'as representative of this association at the Meeting of the Anti-State Church conference' although whether Clapp actually attended or not is unknown. [27] Also at this meeting Clapp was asked, along with two others, to preach to a newly formed congregation at Hartland.

May 1845 saw the birth of a daughter named Paulina or Pauline Deodata to Jerome and Margaret, the first of four children. [28] If Clapp's family was developing so was the village of Appledore. In September 1845 a new quay was constructed by the leading local merchant Thomas Chanter and Clapp was one of those who addressed the enthusiastic crowds at the opening ceremony. [29] A few weeks later, however, a long-simmering problem in the village came to a head. Apparently in 1808 a legacy had been used to purchase £100 worth of 'South Sea Annuities' with the income from them being paid to the 'Appledore Meeting' to help provide an income for the minister. In March 1842 new trustees were appointed at the prompting of Mrs. Rooke, a daughter of the original donor, though the income continued to be paid to Clapp. [30] In December 1845 a letter from Miles Prance to the Bideford solicitor and prominent dissenter James Rooker noted that Mrs. Rooke was 'feeling rather weaker' and was 'very desirous of settling at once all her worldly affairs'. As Prance went on to delicately express it the reading of her will 'may possibly occasion great inconvenience and surprise to the parties interested in the £100 Trust Money now standing in her Name'. It was then discovered that Mrs. Rooke didn't actually have the power to alter her mother's bequest and nothing seems to have happened until September 1854 when the choice of new trustees lead to a violent confrontation and a major schism in Clapp's congregation. It is worth noting that Clapp at this time clearly had the support of his fellow ministers, as in the minutes of the North Devon Congregational Association for 3 June 1846 it was recorded that he, along with five others, was requested to form a sub-committee 'to revise the rules of this Association'.[31]

No references to Clapp have been found between the opening of the new quay and June 1847 when the bitterly disputed Education Act was being discussed in Parliament. A meeting was held of the non-conformist ministers in North Devon where a motion was passed, with Clapp as seconder, requesting all dissenters not to vote for any Parliamentary candidates who supported the passage of the Act. [32] The minutes of the meeting note 'That an address to the dissenting electors of N.D. explaining of the course recommended in the preceding resolution be prepared by the Rev. J. Clapp and submitted previous to publication to a sub committee composed of Rev. Kent, Thomson, Clapp & the Secretary.' [33]

In December of the same year Margaret Clapp gave birth to a second daughter. [34] This child was given the odd names of Blandina Dominica whilst the announcement of the birth gives the family's address as Odun House.

In April 1848 he was invited to address the 3rd AGM of the Bideford and North Devon Building Association held in the Wesleyan school room in Bideford. [35] This group had been formed to allow working men and small traders to borrow money in order to buy their own houses. It still continues today as a constituent part of the Portman Building Society.

This year also saw Clapp travelling overseas to the Brussels Peace Conference in September. Following the 'Year of Revolution' of 1848, when Europe erupted in a series of revolutions, locally based Peace Societies were either formed or re-invigorated in many countries. The first international meeting had been held in 1843 in London to be followed 5 years later by the Brussels meeting. Clapp was one of a party 150 strong from Britain. [36] A fellow delegate was James Passmore Edwards who came from Cornwall and later became MP for Salisbury. In his autobiography Edwards wrote, 'The Brussels Congress was a success. It received the active support of the Belgian Prime Minister, the patronising smile of the Belgian King, a considerable share of public attention, and the good wishes of the lovers of mankind everywhere. That Peace Conference, though it encountered opposition, and got pelted with sneers, was historic, as it was the first of its kind, and it sowed seed which has since germinated, and from which may now be seen the prospect of an international harvest.' [37] In January a meeting was held in the Barnstaple Guildhall where Clapp and Edmund Fry, another of the British delegates, explained the decisions taken by the Congress. Clapp ended his speech with a ringing call reported verbatim in the *Journal*. 'Let the present generation profit by the follies of the past. Let the future mark no such crime – no such madness. Let theirs be the high and holy satisfaction of establishing a purer law for the government of the nations – a law in which honour, honesty, morality, humanity, and religion, would alike concur – the law of national arbitration in national wrongs. (Cheers)' [38]

Another Congress was held in Paris the following year and Clapp seems to have attended this as well – though on this occasion he was accompanied by E M White a Bideford builder and one-time Mayor. In November 1849 the *Journal* carried an account of a public meeting held in Bideford by Clapp for 'explaining and advocating the Principles of the Peace Society, and of giving some account of the late assembling of the Peace Congress at Paris'. [39]

One wonders whether all this activity overtaxed Clapp as in October 1850 he was excusing himself from a meeting of North Devon Congregational ministers 'on account of illness'. [40] The lack of public notices concerning Clapp over the next few months suggests he was taking life more easily. In March 1851 the census enumerator gives us a glimpse of his family even if Clapp was away from home on census night. [41] His 32 year old wife is there with Pauline and Blandina. Also present was Margaret's older sister Francis (sic) Tucker Jones plus four servants including a governess, cook and maid. Clearly the Rev. Clapp was not a poor clergyman. Indeed in August 1851 we find him spending £250 on the purchase of two houses in Bude Street, Appledore from Joshua Williams. [42]

Clapp's ill health that had been noted earlier seems to have got worse and led to a major change in his life if we are to judge from an entry in the minutes of the North Devon Congregational Association. This notes a letter apologising for his non-attendance with the words 'Also from Mr.Clapp excusing his absence on account of his no longer sustaining the Pastoral Relations with the church at Appledore.' [43] He may have stopped his active ministry but he continued to attend the meetings of the Association.

Clapp's wealth and illness unfortunately seems to have attracted some professional fraudsters. In December 1851 the *Journal* carried a long report on a projected rail link to Bideford in the middle of which occurred the following: 'From what we have seen at Hupplestone, and from what we have heard, we are warranted in predicting that the Bidefordians may be awoke one day by the startling announcement that an Eldorado has been discovered in their own locality. Suffice to say, that a drift has been made, and that tin, copper and lead, have been found, of which more next week.' [44] Hupplestone, or Hubbastone as it is known today, was owned by Clapp and he presumably had been impressed by what the miners had told him existed on his land. The *Journal* carried its promised further report two weeks later on 'The Mine at Hupplestone' which again was very optimistic in tone: 'The reports from the above are still very encouraging. In the words of those engaged, they never saw a speculation looking more kindly. We congratulate the Rev. Jerome Clapp, the owner of the land, on his very good fortune; and trust that such a mine will be discovered, as shall not only benefit the proprietors of the soil and company engaged, but the neighbourhood generally.' [45] Sadly this is the last positive notice of the mine, indeed in October 1852 the *Journal* carried two sentences which tell us all we need to know about the operation: 'The works at the Silver and Lead Mine at Ubbastone, in this place, are at the present suspended. They will be again resumed, we hear, as soon as a company can be formed.' [46] In his autobiography, Clapp's son writes laconically of his father's action over this fraudulent mine by saying that he 'started a stone quarry'. This may well have been a face-saving device or perhaps Jerome junior was never told the truth. A 1904 article on the history of Appledore records that 'The entrance to the mine was from the beach, and was tunnelled for some distance under the field where the tower of "Chanters Folly" now stands, and then a shaft sunk.' [47] The article also refers to the 'Mine Captain' fraudulently 'salting' the shaft with real silver ore to convince Clapp to carry on work.

The 1852 references actually begin in January when Clapp organised a temperance meeting at Appledore at which the principal speaker was F W Kellogg from the USA. [48] The Kellogg family were famed advocates of temperance and one of them later invented the famous breakfast cereal though how this Appledore visitor was related to the famous inventor is unclear. This new burst of activity suggests Clapp's illness was improving but perhaps not enough for him to restart his ministry in Appledore. In the same issue of the *North Devon Journal* carrying a report of this meeting is an odd little item to the effect that Clapp's dog called, grandly, *Canino Fidel*, had died. [49] This apparently was cheering news to the local women and children to whom the dog had been a 'terror' for many years.

On June 1, 1852 a Wesleyan Reform meeting was held at the Independent Meeting House (the present-day Lavington chapel) in Bideford. [50] Clapp as a Congregationalist seems to have been invited along to be a neutral chairman and keep order between two groups of disputing Methodists. This sounded innocuous enough but religious passions ran high in mid-nineteenth century England and the actions of Thomas Evans 'late Mayor of Bideford' (in 1849 and 1850) led to Clapp publishing the text of 'A Correspondence' between him and the local councillor. [51] It was published by 'The Committee of the Bideford Wesleyan Reform Association' and although no printer is listed we can assume it came from Clapp's own press. The price was a nominal 'One Halfpenny' – evidently Clapp was hoping for a wide sale.

The introduction notes that Clapp had to deal with two disruptive members of the audience at the meeting. The first, John How, 'had 'utter'd a malignant fabrication against the Rev Gentleman [Clapp] before the teachers of the Sunday School' which he later denied and on 'being invited to meet those who heard him he refused; preferring to write a series of letters, which the Committee for their Chairman's sake hope may soon be published'. The second was Evans who at the meeting caused 'the greatest disturbance by his perverse and disorderly conduct'. Two days after the meeting he wrote to Clapp and this letter, along with the latter's reply, formed the text of the pamphlet. Both How and Evans were said to be 'advocates of Conference Methodism' – i.e. Methodists who were willing to accept centralised control as opposed to local independence. As part of this they supported the exclusion of a Mr. Dunn from the ministry even though he had worked throughout Britain for the church for 35 years. The majority of Bideford dissenters seem to have disagreed with his suspension and let their feelings be known at the meeting.

The kernel of Evans' complaint in his letter was that Clapp had not been neutral but instead had chosen to throw his weight behind Dunn's supporters. Evans at one point wrote rhetorically, 'I would ask whether the antecedents of the Rev. Jerome Clapp are such to show that he is a man to whom we may look, as a competent authority, to lecture the Wesleyan community on matters of Church Government.' As if this wasn't enough he went on to question the success of Clapp's ministry. After pointing out that 'I have known something of the Independent Church and its members at Appledore for the last 30 years', he went on to ask 'for proofs of the flourishing state of your Church after many years of your Ministerial labours among them'.

Clapp's reply was three times as long as Evans' letter and dwelt in detail on what had happened at the meeting. He notes, for example, that Evans was hissed by the audience, refused to answer questions and overwhelmingly lost the eventual vote. In passing, Clapp also attacked 'Mr. Avery' who, from internal evidence, was probably William Avery, the then Mayor of Barnstaple and editor of the *North Devon Journal,* who was also present at the meeting. The letter ended with a ringing series of phrases: 'I thank God I am an Independent and not a Wesleyan Minister. And let me devoutly thank God also, that I am not a Bideford labourer wanting Methodist work; nor a Bideford mechanic seeking Methodist employ; nor a Bideford tradesman observing Methodist custom, upon whom more persons (let me hope that are but few) of the Bideford Conference party might turn the screw in the spirit developed in the late meeting.' I have been unable to trace any further repercussions of this exchange of letters and, though such religious disagreements were common, Clapp's conflict with such prominent adversaries can't have endeared him to powerful elements in the local population,

In answer to Evans' mocking question re the success or otherwise of Clapp's ministry he vehemently replied: 'All the disasters and contentions which have arisen here and which you in the spirit of the Evil One seem to gloat over, have occurred *only since, and only because* I closed my ministry, and through ill health terminated that pastoral relation which for 10 years secured the very highest approval of those, who seized the occasion of its close to risk so much evil, (I hope not by your encouragement, though perhaps for the sake of drawing them to Methodism you became a consenting party) and exhibited so much evil, in an ungodly struggle *(like your own)* for unscriptural and dangerous power.' Whether Clapp ever resumed active proselytising in Appledore is hard to say as the records covering his period in post are missing – presumably removed by Clapp himself when he eventually left the village. This illness could also explain some later events connected to the endowment of the Appledore Independent chapel.

In September 1852 the *Journal* printed a letter from the Appledore clergyman concerning the proposed railway line between Bideford and Barnstaple. [52] Given Clapp's progressive views we should not be surprised to find him advocating its rapid construction. Intriguingly, he ends his letter by quoting the words of 'Mr. Evans' (presumably the Bideford Mayor with whom he had had the public disagreement) to the effect that 'the town that consents to be without a railway, consents so far to its obscurity and ruin'. Another indication of both his interest in railways, and the wealth his wife brought him, comes in October 1852 when, in an advertisement on the front page of the *Journal* seeking investors into the proposed Bideford-Okehampton railway, Clapp's name is listed in the 'Committee of Shareholders'. [53]

Again in September 1852 Clapp spoke at a meeting in Bideford called to discuss moves to persuade local traders to close early for half a day each week. [54] Clapp took the position that such free time was essential to the shop assistants. He actually hoped they would use it to educate themselves – a need he illustrated by an odd story: 'He was at this moment deprived of the services of a valuable servant because he would not sleep in a room which he said was haunted by a ghost. He had talked with him and tried to shame him out of it, but it was of no use.' He went on to suggest two positive moves – that 'ladies' should boycott shops that stayed open late and that a committee be established to implement an early closing agreement in the town. The latter was carried and indeed early closing became the norm in Bideford.

This was the same month that Clapp's silver mine finally faded away and speculation that he lost heavily in this debacle is hinted at by an action brought against the clergyman in February 1853 in the Bideford County Court. [55] A Mr. Clibbett sued Clapp over an unpaid account for £2.5s.9d. Clapp denied he owed the money, saying the bill was a fabrication and that in any case some of it extended over 12 years and was thus ruled out by the statute of limitations. He went on to claim that the case had only been brought owing to 'an unpleasantness that had occurred between them' though what this was is left unstated. The judge seemed to accept these points but still ordered Clapp to pay 3/9 to Clibbett.

Only a week later Clapp was present at a public meeting in Appledore to consider the proposal of local merchant and shipowner William Yeo to build a dry dock in the village. [56] Clapp we read 'moved a resolution, expressive of the most cordial concurrence in Mr. Yeo's public spirited proposal which being seconded by Mr. Lake, was carried by acclamation'. The dock was completed in 1856.

A month later the *Journal* published a letter from Clapp on the Bideford British School and the 'Voluntary Principle' of support for such nonconformist-run schools. [57] Clapp championed this and denounced the fact that fund raising sermons in 'two highly respectable had important congregations' in Bideford only raised a paltry £3 and evidently the school had to be sustained by Government grants. A reply come the following week from Bideford solicitor W S Rooker which reckoned Clapp's complaint rested an 'an entire mistake' – one which is exceedingly surprising from his well-known intelligent discrimination and large information'. At some length Rooker spelt out the finances of the school and the inadequacy of Government funding, though he does not address the point about the miniscule collection. Clapp chose not to reply but clearly he had upset Rooker and his fellow school governors. Clapp's views were further challenged at a meeting of the Bideford Mutual Improvement Society which, although mentioning the 'defunct state of the British Schools in the neighbourhood' reckoned reliance on State payments to keep such schools going was perfectly acceptable to nonconformists. [58]

After this concentrated burst of publicity we have to wait until December 1853 to find Clapp again making news. [59] In this month he chaired 'A working men's demonstration in favour of Total Abstinence' in the Bideford Mansion House. The meeting began with Clapp declaring 'that if ever he felt proud in his life it was on that occasion, surrounded as he was by a company of working men, who were there to testify as to the benefits they had received from abstinence principles'. Interestingly the *Journal* chose to report Clapp's speech at length but ignored 'The powerful arguments adduced' in favour of teetotalism by the working men present – a reflection perhaps of its perceived class of readers. A further temperance meeting followed in February 1854 in Appledore where Clapp was 'unanimously called to take the chair'. [60] He then introduced six speakers including Edward Capern (Bideford's 'postman poet') and a Mr. Thoroughgood who proudly exhibited a 'handsome watch' he had purchased by saving 'the cost of a pint of beer a day' over 18 months.

The following month saw Clapp lecturing on 'Anglo-Saxonism' to the Appledore Mutual Improvement Society. [61] He was according to the *Journal* report, 'listened to with marked attention' especially when he gave 'a bird's eye view of the future' of England. Sadly, what this might have been is left unstated though given Clapp's dissenting background these would probably have included aspects of social justice and reform. He also appeared at this Society in May 1854 when 'Poetry' was the subject under discussion. [62] A month previous to this Clapp was in the news following the discovery of a 'chalybeate spring' on his land. [63] This was a flow of water heavily impregnated with iron – and presumably seen as a 'mineral' water although there is no indication it was ever used as such.

This was one piece of good news in what was a trying time. In May a meeting of local Congregational ministers at Bideford noted that this was their first meeting for two years owing to 'the peculiar state of the churches' in that Bideford, Ilfracombe, Appledore and Chulmleigh had no pastors and the Barnstaple minister was very ill. [64] In order to reinvigorate the cause, a six man committee was set up 'to visit Appledore and confer with the friends upon the present state of things & to arrange for holding the Autumnal meeting at Appledore'. This meeting was actually held in Barnstaple – and Clapp attended.

At this time Clapp's interests were moving away from the church and becoming focused elsewhere. In June 1854, a Mr. Gough, who had achieved fame as a public speaker on the evils of drink, came to Bideford and gave a very well received lecture on the subject. [65] Clapp seems to have been the organiser of a follow-up meeting when about 1,000 'working men' came to hear Gough in a large marquee. Clapp took the chair and he 'congratulated the working men of Bideford on their public spirit'. This meeting went so well Clapp organised another at Buckland Brewer near Bideford. Again a marquee was erected and, surprisingly perhaps, in this very rural area, some 800 people turned up to listen to Clapp and other speakers support the temperance cause. These two meetings can be described as the last high points in Clapp's career in North Devon; never again was he to have the support of so many.

The decline began in September 1854 when a case 'which has excited public curiosity' was heard in the County Magistrates Court in Bideford. [66] Clapp, 'described unexpectedly as 'a gentleman of some notoriety in the neighbourhood', charged both Thomas Cook senior and junior of Appledore with an assault. On the 3rd of September Cook senior, who was 'a leading member' of Clapp's congregation, affixed a notice on the chapel door about a meeting to choose new trustees to manage shares and the property of Mrs. Betty White which formed the endowment of the chapel. These shares have been mentioned earlier when new trustees were chosen in 1842. Clapp came by his chapel with his wife, two children and niece, saw the notice – and ripped it down, The older Cook then, according to Clapp, 'took hold of my neckcloth, and pressed his knuckles into my neck, producing a painful sense of strangulation'. Margaret Clapp then ran to them and exclaimed, 'You dare to strike him.' Cook ignored her and according to the clergyman's evidence said 'Hell was too good for me.' At this point Cook junior had arrived and 'placed his back against the wall on which the notice had been affixed, took off his gloves, squared his fists in a threatening manner, and said 'Shall I strike him father?' His father replied 'I am man enough for that, and for two pins I would kick him down the steps.' Another younger Cook then turned up and began shouting 'Go it father, go it father!' This account formed the basis of Clapp's evidence and he was supported by James Clannan, the sexton of the chapel, who was heard to mutter that 'it was a rough piece of business altogether'. Two other witnesses appeared including Jane Turner who worked for Clapp. She had heard one of the Cooks call her employer 'a d__ n rogue, and that hell was too good for him'.

The Cook's defence was summed up in a paper which their solicitor read to the court 'detailing some circumstances connected with Mr. Clapp's relation to the Independent Congregation, and the appointment of trustees' which concluded with the statement that 'a meeting we want and a meeting we will have'. They called James Kiell as a witness who recounted how he had seen Clapp pull the notice down 'like an infuriated demon'. The Cooks had not assaulted the minister and he had heard no abusive language used.

Faced with such directly contradictory evidence the magistrates were clearly in some difficulties. They only took a short while, however, to return the judgement. They reckoned Clapp 'had used strong provocation in pulling down the paper, and that Mr.Cook had used violence which he had no right to do'. They therefore fined both parties a risible 6d each and made each responsible for their own costs in the case. Unfortunately for the historian nowhere is it stated what the underlying facts of the case were; was it a simple disagreement over who had the right to call a meeting, was it about the choice of trustees or was it, given the strength of Cooks' denunciations, a case of peculation of the chapel funds? One possibility is that even though Clapp gave up his active ministry around 1850 he was still drawing on the chapel's endowment funds. At this distance in time it is impossible to discover but whatever it was it began Clapp's downfall.

Within a few days Clapp's opponents had moved against him as a report in the *Journal* shows: 'Appledore. A public meeting was called on Wednesday last, to be held in the Independent chapel, for the purpose of appointing trustees for that building, and for the property by which it is endowed. Admittance, however, into the chapel for that purpose was refused by the minister; the meeting was, consequently, held in the Bethel, when fourteen persons from this and the neighbouring towns were appointed to act as trustees. The deed is now in course of execution, after which it is to be hoped things will take a more pacific turn, and no more work be made for the magistrates, to the great scandal of all that is good.' [67] Clearly Cook and his party had circumvented Clapp by completely legal means and in so doing had highlighted the traditionally precarious position of nonconformist ministers when compared to Church of England clergy.

Before Clapp could react he had to deal with another case when he was summonsed to the County Court, this time as a defendant in a case over trespass. [68] Frederick Thorold rented an estate known as Bidna from the Cawsey family and he complained that Clapp, who owned the neighbouring estate known as Berners, had illegally 'opened the hedge' separating their landholdings, put up a stile and cut down an oak tree. The magistrates soon dismissed the case, finding in Clapp's favour and awarding costs against Thorold.

Once this was out of the way Clapp could return to the more pressing matter of the chapel dispute and on 26 September 1854 he called a meeting 'in opposition to the one held the other week, in the Bethel' but 'for the same purpose as the other', i.e. to choose new trustees. [69] Whereas the first meeting had been open to the public this one was by ticket only. The Rev. S Kent of Braunton chaired the proceedings which saw the nomination of trustees but, as the *Journal* noted, 'what was thought rather extraordinary, they were all persons living out of the neighbourhood'. In addition 'Constables, it is said, were stationed at the door to prevent the entrance of persons inimical to the proceedings. Lovely.' This last detail suggests a growing paranoia on the part of poor Clapp. What is certain, however, is that the trustees nominated at this meeting never took up their posts – indeed a set of new trustees were finally appointed in 1856. [70] In the next few months the minister seems to have tried to marshal support. Only a month after the assault case he hosted a 70 strong tea party in the Independent chapel. The *Journal* noted that 'The sale of tickets was restricted to the limited accommodation, or many more would have been present' which strikes one as odd given that the chapel could hold 570 people! [71] After a series of congratulatory speeches 'the party separated with mutual expressions of gratification'.

That Clapp was under pressure is shown by the minutes of the North Devon Association of Congregational ministers which, in November 1854, records, 'The subcommittee appointed to visit Appledore having declined presenting any report, Mr.Buckpitt referred to circumstances which satisfied him that Mr.Clapp had met with much unkind and ungenerous treatment from individuals where hostility was as unprincipled as imoderate while the state of affairs at Appledore was as low and deplorable as it well could be. It was resolved after remarks by Mr.Clapp & others to pass to the next resolution.' [72] For the moment Clapp's position seemed to be secure if shaky.

In February 1855 Clapp chaired both a temperance meeting in Bideford and a lecture on Chaucer to the Appledore Mutual Improvement Society. [73] In March he gave an extempore lecture on 'Water' to the Bideford Mechanics Institute where 'the interest of a large and respectable audience' was 'maintained to the end'. [74] In the same month he led the vote of thanks to a speaker at the Appledore Mutual Improvement Society whilst in April he, along with Edward Capern, was lecturing in Buckland Brewer. [75] To round off a busy 6 months the *Journal* in June 1855 carried a notice that the Clapp family of 'Odun House' had been enlarged by the birth of a son. [76] Named Milton Melancthon either after the poet or his father's farm, he died aged 6. [77] Given this concentrated burst of activity and a new child it is rather surprising that, only a few weeks later, the *Journal* carried a large advertisement notifying the public that Milton Farm plus 50 acres of land was to be auctioned in August. [78] The auction, however, was unsuccessful and the property was again put on sale in October, although this time it was split into 16 lots. [79]

In October 1855 a small note in the *Journal* records the re-opening of the Independent Chapel at Appledore 'after a period of "suspended animation"' when a Mr.Haycroft, 'late of Bideford and now of London', and presumably the same person who had acted as Treasurer to The Congregational Tract Society, preached. [80] Two days later several local Congregational preachers held a service when 200 worshippers turned up. Also in February 1856 'a social Tea Meeting' was held in the Appledore Bethel where 120 people attended being described as 'the friends of the Independent Chapel in that place'. They heard two clergymen and three lay people deliver speeches which 'were expressive of a strong desire for the restoration of that peace and union which had been formerly enjoyed by the Church – but which has of late been interrupted by many unhappy circumstances.'[81] Apparently the entire gathering was 'cheered with the hope of soon seeing a Minister established among them'. The North Devon Association of Congregational ministers meeting at North Tawton in November 1855 noted Clapp's 'retirement' and that Messrs Corke, Peacock and Young had offered to preach 'the fourth Sabbath in January, February and March [1856] respectively' so their hopes seem to have been met. [82] From the above it is clear that sometime between July and October Clapp had precipitately left Appledore with his family. In fact he had gone to Walsall, where he altered his name to the grander sounding Jerome Clapp Jerome and carried on preaching in local Congregational chapels – and lost most of what remained of his wife's fortune in digging coal pits and trying to run an iron foundry. [83] What, however, had prompted his move?

In a series of notes on the history of the Appledore United Reform Church there is a short entry that reads 'Dark Period. Apparently church full. Jerome Clapp. Fine figure of a man. Intellectual – Scandal.' [84] In addition *The North Devon Congregational Magazine* from 1888 [85] printed a short piece on the history of the Appledore chapel which mentioned Clapp 'during whose ministry a succession of untoward circumstances reduced the cause to a very low ebb, and at last, in 1855, he retired under a very dark cloud, and the chapel was closed for a very short time, the few people who had remained dispersing themselves amongst the other congregations in the town'. [86]

So what was this 'scandal' and 'very dark cloud'? Clearly Clapp had upset people and there were unanswered questions about aspects of the chapel finances, but what brought it to a head? There is, in fact, still an oral tradition in Appledore that Clapp was the father of at least one illegitimate child – reason enough for a rapid departure and a decline in the chapel membership. [87] Whether the story is true or not it is clear that Clapp's enemies were actively spreading damaging rumours against him. A printed letter dated 'Walsall, December 26, 1856' and addressed to 'J C Jerome Esq' reads, 'We the undersigned, having thoroughly and carefully investigated the reports which have been so industriously circulated against your moral character, have, by the most abundant and conclusive evidence, proved, to our unanimous satisfaction, that the same are wicked and malicious untruths, originated by base men to gratify private revenge. We therefore take this opportunity of expressing our Christian sympathy with you, under these severe trials, hoping that God, who sees all hearts, will, in his own good time, confound and bring to nought their wicked counsels. This sympathy of ours we would doubly tender, as it is with feelings of great regret we find that certain individuals, from whom, as members of the same church, you ought to have expected Christian help and assistance, have given such ready and willing credence to the slanderous reports of your known enemies.' The list of 16 signatories is headed by Samuel Stephens 'Magistrate and Alderman of Walsall'. [88]

It is true that in January 1857 Clapp and 20 others seceded from the Bridge Street Congregational chapel in Walsall and this letter might refer to some long forgotten religious dispute but the reference to 'moral character' seems to tie it in with the Appledore story – and the fact that the letter is preserved in the archive of a Bideford organisation suggests it relates to a North Devon event. [89]

Further light is thrown on these events in the minute book of the North Devon Association of Congregational Ministers. [90] Meeting at Chulmleigh in April 1857 the 18 men present discussed a letter they had received from Walsall and minuted the following, 'Letter having been read from Dr. Gordon and the church at Walsall containing certain statements and making certain inquiries relating to Mr. Clapp late Minister at Appledore and a member of this Association but now of Walsall and known there as Jerome C.Jerome Esq. Also: A copy of the Secretary's reply and a letter signed E H Holden addressed to several Ministers of this Association the object of which appears to be to discredit the reply of the Secretary.'

After discussion the meeting passed the following motion, 'That this Association approve the letter of their Secretary addressed to the Pastor & church at Walsall under date 29 December last and adopt it as their own. That they deem it the solemn duty of Mr. Clapp to make every effort to disprove the charges so seriously affecting his moral and Christian character, referred to in this correspondence. That in the event of no sufficient steps being taken by Mr. Clapp for the clearance of his character from those charges previous to the next meeting it will be the painful duty of this Association to consider the propriety of removing Mr. Clapp from their fellowship. That copies of these resolutions signed by the Ministers & Delegates present be transmitted to the Church at Walsall and to Mr. Clapp. That this Association desire to convey to the Minister & Church at Walsall the expression of their deep sympathy in the troubles occasioned by Mr. Clapp and their fervent hope that by the overruling Providence of the great Head of the Church what has happened may be followed by a great and lasting blessing.'

Some seven months later in November 1857 the Association met at Barnstaple and noted that a copy of their resolution regarding Clapp had been sent to him and the Walsall church. Clapp had not replied but the Walsall congregation had sent their 'resolution' which was copied into the North Devon records. It reads, 'Resolution passed unanimously at a Meeting of the Congregational Church Walsall October 1 1857 with a request that it be transmitted to the Secretary of the N.Devon Association of Congregational Ministers. Resolved unanimously That the Church feels truly thankful to the N.Devon Assoc. of Congregational Ministers for their kind expressions of sympathy in reference to the severe trial of principle which this church has been subjected by the conduct of the Rev. Jerome Clapp and trusts the Great Head of the church may overrule these trials for his own glory and the ultimate good of his Church; and while expressing this hope this Church would also express the assurance that as they have done their duty irrespective of consequences confiding in God and vindicating the principle of a pure fellowship, the Congreg. Association of Devon will not shrink from them, but take such steps in due course as a regard to their own Association as Ministers of Christ and the interests of the cause of the divine Lord so manifestly demands.' It is signed by Pastor A Gordon and five deacons.

When this was read to the North Devon meeting it gave rise to 'anxious deliberation' – so much so that 'It was at length suggested by the Secretary that in so painful a case Special prayer should now be offered seeking Divine Guidance in this matter whereupon Revd. Mr. Whiting offered solemn prayer to God.' This seems to have worked as the group decided that Clapp, having not replied to their letter 'has thereby deprived himself of the fraternal confidence of the Associated Churches and brethren'. More tellingly they went on to add 'That regarding it to be their imperative duty to countenance in the ministry no man whose moral and religious character is not free from all reasonable suspicion this Association is unhappily compelled to carry out the Resolution IX of last meeting.' Copies of this decision were then sent to Clapp and the church at Walsall.

The next Association meeting was held at Appledore on 28 April 1858 with the Rev. Edward Hipwood, Clapp's replacement, in the chair. This heard, and minuted, a letter from Walsall thanking the North Devon churches for their 'fidelity' in expelling Clapp.

On this inconclusive note Clapp passes from North Devon history. There is an odd reference in his wife's diary to him returning to Appledore in August 1866 for a week – possibly to tie up some loose financial ends? Additionally his wife and son visited Appledore in July 1868 but nothing is known of this other than that various locals welcomed them and seemed to show genuine warmth to Mrs. Clapp. [92] In conclusion, Clapp's time in Devon can best be described as 'interesting' and 'varied'. Those wishing to follow Clapp's life up to his death in 1871 are referred to a paper by Alan Argent. [93] It is worth noting, however, that Joseph Connolly in his introduction to a 1992 edition of Jerome K Jerome's autobiography highlights the son's curiously intense efforts to retain his family's privacy – especially with regard to his stepdaughter and natural daughter along with his own marriage to a divorcee. [94] One wonders if this 'intensely private man' felt further burdened by his father's secrets? Connolly in a postscript ends with the comment 'If Jerome had secrets, they have all been kept'. The article you have just read perhaps draws back the veil to a certain extent.

APPENDIX 1

Each measures 75 mm by 120 mm and are printed on thin paper. No. 1 is entitled 'An address on the duty of diffusing Congregational Principles', consists of 12 pages and was sold at the nominal price of 1/6 per hundred. No author is given but the Rev. Jerome Clapp of Marine Parade, Appledore is given as the publisher. The author states in the preface that 'Infidelity taking advantage of the times is using the Printing Press to overthrow the pulpit, and High Churchism is employing it also to rivet the chains of superstition upon prostrate conscience. To those it must not be left. True piety must engage it in her service to enlighten and to bless the world.' No.4 in the series carried the title 'The Voluntary System explained in a Letter to the Lord High Chancellor of England'. Again no author is given and it is the same size and price as No. 1. The booklet exists in two different coloured covers. The third survival is numbered 19 and address 'The Practical Evils resulting from the union of Church and State'. The author is given as Edward Miall, who took 24 pages to explain his argument.

It is also worth noting that Clapp apparently produced other material on his press. A letter to the *Western Daily Mercury* which was reprinted in the *North Devon Journal* reads, 'An Appledore correspondent writes – In your issue of the 22nd mention is made of the Appledore hymn book, published by the late Rev. Jerome Clapp. It is quite true, as a reader of the *British Weekly* says, the hymn book was well known and widely used. About the same time, too, Mr.Clapp printed and published a book of tunes for the hymns, many of them being named after members of his family or members of his congregation.' [91]

NOTES

1. *Jerome K Jerome – A Critical Biography by Joseph Connolly* (Orbis 1982). A search of the *Register of the Scholars Admitted to Merchant Taylors' School from AD 1562 to 1874* edited by C.Robinson (1882–3) reveals no Clapp – personal communication from Frank Rodgers
2. North Devon Journal 20.8.1840 3a [Hereafter NDJ]
3. 1841 Census – Appledore, NDRO
4. NDRO B560/1
5. *Report of the Conference of Ministers of all denominations on the Corn Laws 1841, Manchester* – NDRO B151 add/42
6. NDJ 9.6.1842
7. *My Life and Times* by Jerome K Jerome. (London 1926/1992) The son calls his grandfather a solicitor but he appears as a draper on the wedding certificate – personal communication from Frank Rodgers
8. *My Life and Times*
9. NDJ 31.1.1850 1b
10. NDJ 12.7.1855 4c; 26.7.1855 4c; 25.10.1855 4c
11. NDJ 29.10.1857 1a
12. *My Life and Times* by Jerome K Jerome (London 1926/1992)
13. NDJ 23.9.1841 3d
14. NDRO B151 add/28/32 15.
15. NDRO B560/1
16. NDRO B151 add/28/29–32
17. NDJ 16.12.1847 3f
18. NDJ 31.7.1856 1a
19. *My Life and Times* by Jerome K Jerome (London 1926/1992) + *Journal's 175th Anniversary* by P.Christie in NDJ 1.7.1999 – 29.7.1999
20. NDJ 4.5.1843 2f–3e
21. NDJ 8.6.1843 3c
22. NDJ 31.8.1843 3b
23. NDJ 15.2.1844 3c; 22.2.1844 3e
24. NDJ 28.3.1844 3a

25. NDJ 4.4.1844 3b–c
26. NDJ 11.4.1844 4b–d
27. NDRO B560/1
28. NDJ 15.5.1845 3a
29. NDJ 18.9.1845 2g
30. NDRO B151 add 48/22
31. NDRO B560/1
32. NDJ 10.6.1847 2c
33. NDRO B560/1
34. NDJ 16.12.1847 3f
35. NDJ 27.4.1884 3d
36. NDJ 28.12.1848 3a
37. *A Few Footprints* by John Edwards (Privately published 1905)
38. NDJ 4.1.1849 3b–c
39. NDJ 4.1.1849 3b–c; 1.11.1849 5c
40. NDRO B560/1
41. 1851 Census Appledore – NDRO
42. Alison Grant – personal communication
43. NDRO B560/1
44. NDJ 18.12.1851 5a
45. NDJ 25.12.1851 8b
46. NDJ 21.10.1852 8a
47. Bideford Gazette 17.5.1904
48. NDJ 15.1.1852 5c
49. NDJ 15.1.1852 5d
50. NDJ 3.6.1852 8b–d
51. *A Correspondence between Thomas Evans Esq (late Mayor) of Bideford and the Rev. Jerome Clapp of Appledore respecting the late public meeting on Wesleyan reform held at the Independent Meeting House, Bideford; June 1st 1852.* No printer stated. Copy held in NDRO.
52. NDJ 2.9.1852 6d
53. NDJ 14.10.1852 la
54. NDJ 9.9.1852 8b–c
55. NDJ 17.2.1853 8c
56. NDJ 24.2.1853 8b
57. NDJ 3.3.1853 6b
58. NDJ 17.3.1853 8a
59. NDJ 15.12.1853 8a–b
60. NDJ 9.2.1854 8b
61. NDJ 9.3.1854 8a
62. NDJ 18.5.1854 8a
63. NDJ 20.4.1854 8b
64. NDRO B560/1
65. NDJ 22.6.1854 8b
66. NDJ 7.9.1854 8b–c
67. NDJ 14.9.1854 8a
68. NDJ 14.9.1854 3b
69. NDJ 28.9.1854 8b
70. NDRO B151 add 48/22
71. NDJ 12.10.1854 8b
72. NDRO B560/1
73. NDJ 8.2.1855 5d; 22.2.1855 5e
74. NDJ 1.3.1855 5d
75. NDJ 5.4.1855 7e

76. NDJ 14.6.1855 5e
77. *My Life and Times* by Jerome K Jerome (London 1926/1992)
78. NDJ 12.7.1855 4c; 26.7.1855 4c
79. NDJ 25.10.1855 4c
80. NDJ 11.10.1855 8b
81. Bideford Gazette 5.2.1856 la
82. NDRO B560/1
83. *My Life and Times* by Jerome K Jerome (London 1926/1992)
84. NDRO B151 add 28/6
85. The North Devon Congregational Magazine 1888
86. NDRO B151 add 28/17
87. Alison Grant – personal communication
88. NDRO B66B/1/1
89. C Yates, Librarian of Walsall Local History Centre – personal communication
90. NDRO B560/1
91. NDJ 25.10.1900 8b
92. *My Life and Times* by Jerome K Jerome (London 1926/1992). Frank Rodgers of Guatemala who now owns Marguerite Clapp's diary kindly supplied this entry from it which refers to Marguerite's trip: '1868, July 18. This morning we start to pay our long talked of visit to Devon and altho' we anticipated much pleasure I had no idea realysing half the kind attention and reception I and the dear children received. They seemed to remember all my acts of kindness which I had long ago forgotten and quite overwhelmed me with their love and affection. We enjoyed ourselves excessively. My visit has been to me like the refreshing rain after a long and dreary drought. August. Papa met us and we all came home safe again tho' we left Jerome behind at Salisbury. They forwarded him by express and we met on the Platform.'
93. Alan Argent *The Tale of an Idle Fellow, Jerome K.Jerome* in Congregational History Circle Vol.3 no.4 pp.18–30 1996
94. *My Life and Times* by Jerome K.Jerome (London 1926/1992)

* * *

Peter Christie gave a talk about the Reverend Jerome Clapp to the Appledore Book Festival in 2007 and was astonished to be approached at the end by lifelong Appledore resident Jenny Arnold who told him of a lengthy skipping rhyme her grandmother had taught her which apparently referred to Clapp's illegitimate child. Sadly she could only recall the first verse and an appeal he made in the local newspaper did not elicit any others. It reads:

Miss Mary had a baby
She dressed him all in white
And took him out to Shilford
To keep him out of sight

(Silford is a tiny cluster of houses in the same parish as Appledore but about as far away from the village as you can get.)

Two years later, Peter Christie came up with even more news of the allegedly errant Rev. Clapp:

The third piece of information follows detective work by local resident David Carter which revealed that a child born in Appledore in the 3rd quarter of 1855 was given the very suggestive name of Jerome Clapp Fursey. The naming of illegitimate children with the names of the father was a common occurrence in the eighteenth and nineteenth centuries but this boy was actually the ninth of his mother's children! She was called Susanna Fursey and her husband was Samuel. Their first child had been born in 1838 and Samuel became Postmaster of Appledore in 1860 and was President of the local Independent Order of Rechabites in 1876. Jerome Clapp Fursey (or Thursey) went on to become a shoemaker. He is listed as such in the 1891 Census for Appledore but by 1901 he was in Pontypridd where he died, apparently unmarried, in 1926.

Jerome Clapp Jerome, JKJ's father

The timing of his birth is, as said, very suggestive and his naming is also very odd given that the Reverend Clapp was clearly not a popular man in the village by this date. I have never come across a married woman naming an illegitimate child in this way and I do wonder whether the child was born to an unmarried female relative of Susannah and passed off as hers to try and avoid the shame associated with illegitimacy at this date.

Jerome K Jerome (age 2 years) and nurse

WHEN PASTOR JEROME CAME FROM APPLEDORE IN DEVON

by Pitman (M Wright, J P)

from The Friendship of Cannock Chase

When the Rev. Jerome Clapp Jerome migrated from Appledore, in Devon, to Staffordshire in 1855, it was chiefly because he felt the glamour of the coal and iron of Cannock Chase and the adjoining industrial districts. He had heard of the beauty of the thousands of acres of heatherland, and alluring information had come to him of the riches that were to be made from the seams beneath the wild lands in the middle of the county. He hoped to blend his pulpit work with his prospecting in minerals, and while he was active in promoting spiritual progress in Walsall Congregational circles, he had business concerns with the Birchills Ironworks. It was coal, however, that gripped his attention most.

Brownhills and Norton Canes – otherwise Norton-under-Cannock – was a united neighbourhood in the great developments which were taking place, and the men who were hoping to turn the Conduit Colliery into a gold mine were glad to receive the investments of the energetic Independent pastor. Eloquent a preacher though he had proved himself to be, he had not found the calling to be plentiful in remuneration, but his wife, Marguerite, had inherited a handsome fortune from her father, a Swansea solicitor named Jones. In what more promising venture could her money be placed than in assisting to produce the coal which was to be the life-blood of the industrialism of Mid-Victorian England?

For three hundred years extensive areas of land in the Norton Canes district had been in the possession of the Lichfield Conduit Trust, the income derived therefrom being used for the repair of the Trust conduits and the maintenance of the feeder water-courses in and around the city. Thus it was that the first ambitious mining enterprise at Norton Canes was called the Conduit Colliery. The Bottom Cathedral pit and the Top Cathedral pit were names which also had reference to the Lichfield Trust associations.

Great hopes were held that success would reward the sinkers at the Conduit, and it was an anxious Marguerite who waited for the news of progress brought by her husband when he returned home from Norton day by day.

Pastor Jerome had a courageous enthusiasm, and he kept his preaching appointments on Sundays in spite of his tired and worried body and mind. He had capable and experienced men to help him, but difficulties were constantly arising, and he realised that capital at his disposal was melting away before the turn of fortune had been reached. Water and running sand had swept more than one man of Cannock Chase to ruin, and Jerome found himself engulfed in such a tragedy.

Late one night, when all at home had gone to bed, the pastor-prospector returned from Norton Canes bearing the bad tidings, the fear of which had haunted his wife like a spectre for weeks. He sat himself on the edge of the bed and broke to Marguerite, as gently as he could, the news that the pit was flooded, and that he was a ruined man.

May 2nd, 1860, was the day of disaster. Some days later Pastor Jerome, leaving the family fortune lost in the rush of waters and his own surname written in large letters on the pit for future generations to read, went to London in the hope that he would be able to get on his feet again. In due course, he was joined in London by his wife and children, including the four-year-old son, Jerome K Jerome, who was destined in subsequent years to win considerable fame as the author of *Three Men in a Boat* and *The Passing of Third Floor Back*.

'Papa's railway', as it was termed in the Jerome family circle, was a later venture of the ex-colliery owner. It led 'from Poverty to the Land of Heart's Desire', said Jerome Jerome the Second. It did not pass beyond the stage of phantasy, and when bad news was once more told to the ever-hopeful wife, she wrote in her diary: 'Every effort my dear husband makes proves unsuccessful. We seem shut out from the Blessing of God.'

The name 'Jerome's Pit' has stuck to the Conduit as the most frequently used of the two. The miners have never tried to pronounce the name in the three-syllable form which the pastor from Appledore declared to be the correct one.

'He used to call himself something like "Jerrymy"', said an old miner whom I met one day in Norton. This veteran was born in 1846, and he described to me how he saw Jerome many times on the pit-bank, where there was a lot of bustle and noise when the sinking was going on.

'A nice gentleman, but he was quiet and used no bad language,' was the old miner's single sentence summing-up of Jerome.

Men with deeper pockets than Jerome took over the Norton Canes sinkings. They triumphed where their predecessor came to grief, and the Holcroft family were able to establish Jerome's pits in the forefront of the undertakings of the Cannock Chase coalfield.

THE OLD PHILOLOGIANS
by Ivor Hussey

Hon. Sec. of The Old Boys' Association of St Marylebone Grammar School (formerly called The Philological School)

Jerome K Jerome was for a very short time a pupil of what was then known as the Philological School. It wasn't until I heard JKJ's biographer about a year ago being interviewed on the radio that I knew that JKJ had hated his school (if indeed that was so) or that he spent at most two years there.

Nevertheless, he is now commemorated there in bricks and mortar. The buildings of The Philological School were reconstructed between October 1856 and June 1857. It stood at 248 Marylebone Road in London and the building which JKJ knew became 'listed'. In 1901 the school's name was changed to St Marylebone Grammar School for Boys and on the first day of 1909 it became a County Council School. In 1926 (I think) new adjacent and connecting buildings substantially increased the accommodation. In 1981 the school closed down.

The buildings remained empty for some seven years, passing through the hands of several owners who both neglected to secure the premises (thus permitting much vandalism) and failed to obtain approval for 'development' on the lines which they wanted. Eventually, the site was bought by Gaseley Properties Ltd., a company in the ASDA Group, who secured planning permission to (a) rehabilitate the listed building for conversion into ASDA's London headquarters and (b) demolish the 1920s additions and replace them with (i) a block of offices to be let out and (ii) a block of flats – on the site of what had been the school's gymnasium with the hall above it.

ASDA's London headquarters was finished and first occupied in September last year: the building has been named Abbott House after one of the Headmasters of The Philological School, Edwin Abbott from 1827 (when he was not quite 19 years old, and an ex-pupil) until 1872: he would therefore have been Headmaster during JKJ's time as a pupil, which would seem to have begun in January 1869. The office block (named Grove House: it has its entrance in Marylebone Road but most of it fronts Lisson Grove, at right angles to Marylebone Road) was finished a few months ago and tenants are moving in. The block of flats has been named Jerome House. When I was last in the vicinity, at the beginning of July, there was still quite a bit of work to be done there.

ON THE RAILS AND OFF

A SMALL CENTENARY ITEM – WITH COMMENTARY

by David Fink

In 1889 Jerome wrote to G P Neele, Superintendent of the Line to the London and North Western Railway. This letter is quoted by Neele, to whom we are most grateful, in his *Railway Reminiscences* of 1904. Here it is:

SAVAGE CLUB,

SAVOY, W.C.,

24th September, 1889.

Dear Mr. Neele,

Finding myself writing to you on a matter of business – about an unfortunate Gladstone Bag full of luggage that your people seem to have lost for me – I am tempted to write a few private lines, that I have often thought of writing, but wanted some excuse, as without one it seemed making a business of it, to thank you for your kindness to me in the past. I sadly fear you must have been disappointed with me, and thought me an ungrateful youngster after the trouble you had taken, but I was never fitted for business, and the more I tried, the more unsuccessful I became.

Having seemingly found now what Carlyle says is the great object of every man to find — the work he is meant for — I am sure you will be glad to know I am settling into my groove very comfortably, and as far as worldly condition is concerned, I suppose I ought to consider myself, at my age, lucky enough.

I never come to Euston Station — which in the way of travel I do pretty frequently — without pleasant thoughts of the time when it fed and clothed me.

Trusting sincerely that all goes well with you and yours in all things,

I remain,

Very truly yours,
Jerome K Jerome

JKJ had certainly settled into his groove by 1889, having published *Idle Thoughts* (the original!) and *Three Men in a Boat*. Further, as a member of the prestigious Savage Club he moved in high artistic circles. Founded in 1857 at the Grown Tavern in Drury Lane, the Club had premises at 6 and 7 Adelphi Terrace until the Terrace, vaingloriously named after its architects, the Adam brothers, was demolished in 1937. The present premises off Berkeley Square cater for about 1,000 members who qualify, as stars of the literary, musical and scientific firmament, together with others whom it is desired to honour. In 1936 three 'Savages' occupied the throne, George V, Edward VIII and George VI.

Neele introduces JKJ's letter with the words:

'The indoor staff at the time included Mr. G W Pope, who has since entered the ministry … also the better known Mr. Jerome K Jerome. The following note will give some pleasant idea of his own views of his railway career.'

The main purpose of JKJ's note to Neele was clearly to recover his Gladstone Bag. In the course of his appeal to the top man, Superintendent of the Line, no less, he also felt impelled to express regret and repentance at what he felt might have been a lack-lustre performance as a railway clerk, and also gratitude to the great man for his help. Further he felt an impulse, after a lapse of sixteen years to say how much he had enjoyed his days at Euston. Well, with the Gladstone Bag in mind, he would, wouldn't he?

Jerome's scattered comments in *My Life and Times* (1926) throw some light on this phase of his life. He was at Marylebone Grammar School from 1869 to 1873. Leaving school at the age of fourteen he took up a clerkship at Euston, which he obtained through the help of an old friend of his father, J C Jerome, who had died two years earlier. The 'old friend' is presumed to be Neele himself, and the family connection will become clear at the later stage of this article. JKJ's salary was £26 a year with an annual rise of £10. He also had plenty of overtime pay at 21/2d till midnight and 4d afterwards, with the result that he often went home on Saturdays with six or seven shillings extra in his pocket. Further, he was entitled to four free passes a year.

His work in the advertising department took him out and about around London to see that bills and timetables were properly displayed. He was thus able to take time off and (conscientiously) make it up without anyone being the wiser. Time off for what? For rehearsals in the theatre, his recently discovered love, specifically Astley's across Westminster Bridge, where among other parts, he played a 'great swell', a role for which he had to purchase a dress suit in Petticoat Lane from an 'old Sheeny' (his words in 1926) who gave him credit. Literature was his goal and stage experience would be useful.

Also useful to a youth's career was his acquisition of the vices, without which one was a milksop, he tells us. Smoking needed pluck and perseverance; drink presented greater difficulty, and there was also (most delicately phrased) the 'vice that does not have to be acquired' and JKJ wished that men of 'good-feeling' would treat 'this deep mystery of our nature with more reverence'. One feels that all this moonlighting served to alleviate the tedium of railway clerical work, and that, if the Jerome of 1889 could reflect on his Euston period of 1873 with 'pleasant thoughts', this was not entirely due to his railway work. However, we must not be too pious and censorious. The railway was not to be his chosen career. He gave value for money, searching elsewhere meanwhile for fulfilment. After all, he was only fourteen years old when first exposed to a harsh world.

The addressee of JKJ's letter was George Potter Neele, LNWR Superintendent from 1875 to 1895. In this capacity he escorted Queen Victoria on 112 journeys on the line, many from Windsor or Osborne to Ballater (for Balmoral) and back. On the last of these journeys 'she accorded me a most pleasing smile' and sent him souvenir gifts of a signed painting of the royal family and a large inscribed silver tray.

In the Winter 1989 number of the *Blackcountryman* Charles Elwell explains in lively and careful detail why and how the Neele family came to Walsall. Entitled *A Nobleman's Agent and his Family* his article deals with the Potter family who were Lord Bradford's agents for his Walsall estates. George Potter Neele's mother, Elizabeth Potter, married a Bank of England employee, George Neele, who died in 1838, whereupon the widow left her Kentish Town home and came to Walsall with her family to be with her brothers and sisters. Being evangelically inclined she was entirely content to entrust her three sons, including GPN, to the care of the godly and severe Rev C F Childe, Headmaster of the Grammar School, which was then in Park Street on the site of the present Saddler Centre and Station. GPN later described Childe as an iceberg.

GPN left Queen Mary's Grammar School (this title came later) as Head Boy in 1842 at the age of seventeen and after a spell in his uncle's office embarked upon a career in railway administration. By 1849 he was Superintendent of the new South Staffordshire Railway, with headquarters in Walsall's Station Street. GPN along with the SS Railway was taken over by the LNWR in 1861, and by 1875 was its Superintendent, as noted above. It would be during his Walsall period that he became a friend of JKJ's father, Jerome Clapp Jerome, the Nonconformist Minister and mine-owner, who designed the Wednesbury Road church in 1859, the year of JKJ's birth.

Distilling the evidence given above, we may say that the convergence and interaction of Potters, Neeles and Jeromes in Walsall in the 1840s and '50s resulted in JKJ's Euston job in the '70s. This afforded him time, opportunity and indeed, motive for a youthful entry into the theatrical and literary world, and set him on the way to his true career. Perhaps in the light of this evidence a re-reading of JKJ's letter to Neele would suggest that Walsall had rather more influence on his career than his brief sojourn in the town would indicate.

ACKNOWLEDGEMENTS

G P Neele – *Railway Reminiscences* (1904) (The author thanks John Whiston for a long loan of this rare book)

J K Jerome – *My Life and Times* (1926) (reprinted by Alan Sutton Publishing Limited, 1984)

D P J Fink – *History of Queen Mary's Grammar School* (1954)

C J L Elwell – *A Nobleman's Agent and his Family* (1989), an article in the *Blackcountryman* Vol. 22 No. 1, Winter 1989

JKJ ON THE STAGE
by Peter C Hall

of Miami University, Oxford, Ohio

In *My Life and Times* Jerome relates some interesting details of his first acting experiences at Astley's with Murray Wood's company. The exact dates of his first engagement, however, are not supplied and the authors of subsequent books about Jerome have been quite content to give only a general time-frame for his acting days – the late 1870s. The recent increase in scholarly interest in Victorian and Edwardian theatre has made the records of the London stage much more readily available to researchers, and it is now possible to use the scant details supplied by Jerome himself to date his first acting experience.

Jerome mentions that the first play produced by Murray Wood when Jerome joined the company was *Dolly Varden*. Theatrical records show that Wood's adaptation from *Barnaby Rudge* was first produced at the Surrey in October of 1872, and that his four act melodrama was revived at Astley's in April of 1878. The cast list for this production includes Virginia Blackwood as Dolly Varden, just as Jerome states in his autobiography. This date can be taken, then, with some degree of certainty, as the beginning of Jerome's acting career.

According to Jerome, the season at Astley's ended in November, and by that time he also had been assigned roles in Wood's *Little Nelly*, Watts Phillips' *Lost in London*, and a play by George Manville Fenn. The Manville Fenn play, which Jerome does not mention by name, would have been *Land Ahead! or The Irish Immigrant*, which was first produced at Astley's in October of 1878.

Not being a principal player, Jerome's name does not appear in the cast lists for the productions of *Dolly Varden* and *Land Ahead!* at Astley's. From

Jerome's own descriptions in his autobiography and *On the Stage – and Off* it can be assumed that he appeared mostly as a 'Walking Gentleman' or what we now know as a bit-player. His mention of playing a 'wicked swell' in *Lost in London*, suggests that he might have advanced enough in the company to play the villain, Gilbert Featherstone, in this melodrama, but I have not yet found a cast list of the revival of this play at Astley's in 1878, and am not sure if this is indeed the role to which Jerome refers.

All the details Jerome relates in *My Life and Times* fit together quite nicely with theatrical records I have access to at this point and it can be taken as quite definite that Jerome's first acting experience spanned the season at Astley's from April to November 1878. After the end of the season at Astley's Jerome joined the first of several touring companies and his acting career becomes very difficult to trace – for details from that period we are all still dependent on the anecdotes related in *On the Stage – and Off*.

Note: I have found a recent reference work compiled by Donald Mullin, *Victorian Plays: A Record of Significant Productions on the London Stage, 1837–1901* (New York and London: Greenwood Press, 1987), to be very useful in my work on Victorian and Edwardian theatre.

4
EARLY JEROME STORIES

In *My Life and Times*, Jerome describes his efforts to have his writing published: 'I had tried short stories, essays, satires. One – but one only – a sad thing about a maiden who had given her life for love and been turned into a water-fall, and over the writing of which I had nearly broken my heart, had been accepted by a paper called *The Lamp*. It died soon afterwards.'

Later, in an article entitled 'My First Time in Print' in *Grand Magazine* (July 1905), Jerome offers a somewhat different recollection of his first published work. The piece, he remembered, was 'a short story of somewhat ambitious intent – an allegory commencing with "Once upon a time". It was all about a prince who wandered the world seeking for Love (with a capital L) and, returning disappointed to his own palace, found it waiting for him there. It was meant to teach a useful and cheerful moral lesson. I hope it accomplished its end.'

In both instances, Jerome's memory is at fault. The latter piece is clearly 'The Prince's Quest' (reproduced below). The former has not been identified, but our indefatigable patron, Frank Rodgers, tracked down the only story contributed by Jerome to *The Lamp*, an obscure monthly Roman Catholic magazine. It appeared in the July issue of 1881. 'Jack's Wife' is, without a doubt, Jerome's first published work.

JACK'S WIFE
by Jerome K Jerome

You don't know anyone who wants a set of chambers, do you? These nice large rooms, sitting room, bedroom and another smaller one – do for a study. All well furnished; linen, china and everything complete, and only up six flights of stairs. It's not much of a look out at the back certainly, but there's the garden in front. They are going to do it up and put a fountain there, so I hear. It isn't half bad even now when the sun shines on it, and looks quite pretty through a pair of opera-glasses turned the wrong way; you can imagine the trees are green, and you don't notice the dead cats and the brick-bats. Mrs. Cutting would 'do' for you. She is an excellent woman. She has seen better days though and is consequently given to occasional lowness of spirits, at which times she sits down at the top of the stairs and cries; but you would soon get used to this. A stiff glass of brandy and water is the best thing for it you will find. You couldn't have a better set of chambers for two fellows. It's lovely for one though and that's the reason why I want to get rid of them. I don't care to stop here by myself now Jack's gone. We lived together for four years, you know; Jack and I, and without him the place seems empty and ghost-like. What jolly times we used to have here to be sure. Ah, well; poor fellow; he's done for now.

I can't help laughing when I think of it. The way he used to talk, too, though he doesn't like to be reminded of that now. I remember the very last time we ever discussed the subject – discussed it sensibly that is. I don't count, of course, the time when Jack used to walk up and down the room and rave, or when he used to come home about twelve o'clock and bore my life out with what *she* said, and what *he* thought, until I would sneak off to bed and leave him, making an ass of himself over some limp looking flower or dingy glove. No, I pass over all that. The last time we ever talked like reasonable beings upon the question was just about a year ago. We had been arguing about a good many things that evening – politics, literature, art, and the stage were a few of them I know. 'Hamlet' came up somehow, and from that we got into madness and so on to love and marriage, and all that sort of thing. We considered the whole matter carefully, and both of us agreed that there was no such thing as love, and that it was all a bit of humbug got up by the poets. As Jack said, it was all very well for sentimental young milksops and silly, idling girls to fancy themselves in love, and to go sighing and mooning about, but it was absurd to suppose that *men* would give way to such imbecility. If not, why hadn't either of us ever fallen in love? 'Here am I,' said Jack, 'over twenty-two and you close upon it, and we have never had it.' Was it at all likely that if there was such a thing we should have escaped it all those years?

Jack didn't go so far as I did even at that time, but though he didn't disagree with marriage entirely, he had some very sensible views about it. He maintained that it was a very good institution if looked at practically and entered upon with judgement. Marriage was right enough, he said, if you only went about it the right way. Let a fellow make his way in the world first, and then, having fully thought it over and made up his mind as to what kind of woman would suit him – 'There's the great point,' said Jack, in an impressive manner, "*suit him*". It's just because people don't pay enough attention to this that marriages are so unhappy. There should always be a similarity of disposition, a harmony of thought, and a general accordance of character. A man will take any amount of trouble to get a pair of boots the right size for him, while he never thinks to see that he gets a wife that fits him. A man ought not to take such a step as this rashly. He should first of all carefully examine himself and then he should think out the kind of woman that would properly match with him. 'By Jove!' exclaimed Jack suddenly jumping up and putting down his pipe, 'I'll tell you what I'll do. I'll just jot down a rough outline of the woman I intend to marry – that's it, if ever I do marry – and I'll keep it by me, so that if I come across anyone that I think will do I shall be able to check her off by it, and then there can be no mistake.'

I've got it by me now. Jack laughingly gave it me when he went away. He said it might come in useful to me some day, but that he didn't think he should ever want it. Wait a minute and I'll get it out. Yes, here it is, neatly folded and endorsed in the dear old fellow's business-like way. 'Jack's Wife. Rough dft. 1/4/80. Personal attractions – She must be handsome (this is written in a bold, decisive hand) not a mere pretty doll-faced girl, but a beautiful, stately woman, her figure tall and graceful, and her lithesome form (by-the-bye, what is lithesome? I can't quite make it out. Dictionary says 'loose, easily bent, or pliable limber'. I suppose it's all right), and her lithesome form will be undistorted by the absurdities of fashion. She must be a blonde, with deep, blue tender eyes like a startled fawn's (wonder if a startled fawn has deep, blue tender eyes. The only fawn I ever saw butted me. It didn't seem at all startled. I was though. I never noticed its eyes) and wavy hair that will fall like a golden cataract over her ivory shoulders. A rare smile will now and again illumine her thoughtful and expressive features with a look of ineffable sweetness and her voice must be musical and low. (An excellent thing in women provided always that you don't get too much of it). 2. Character, manner, etc. – She must be dignified almost to *hauteur*, and yet have about her a certain indescribable charm of manner (we said 'indescribable' after we had spent ten minutes trying to understand what we really meant ourselves. Jack waved his arm about and said 'You know' and I jerked my head and remarked, 'Exactly'. Under the circumstances 'indescribable' seemed to be the very word. Besides, there's a freedom about it. It doesn't tie you down strictly), and though cold and proud to all else around, submissive and loving to me (Jack, you know. Jack said he thought it quite natural she should love him. At least when he said 'love' he meant have a warm affection for him. Of course he didn't believe in what silly people called 'love' but a woman's nature, so he said was affectionate. She required something to cling to and to look up to. She would cling to and look up to him. He should make a very good husband. He must be master; that would have to be understood from the first but he should be kind and indulgent and easy-going enough if not thwarted). She must be cheerful, amiable and not quick tempered. ('I'm quick tempered myself,' explained Jack, 'and it would never do for her to be the same. I don't mind her having a little temper of her own,' he added, 'so long as she keeps it.' I pointed out that this would not tally with the harmony of disposition that he had insisted upon. I suppose I must have said 'that it would not accord with the harmony' for I know he replied that it would be better to have discord that would produce harmony than harmony that would produce discord. I didn't think it worthwhile to say any more about it after that.) She must be modest and retiring, and above all not a flirt. (No, he couldn't stand a flirt at any price. A flirt was frivolous and vain and conceited and foolish. 'A flirt' – he got quite excited – 'has no real depth of feeling, no truth, no modesty, no womanliness, no – no anything, and I would shun one as I would a serpent.' No, he could *not* stand a flirt.) 3. Character and mental development – She must be thoroughly well educated, not the education of the ordinary school miss who is considered 'finished' when she has a smattering of bad French and worse English, and can make a noise upon the piano. What I mean by a well educated woman is a woman who, beside having a thorough ground work of knowledge on most subjects, is well up in all standard and classical literature, understands and can take an interest in science and art and who is capable of conversing about all general topics, such as theology or politics etc. (In short, a clever, sensible woman who would be a companion to him, who would appreciate and comprehend him and to whom it would be a pleasure to talk and to instruct, one who could sympathise with his aspirations, and assist him, in a small way, towards his ambition. That was his idea.) She must also be domesticated and homely, understand cooking and all such like details of household economy and take a pride in her home, and see to the comfort of her husband and her family. For what higher ambition can a woman have than to be the ministering angel of a home? (That was mine that last bit. I rather like it. I'll write a novel or a play, or something, one of these days and bring that in. The hero might say it at the end of the last act, with his left arm round the heroine's waist and his right hand pointing to the ceiling.) 4. Higher mental attributes – High intellectuality tempered with calm judgement, deep thought, relieved by lively wit, dispassionate justice combined with all a woman's gentleness and mercy, her tender pity, her sweet charity.

That was the sort of wife he wanted.

He said he should not marry for a good many years yet. He thought thirty-five or six was a good age and by that time he would have made his way and be able to afford it, and in a position to keep a carriage and have plenty of servants and go into good society, etc. Whatever could induce a fellow to marry on anything under two thousand a year he could *not* make out.

I was there – Tuesday evening – at Jack's I mean. They live in a six roomed cottage at Highgate. A charming little place just as you turn down the hill by the waterworks, they keep one servant and Jack comes to town of a morning on the top of a threepenny bus. She is a bewitchingly pretty little thing, stands four foot nine and orders Jack about in as authoritative and peremptory a manner as can possibly be assumed by a saucy little dot that cannot keep still for ten seconds and whose hair is always falling down into her eyes. She's dark, with nut brown hair that is ever out of curl, and big round childish eyes and a tiny bud of a mouth that is always laughing or pouting and you can't tell which make it look the prettier. She is the most desperate little flirt – and knows it. She used to send Jack half mad with jealousy about three times a week before they were married; but he has got used to it now. He says 'you can't have everything you know.'

She has had a most expensive finishing education, including all 'extras', at a fashionable Brighton seminary. I have a letter from her by me now, asking me to come down on Sunday. She dispenses with stops altogether, underlines every other word, and spells 'manage' with two n's. Her favourite literature is the 'Family Herald', with an occasional 'Young Ladies Journal', which she hurriedly sits upon whenever she hears Jack coming.

She's very frightened of cows and mice, and will faint at the sight of blood. She is not what you would call a first-class cook. She made a pie once, but has kindly consented not to attempt another. She rather prides herself on her needlework, though she has worked Jack half a dozen pocket handkerchiefs with his initials in blue silk, very big in the corner. They are made of very fine cambric and measure just nine inches square. She started some dusters a week ago, great big things almost as large as herself. She brought them out every evening and sewed a few stitches. Then she'd tie one of them round her head and ask how she looked, and then she'd tie it round Jack's head and laugh at him, then she'd sew a bit more, and then come over with a pitiful grace to show Jack the marks the needle had made on her finger, so that when she'd hemmed about two sides of the first one he took them away, saying that her hands were not big enough to work, and were only meant to be kissed.

She has not quite mastered all the details of book-keeping yet. Jack tells me he came in one day and found her sobbing most bitterly over a little pile of coppers, a miniature account book scored all over with the most remarkable hieroglyphics, and a broken lead pencil. She had started with the best intentions, and had bought a beautiful gilt-edge book, all rules and dates in which to put down everything she spent. But the 'stupid old thing' wouldn't come right. Her accounts conclusively proved that she had spent three shillings and a penny more than she had had, and that there ought to be a balance of four and sixpence, whereas all the money she had left was eightpence halfpenny.

I believe she *thinks* Jack clever, but she *calls* him 'an old stupid'; 'it sounds different though when she says it.' She fell in love with him because he had fair hair, and she likes me, she told Jack, because I've got a nice nose.

As to him he is a perfect slave. Why, he has shaved his whiskers off to please her, I do believe he'd walk on his head if she told him to, and if she expressed a wish for the moon I'm certain he'd start off immediately in a balloon to try and get it for her. He looks upon her as a sort of Fairy Queen, to be worshipped and waited on as a child, to be petted, spoilt and loved.

How ridiculous it is. I am thoroughly surprised at Jack, thoroughly, and yet somehow or other I like him ever so much better now than I did when he was sensible. I don't know what it is, I can't describe it, but it has made a wonderful change in him. It may be that it has taken a little of the conceit out of him. He used to be very conceited. I've told him of it often – or the obstinacy perhaps. At all events it's certain that he is more agreeable and pleasanter altogether, though I can't for the life of me make out how or why. But it's very absurd the whole thing.

I don't see what I've got to laugh at after all. He seems jolly enough, and it's precious dull in these old chambers all by one's self. Perhaps a smooth little face with curls all round it does make a place look more cheerful, that is to those who like such things. It wouldn't suit *me*. Anything would be better though than that big empty chair staring one in the face. How dark it's getting. What a long way off that old chair seems. I wonder if I'm getting sleepy. I can fancy there's somebody in it. I can see a pair of dark brown eyes instead of the two old buttons now, and the bit of torn covering has changed to two little white hands, folded demurely over a neat fitting black dress. Yes, there's the white lace collar and cuffs and the little shoes peeping out underneath. She is sitting there with that laughing look in her eyes, just like she sat last night. She is pretty – very.

'Come in. Boy waiting for an answer? Who is it from? Just light the lamp will you?'

Thursday

Dear Mr. Hartland, – If you have nothing else to do, mamma says will you escort us to the opera tonight – mamma, Ettin and me. It is "Aida". You said last night you would like to hear it. It is a shame to trouble you, but papa cannot come. Oh, mamma's compliments of course. I ought to have begun with that.

Yours sincerely,
Comsie Millingham.

Mamma says I ought not have asked you, I ought to have asked Cousin Tom. Ought I?

'Here, put those things away, Mrs. Cutting. Tell the boy "Mr. Hartland's compliments, and he'll be there in five minutes." What's the time? Give me a candle. Oh, Mrs. Cutting, if Jack should happen to look in tell him I was suddenly called away on business. I don't know what time I shall be back.'

THE PRINCE'S QUEST
by Jerome K Jerome

This early story appeared in Pot Pourri of Gifts Literary and Artistic, *'contributed as a souvenir of the Grand Masonic Bazaar in aid of the annuity fund of Scottish Masonic Benevolence, Edinburgh 1890'. Other contributors to this strange publication included John Stuart Blackie, W E Henley and J M Barrie.*

Once upon a time, in a far-off country, there lived a Prince who ought to have been very happy but wasn't. He reigned in a gorgeous palace, and was rich, and powerful, and great, and had everything he wanted – that is, at least, he had everything he wanted, except the one thing that he wanted more than anything else on earth, and to obtain which he would have given half his kingdom. He would have given the whole for the matter of that, only he had already promised the other half to any one who would tell him what it was he wanted.

Everybody had a guess at it, but nobody seemed able to hit upon it. Everything that was suggested he had; everything that wealth could buy, or skill procure, was his already. So at last he appealed to the wise men of the city, and they put their heads together, and found out the wrong thing, and the Prince became more despondent than ever.

In the palace his jovial companions made laugh and jest, and kept the walls for ever echoing to the tune of their noisy merriment. All day long they hunted the deer through the forest glades, or rode a-hawking in gay cavalcade; and at night there were feasting, and dancing, and song, and the wine ran free, and the mirth ran high, and happiness beamed on every face except the Prince's. In the midst of all the revelry he sat silent and apart, or shunned the chase to muse alone on what this thing could be, the want of which, with all his wealth, made life seem so unfinished.

'Oh, is there no one who can tell me what I want?' sighed the Prince aloud, one day, as he threw himself down on the ground beside a fallen tree.

'I can.'

It was a little old man that spoke; a little bent, withered old man, with wrinkled face and snow-white hair; but his eyes were brighter than a boy's, and his voice was as clear as a sweet-toned bell, and, as he looked down at the Prince from his seat on the tree, he laughed a merry, childish laugh.

The Prince looked up at him, and wondered how he got there, but was too surprised to speak, and only stared in silence at the merry, twinkling eyes.

'Well,' said the little old fellow after a while, 'shall I tell you? Would you like to know what it is you want, or have you come to the sensible conclusion that after all it is not worth the knowing? I think you had better not know,' he went on, changing from gay to grave. 'It may make you only more unhappy. It will bring you pain and trouble. You are young and weak – why seek to know? Rest with the happiness you have, child. Joy is only reached through sorrow.'

But the Prince heeded not the warning. All eagerness and hope, he started up, and caught the old man by the hand, and would not let him go.

'Tell me, you who are wise, and who know,' cried he; 'tell me and I will seek for it through fire and water. I am strong, not weak – strong to dare, to suffer, and to win. I will find it, if it take me all my life, and cost me all my treasure.'

The old man gently laid his hand upon the Prince's head, and a look of pity was in the bright, quick eyes.

'Lad,' said he, and his voice was grave and tender, 'you shall seek your wish. You shall toil for it, and your brain shall ache. You shall wait for it, and your heart shall pant. You shall pass through sorrow and through suffering on your search; but when you are weary and footsore the thought of it shall strengthen you, when your heart is heaviest the hope of it shall raise you up, and in your darkest hour it shall come to you as the touch of a mighty hand. Prince, it is Love you lack. Go seek it.'

So the scales fell from the Prince's eyes, and he stood as one that has suddenly emerged from darkness into light, half-bewildered before he understood. Then stretching out his arms, he called to Love, as though he would draw her down from heaven, and clasp her to his heart.

'Oh, Love,' he cried, 'why have I been so blind as not to know your messenger, who spoke within me? I might have wandered lonely all my life, uncaring and uncared for, and never dreamed of your dear presence, or ever have known that it was for need of your sweet voice that all the world seemed drear.'

Full of gratitude, he turned to thank his mysterious guide, but the little old man was gone.

The Prince's own sentinels scarcely knew their lord when he returned to the palace, and even the old hall-porter who, twenty years ago, had rocked him on his knee, looked hard at him, and seemed inclined to challenge his breathless entrance. Never was a man so changed in half-an-hour before, Out into the woods had gone a moody, sorrowful youth, with wavering steps and dreamy, downcast eyes, while back had come a gallant Prince, with quick, firm tread, and head thrown back, and eyes that flashed with high resolve. Small wonder if the porter was in doubt.

In the banquet-hall his guests already waited his arrival, and hurrying thither straight, without a word he passed up the crowded room until he reached the dais at the end, and there he turned and spoke:

'Friends,' said the Prince, 'rejoice with me, for to-day I have learnt the thing that I want. To-day I have found out what is the only thing on earth that can make me happy – the only thing on earth I have not got – the only thing I cannot do without, and that I mean to seek for till I have found. Let all my true friends join me, and at to-morrow's dawn we will start to search the world for Love.'

Then one and all cheered loud and long, and swore that each was his loyal friend, and swore that they would follow him throughout the whole wide world, and they drank a bumper to success, and another one to Love, and never in that palace had a banquet been so gay, and never before had such merry guests feasted in that hall. Long into the night they drank and sang, and their loud laughter filled the palace full, and overflowed through open door and window out into the stillness, and the red deer browsing heard it, and scudded away down the moonlit glens, or dreamt then of the time when they would fearlessly crop the grass round the very walls of the palace, and rest secure and undisturbed upon its weed-grown terraces.

But no shadow of the coming gloom marred the glittering pageantry on which the morning sun threw down his glory, as gay with silk, and flashing steel, and fluttering plumes, and prancing steeds the gallant train of knights and squires rode slowly down the hill. And hearts were light and hopes were high, but no heart so light as the Prince's, no hopes so high as his, as he rode at the head of that gay throng, the gayest of them all.

At each place that they came to the Prince enquired for Love, but found, to his astonishment, that, though people talked about her a good deal, hardly anyone knew her. Few spoke of her as a reality. Most folks looked upon her as a joke; others, as a popular delusion; while the one or two who owned to having known her seemed half ashamed of the acquaintanceship. There were shams and imitations in abundance, but the real thing, when acknowledged, was considered vulgar, and no one knew or cared what had become of her.

The first place at which they halted was the town of Common-Sense – a most uncomfortable place, all full of close and narrow streets that led to no-where, and inhabited by a race celebrated for the strength of their lungs, it being reckoned that one man of Common-Sense was equal to a dozen poll-parrots, and could talk down fifty men of Intelligence (their natural enemies) in less than half an hour. The religion of this charming people was touching in its simplicity. It consisted of a firm and earnest belief that they were infallible, and that everybody else was a fool; and each man worshipped himself.

They were quite indignant when the Prince asked them where Love was.

'We know nothing at all about her,' said the men of Common-Sense. 'What have we to do with Love? What do you take us for?'

The Prince was too polite to tell them what he took them for, so merely bidding them adieu with a pitying smile, rode off to seek elsewhere for Love.

But he had no better luck at the next place they came to. This was Tom Tiddler's Land, and the people there were very busy indeed. So busy were they, picking up the gold and the silver, that they had not time even to make themselves respectable, and their hands were especially dirty – but then it was rather dirty work.

'Love!' said the people of Tom Tiddler's Land. 'We don't keep it. Never heard of it. Don't know what it is. But dare say we could get it for you. What are you willing to go to for it?'

'You can't buy it,' explained the Prince. 'It is given.'

'Then you won't get it here, young man,' was the curt reply; and they went on with their grovelling.

At last the Prince came to the City of Science, where he was most hospitably received, and where for the first time he learnt the great truth that everything is just precisely what one always thought it wasn't, and that nothing is what one thinks it is. The inhabitants were all philosophers, and their occupation consisted of finding out things that nobody wanted to know, and in each day proving that what they themselves had stated the day before was all wrong. They were very clever people, and knew everything – Love included. She was there, in the city, they told the delighted Prince, and they would take him to her.

So, after showing him over the town and explaining to him what everything wasn't they took him into their museum, which was full of the most wonderful things, and in the centre was Love – the most wonderful of them all. The Prince couldn't help laughing when he saw it, but the philosophers were very proud of it. It sat upright and stiff on a straight-backed chair, and was as cold as ice.

'Made it ourselves,' said the philosophers. 'Isn't it beautiful! Acts by clockwork, and never goes wrong. Warranted perfect in every respect.'

'It's very charming,' answered the Prince, trying to swallow down his disappointment; 'but I'm afraid it's not the sort of thing I wanted.'

'Why, what's amiss with it? It's got all the latest improvements.'

'Yes,' replied the Prince with a sigh, 'that's just it; I wanted it with all the old faults.'

Again the Prince journeyed on, and came to a town where lived a very knowing people called 'Men of the World', who had the reputation of 'knowing their way about' – a reputation, the acquirement of which it was difficult to understand, seeing they never, by any chance, went outside their own town – a remarkably small one, although the inhabitants firmly believed that it was the biggest and most important place on the earth, and that no other city was worth living in for a day.

A dim oil-lamp burnt night and day in the centre of the town, and the inhabitants were under the impression that all light came from that, for as they crawled about on their hands and knees, and never raised their eyes from the ground, they knew nothing about the sun. When they had crawled once forwards and backwards across their little town, they thought they had seen 'life', and would squat in a corner, and yawn, till they died.

When the Prince mentioned the name of Love to these creatures, they burst into a coarse, loud laugh. 'Is that what you call it?' said they. 'Why, wherever do you come from? We know what you mean, though. Come along.' Any they took him into a dingy room and showed him a hideous, painted thing that made him sick to look upon.

'Let us leave this place quickly,' said the Prince, turning to his followers. 'I cannot breathe in this foul air. Let us get out into God's light again.' So they mounted in haste and rode away, leaving the men who 'knew their way about' crawling about the ways they knew so well.

Farther and farther into the weary world wandered the Prince on his search; but Love was still no nearer, and though his heart was ever brave, it beat less hopefully every day. Time after time he heard of her, and started off, only to find some worthless sham – a golden image – a dressed-up doll – a lifeless statue – a giggling fool. Shams wherever he went, and men and women worshipping, and hugging them close to their breasts, knowing all the while that they were shams; and each time the Prince turned away, more sick at heart than ever.

And now, not a single one of all who had shouted their loyalty so loudly was left, when weary, baffled, and disheartened, the Prince at last turned back. A great longing was upon him to be once more among his own people, and to see his own land again; and so, with this last hope, he still toiled on, and each day pressed on quicker, fearing lest death might overtake him by the way, and that his tired eyes never more would rest upon the old grey towers and sweet green woods of home.

But the dreary road came to an end at length, and one evening he looked down upon his palace, as it lay before him bathed in the red of the sinking sun. Restful, now, he stood for a while, feasting his hungry eyes upon the longed-for sight, and then his thoughts ebbed slowly back to that morning, long ago, when he had bidden it adieu, and had ridden forth in the world upon his quest for Love.

How changed the place! How changed himself since then!

He had left it as a gallant Prince with all the pride of pomp around him, and a gaudy throng of flattering courtiers at his side. He crept back, broken-hearted and alone. He had left it standing fair and stately in the morning light, and bright with life and sound; now it was ruined, desolate, and silent; the bats flew out of the banquet-hall, and the grass grew on the hearths. Another had usurped his throne; his people had forgotten him, and not even a dog was there to give him a welcome home.

As he passed through the damp, chill rooms a thousand echoing foot-steps started up on every side, as though his entrance had disturbed some ghostly revel, and when, having reached a little room that in old times he had been wont to go to for solitude, he entered, and shut himself in, it seemed as though the frightened spirits had hurried away, slamming a thousand doors behind them.

There, in the darkness, he sat himself down, and buried his face in his hands, and wept; and sat there long through the silent hours, lost in his own bitter thoughts. So lost, that he did not hear a gentle tapping at the door – did not hear the door open, and a timid voice asking to come in – did not hear a light step close beside him, nor see a little maiden sit herself down at his feet – did not know she was there till, at last, with a sigh, he raised his head and looked into the gloom. Then his eyes met hers, and he started, and looked down at the sweet, shy face, amazed, and half in doubt.

'Why, you are Love!' said the Prince, taking her little hands in his. 'Where have you been, sweet? I've sought you everywhere.'

'Not everywhere,' said Love, nestling against him with a little half-sad laugh; 'not everywhere. I've been here all the time. I was here when you went away, and I've been waiting for you to come back – so long.'

And so the Prince's quest was ended.

JEROME'S RAREST BOOK – *WEEDS*
by Alan R Whitby

In February 1968 a letter was auctioned at Sotheby's written by Jerome K Jerome to the publisher Arrowsmith, that identified him as the writer of *Weeds* – a story in seven chapters written under the pseudonym 'K McK'. The intention had been to publish *Weeds* as part of the Arrowsmith's Note-book Series for one shilling and sixpence. These were small books about 11 cm by 171/2 cm in size that were bound at the top, rather like a shorthand notebook. This allowed the book to be printed on one side of the paper only. Consequently, a slight tale of 118 pages appears at first sight to be twice as long.

The original publisher's cloth was brown, but the copy in the British Library has now faded to a yellow ochre colour. For some reason it appears to have been withdrawn and never went on general sale. The April 1991 *Book and Magazine Collector* gives it a value of between £50 and £100, but it would be interesting to learn if a copy has ever come on the open market, and if so, what price this rarity fetched.

The title page contains the aphorism, 'Everyone is as God made him, and oftentimes a great deal worse', and then on the following page is a little two line verse that was to prove apt for a book withdrawn from publication:

> Some said 'John print it', others said 'Not so'
> Some said 'It might do good', others said 'No'.

So why was this book written by Jerome under a pseudonym and then suppressed? This writer has no special information, other than having actually read the book. It is not a humorous work at all. It came out (or rather didn't) when Jerome was extremely popular for *Idle Thoughts*, *Three Men*, and *Diary of a Pilgrimage*. What is curious is that the year of intended publication, 1892, found Jerome a married man for a little over three years. *Weeds* is the story of a perfect marriage that founders after three years, when the husband develops a passion for a beautiful young girl of 17 or 18. What would Ettie have thought of that?

The extremely dated approach to the subject matter makes the book a disappointment. Apart from Jerome completionists there would be no demand for it today, but perhaps one day an enterprising publisher could squeeze it into an anthology, whose more popular pieces would ensure a market.

In the meantime, for all Jerome readers who do not have access to the British Library's copy, here is a summary of the plot of *Weeds – A Story in Seven Chapters*. Where possible, the original language is used.

CHAPTER ONE – THE GARDEN

We are introduced to Dick and Daisy Selwyn at the breakfast table. They have been married for three years, and it appears a perfect match. Daisy has received a letter from her cousin, Jessie Craig, who is going to visit them that day. They have not seen her since before they were married three years ago. Dick is not very enthusiastic. He remembers her as a 14 year old who was always there in the way when they were sweethearting. Dick muses on the time he proposed to Daisy, and how before they were married she had been quite ill. Even now she still occasionally talked in her sleep. Making sure the servants are not watching he kisses Daisy and goes off to work.

CHAPTER TWO – OF THE WEEDS IN THE GARDEN

Dick works as the junior partner in a firm of indigo importers. At work he daydreams how, as his fortunes improve, he and Daisy can move to a bigger and better villa. He sees them both old and happy, surrounded by their family. Love is like a flower that grows in a man's heart. However, also in Dick's heart are weeds – evil thoughts that keep appearing. (A coy veil is drawn over the exact details.) But Daisy will never know of this. But he worries – is he worse than other men, or only troubled with a more morbid conscience? At five o'clock he leaves work and goes home to his little suburban house.

CHAPTER THREE – THE WEEDS GROW

When Dick arrives home he meets Jessie, and what a surprise! She has grown up into a beautiful young woman. Jessie does not understand her power. Remarks that previously would have caused her to be scolded and given lines to write out, all of a sudden the menfolk now find witty and interesting. She can't quite understand it ... Some teasing occurs – Dick is teased about his first reaction at hearing she was coming, and Jessie is teased about a possible suitor named Barnard. But at the bottom of Dick's mind, like mud at the bottom of a rippling stream, he is fascinated by Jessie – how white and soft she is. He finds himself watching her more and more. When they momentarily touch, he flushes; and an evening around the piano for a sing–song does not improve matters. But at the end of the evening when Jessie has gone to bed, he holds Daisy so close that nothing could come between them, not even so slim a thing as the shadow of an evil thought.

CHAPTER FOUR – THE VIGILANCE OF THE HUSBANDMAN

Jessie stays for a week and the mutual attraction grows. It is like a weed that should be plucked out. Nothing actually happens, but now there is new meaning in little glances and touches. At night 'Worldly Prudence' visits Dick and talks to him – 'Don't be a fool, don't risk a lifetime's happiness for the gratification of a few chance moments'. He resolves to reform and is deliberately cool towards Jessie the next morning. However, Jessie has no visit from 'Dame Worldly Prudence' and cannot understand his sudden change of manner. Jessie's visit comes to an end and she is leaving for Kent. Daisy suggests that Dick take her to Charing Cross Station in a cab. Dick tries to persuade Daisy to come but she declines, and then – when it is too late – she wishes she had gone. In the cab, Dick and Jessie talk about her trip abroad which will last a year. He puts his arm around her and they have a brief, but interrupted embrace. But once seeing her off, Dick longs to be back with Daisy.

CHAPTER FIVE – THE NEGLIGENCE OF THE HUSBANDMAN

Over the next few months the memory of Jessie lingers. Dick allows his imagination to run away with him a few times, but rationalises that there is no harm in it because the girl is now far away. Daisy gets letters from Jessie that suggest that Barnard is now paying her a lot of attention. But then suddenly a letter comes – Jessie is coming to spend a fortnight with them before going abroad again. Dick tries to put Daisy off the idea of having her come, but is not successful. He wishes he could tell Daisy the truth, but he cannot, his evil thoughts and passions are now deep rooted. So Jessie arrives. After dinner, Dick suggests that they all go to an exhibition, but Daisy has a slight nervous disorder, so she asks Dick and Jessie to go without her. Over the next two weeks Daisy remains ill, and Dick and Jessie are thrown together more and more. The attraction grows, they now have fewer inhibitions when on their own, but they don't go too far! In fact, Dick feels quite virtuous, under all the circumstances he feels he is quite a modern Joseph. (For those who are rusty on their *Book of Genesis*, when Potipher's wife made advances on Joseph, he fled.) But then – it happens. Returning home from the theatre, as usual Daisy has gone to bed unwell. Suddenly – Dick and Jessie embrace. While so entangled, Dick looks over her shoulder into the mirror. The door stands open, and from the glass there looks out at him a face – a face dead, like his own. The door softly closes. Disentangling himself, Dick leaves the house and wanders the streets like a man who has committed a crime trying to escape.

CHAPTER SIX – THE STRANGLING OF THE FLOWERS

Dick returns home at the first light of dawn to be met by a servant. The mistress is unwell. They call a doctor who pronounces that she is very weak and has been overtaxing herself in some way. Dick should take her away to the country when he can. He goes to Daisy but she is in an exhausted sleep, so then he goes to work. At work his mind is in a turmoil – perhaps she will think that what she saw was a dream? Perhaps she was sleepwalking? She used to sleepwalk when she was ill four years ago. He can't bring himself to go home after work, so visits the theatre and then walks the streets until late. On arriving home he goes to Daisy but she is asleep. Suddenly she starts talking in her sleep – 'A dream, I cannot look, I should hate him – don't let me see his face …' She wakes suddenly to see Dick. Was it a dream or was it the truth? Please tell her it was a dream! He cannot answer. In a typical 1890's theatrical moment, he sinks to the floor and bows his head and she gives a cry of despair. 'What do you wish?' he asks her, 'Shall I go away?' She answers: 'I don't know. I cannot think just now. I must wait a little while. Leave me alone.' Dick leaves.

CHAPTER SEVEN – IN THE WILDERNESS

Jessie knows nothing that has gone on between Dick and Daisy. With her inexperience of life she doesn't understand. There is no harm surely? It is only a little flirtation. Why, Dick is like a brother … isn't he? She has been waiting for him, but hears him going to Daisy's room. Suddenly she hopes that Daisy will die. Dick and Jessie meet next at breakfast. They exchange empty commonplaces. He is repulsed. All his pain is for Daisy. Jessie has come between them and ruined their lives – it is all her fault. Jessie realises that Daisy knows. The next day is the day of Jessie's departure. Daisy sends a message down, she is too ill to say goodbye. But then she appears. In her hand is a letter for Jessie that the servant took upstairs by mistake. It is from Barnard. She asks Jessie, 'What answer will you give him?' Jessie raises her head. Daisy sees the face of a woman old before her time. Then suddenly she sees again the shy awkward child in trouble and puts her arms around her. 'May God forgive him,' she says, very low.

One evening, a few days later, Daisy has given the servants a holiday and is on her own when Dick returns from work. She tells him she is going away. It will be difficult for both of them, but more so for her. She has tried to feel differently, but cannot. She does not feel anger for him or sorrow for herself, she feels as if she has been turned to stone. She goes out and he closes the door. As the first drops of rain fall, he wonders does she have her umbrella? Should he follow with it? Suddenly he has the desire to rush out and say all the thoughts in his heart, and starts for the door. But then he checks himself. 'She would not understand,' he says and, returning to the window, he stands watching the dead leaves whirling in the wind.

The originals of the famous Three Men in a Boat: (l–r) Carl Hentschel (Harris), George Wingrave (George) and Jerome K Jerome (J)

Mrs Jerome K Jerome

5
THREE MEN – IN A BOAT
& ON THE BUMMEL

THE STORY BEHIND JEROME'S TWO COMIC MASTERPIECES
by Jeremy Nicholas

Basil Boothroyd, a celebrated editor of *Punch*, once regaled his fellow-humorist, the young Miles Kington, with the story of a disastrous visit to Wigan where he'd been invited to give an after-dinner speech. One terrible mishap had followed another in the course of the trip and the amused Kington asked Boothroyd if the story was true. 'Never,' admonished Boothroyd, 'never ask a humorist if things really happened.' 'Yes, but did they?' persisted Kington. 'Not in that order,' admitted Boothroyd, 'not all on the same day – and not all of it to me.'

That's all you need to know about *Three Men in a Boat* and *Three Men on the Bummel*. Jerome, as he underlines in the preface to *Boat*, recorded 'events that really happened. All that has been done is to colour them; and, for this, no extra charge has been made.' But surely, you ask, the main protagonists are as fictional as Noddy and Big Ears … aren't they? Well, no. There really were three friends – George Wingrave, Carl Hentschel and Jerome himself – on whom Jerome based his main characters, who made literally scores of trips up and down the Thames and cycled together across Europe to the Black Forest. However, to then see photographs of these three 'fictional' characters actually lounging around on the river bank is the equivalent of hearing Noddy speak: it makes you rub your eyes. Only Montmorency never existed. 'Montmorency I evolved out of my inner consciousness,' admitted Jerome. 'Dog friends that I came to know later have told me it was true to life.'

Jerome was acting as a clerk to a firm of solicitors and lodging just off London's Tottenham Court Road when Wingrave entered his life. George was a bank clerk (who 'goes to sleep at a bank from ten to four each day, except Saturdays, when they wake him up and put him outside at two') and was living in a back room of the same house. The landlady suggested that, to save money, the two might share a room. They 'chummed' together for some years – both shared a love of the theatre – and a life-long friendship was formed.

George, who remained a bachelor, rose to become manager of Barclays Bank in the Strand and outlived the other two, dying at the age of 79 in

March 1941. Carl Hentschel, rechristened William Samuel Harris by Jerome, was born in Lodz, Russian Poland, in March 1864, arriving in England with his parents at the age of five. His father invented the half-tone photographic blocks which revolutionised the illustration of books and magazines and Carl left school at fourteen to join his father's flourishing business. At only 23 he set up on his own, the start of a long and distinguished career, one which merited an obituary in *The Times*. Again, it was the theatre that cemented the friendship with Jerome. Hentschel co-founded The Playgoer's Club and claimed that, with few exceptions, he had attended every London first night since 1879. He died in January 1930, leaving a wife and three children. In 1981, during the West End run of his one-man adaptation of *Three Men in a Boat*, the present writer was introduced to a sprightly, elderly lady. She had much enjoyed the performance, she said, and it was a book she knew extremely well. 'You see,' she continued, 'Harris was my uncle.'

So there were the ready-made characters, save one little Jeromian twist. Throughout *Three Men in a Boat*, readers are left in no doubt that Harris is fond of a drink: there is the episode of the swans at Shiplake and the reference to the small number of pubs in the country which Harris has not visited. In fact, Hentschel/Harris was the only teetotaller of the three. There were also ready-made events: for instance, the melodramatic story of the drowned woman at Goring (Chapter 16) is based on the tragic suicide in July 1887 of a Gaiety Girl named Alicia Douglas. Jerome almost certainly read the story in the local newspaper.

It was only in the mid-1870s that the Thames had been discovered as a pleasure-ground. London was expanding at the rate of knots (to use a suitably nautical term) and the middle- and working-class population suddenly woke up to the recreational potential of the great river, with its towns, villages and watering holes lying only a cheap rail fare away. Boating on the Thames became the latest craze: in 1888, the year in which Jerome wrote *Three Men in a Boat*, there were 8,000 registered boats on the river; by the following year there were 12,000. Jerome was therefore writing about the 'in thing' – the book doubtless swelled the number of boating fans – though the three friends had caught the bug earlier than most. 'At first,' recalled Jerome, 'we would have the river almost to ourselves … and sometimes would fix up a trip of three or four days or a week, doing the thing in style and camping out.'

In other words, there were plenty of excursions to provide a writer with plenty of material. Jerome had, by this time, been a journalist, his first published book, *On the Stage – and Off*, had successfully used his all-too-real experiences as a professional actor to great comic effect, and *The Idle Thoughts of an Idle Fellow* had proved his gift as a humorous essayist: a magpie like Jerome would have brought his notebook to the river.

Idle Thoughts had been serialised in the monthly magazine *Home Chimes* and it was its editor, F W Robinson, who took on Jerome's next project, *The Story of the Thames*. 'I did not intend to write a funny book, at first,' Jerome confessed in his memoirs. The book was to have concentrated on the river's scenery and history with passages of humorous relief. 'Somehow it would not come. It seemed to be all humorous relief. By grim determination I succeeded … in writing a dozen or so slabs of history and working them in, one to each chapter.' Robinson promptly slung out most of them and insisted that Jerome came up with a better title. 'Half way through I hit upon *Three Men In A Boat*, because nothing else seemed right.'

The first instalment came out in the August issue of 1888, the last in June the following year. Meanwhile, Jerome was wooing the Bristol publishers J W Arrowsmith who brought out the book that summer. Had Mr. Arrowsmith not accepted, it would have been the literary parallel of Decca turning down The Beatles. Years later Arrowsmith, commenting on the amount of royalties he paid Jerome, confessed he was at a loss to know of what became of all the copies of *Three Men In A Boat*. 'I often think,' he said, 'that the public must eat them.'

Years of struggle, deprivation and uncertainty were over for good. Jerome was thirty in 1889, the year which also saw the completion of the Firth of Forth rail bridge, the Eiffel Tower and London's Savoy Hotel. *Three Men in a Boat* is now just as much part of the fabric as these noble edifices. Twenty years after it first appeared in hard covers, the book had sold over 200,000 copies in Britain and over a million throughout the United States though, as it was published before the Copyright Convention, Jerome never made a penny from the American sales. Only the German translation outsold the inordinately-successful Russian edition. To date it has been published in almost every language in the world including Japanese, Pitman's Shorthand, Hebrew, Afrikaans (*Drie Swape op De Rivier*), Irish (*Triur Fear I Mbad*) and Portuguese (*Tres Inglises No Estrangeiro*). It has been adapted into every performance medium – filmed three times (1920, 1933 and 1956), televised by Tom Stoppard, turned into a musical by Hubert Gregg, made into a stage play on several occasions, read aloud on radio and spoken-word cassette numerous times and, at least twice, done the rounds as a one-man show. *Three Men in a Boat*, incidentally, enjoyed the rare distinction of coming out of copyright (in 1977, fifty years after the author's death), then going back into copyright (for just one year, 1996) after new laws extended copyright to seventy years. It has never been out of print.

In a foreword to the 1909 edition Jerome remained puzzled as to the reasons for the undiminished popularity of *Three Men in a Boat*. He had, he believed, 'written books that appeared to him more humorous'. But then Beethoven could never understand the popularity of his 'Moonlight' sonata, complaining that he had written far better works. Not that Jerome ever occupied the same Olympian heights as Beethoven; no one has ever mistaken him as a great literary thinker. (Somebody once accused H G Wells of 'hiding his intellect and trying to pass himself off as another Jerome'.) He was not a virtuosic comic novelist able to concoct the joyously-improbable plots of a Wodehouse, Waugh or Tom Sharpe (though it is extraordinary how many people assume that Jerome was a contemporary of Wodehouse). Extended forms were not Jerome's forte. He was better at the scherzo than the symphony. Within these limitations he was a master. He knew all about comic timing, how to transfer it intact to the page 'live' – and how to polish. Compare the opening paragraph of *Three Men in a Boat* with the clumsy opening passage as it first appeared in Home Chimes:

'There was George and Bill Harris and me – I should say I – and Montmorency. It ought to be "were": there were George and Bill Harris and me – I, and Montmorency. It is very odd, but good grammar always sounds so stiff and strange to me. I suppose it is having been brought up in our family that is the cause of this. Well, there we were, sitting in my room, smoking, and talking, and talking about how bad we were – bad from a medical point of view, I mean, of course.'

Nevertheless, there are long passages of mawkish purple prose (the end of Chapter Ten, for example, with the 'goodly knights' riding through the deep wood) that must have made readers wince even in 1889. It is as though Jerome felt obliged to insert a four-part fugue in the middle of a popular song, merely in order to give the critics something to chew. The construction of the book, too, is lop-sided: we are nearly a third of the way through the book before anyone rows a stroke, and the return journey is accomplished in eleven brief pages (out of 315). Its shortcomings have never mattered one jot to succeeding generations of devoted fans.

What was entirely new about *Boat* was the style in which it was written. Conan Doyle, Rider Haggard, Rudyard Kipling and Robert Louis Stevenson were widely read and highly popular but Jerome differed in two respects: his story was not of some fantastical adventure in a far-off land, peopled by larger-than-life heroes and villains, but of three very ordinary blokes having a high old time just down the road, so to speak; and, in an age when literary grandiloquence and solemnity were not in short supply, Jerome provided a breath of fresh air. In the preface to *Idle Thoughts*, Jerome had set out his stall: 'What readers ask now-a-days in a book is that it should improve, instruct and elevate. This book wouldn't elevate a cow.' He used everyday figures of speech for the first time ('colloquial clerk's English of the year 1889' as one critic described it) and was very, very funny. The Victorians had simply never come across anything like it.

Jerome was taken to task by the serious critics. They hated the 'new humour', the 'vulgarity' of the language and its appeal to the 'Arrys and 'Arriets (a term coined by the middle-classes to describe the lower-classes and those who dropped their aitches). *Punch* dubbed Jerome ' 'Arry K 'Arry'. 'One might have imagined,' JKJ recalled, 'that the British Empire was in danger … *The Standard* spoke of me as a menace to English letters; and *The Morning Post* as an example of the sad results to be expected from the over-education of the lower orders … I think I may claim to have been, for the first twenty years of my career, the best abused author in England.' Perhaps the most remarkable thing about *Boat* is that, compared with almost all its contemporaries and despite Jerome's wide use of then-fashionable colloquialisms, the book has dated very little.

Three Men On The Bummel (*Three Men on Wheels* as it appeared in America) is often unfairly chastised as being an ineffectual afterthought. True, it is not on the same exalted level, but it is written with the same verve and energy, and the set pieces (the boot shop, Harris and his wife on the tandem, Harris confronting the hose-pipe, the animal riot in the hill-top restaurant) are as polished and funny (funnier, some would say) as anything in the earlier book. Much time is spent, to the reader's smug self-satisfaction, observing the peculiarities of the German nation and its people with wry amusement and not a little affection (the schools of Imperial Germany, with characteristic earnestness, adopted it as a textbook). Jerome is also uncannily perceptive about the political catastrophes that were so shortly to overtake the country. But too often one loses sight of the *bummel* itself, the book's *raison d'être*.

The trump card that *Bummel* lacks, and which makes *Three Men in a Boat* what it is, is the River Thames. It provides the framework for Jerome's discursive narrative. He can stray from the present adventure as much as he likes, he can stop for his set pieces whether they be on the river or elsewhere, he can recall events from previous trips (the cheeses taken from Liverpool to London, the visit to Hampton Court maze), but the river holds the whole thing together and gives the book its satisfying unity. The best television situation comedies rely on this same device, a world with clearly-defined parameters. A ramble through Germany and the Black Forest does not provide that.

None of this fully explains the popularity of Jerome's masterpiece. Perhaps it's a pointless exercise, like pulling off the wings of a Red Admiral to see how it flies. Jerome concluded that 'be the explanation what it may, I can take credit to myself for having written this book. That is, if I did write it. For really I hardly remember doing so. I remember only feeling very young and absurdly pleased with myself for reasons that concern only myself.'

Miles Kington told another Boothroyd anecdote that encapsulates perfectly the art of the English humorist as personified by Jerome and exemplified in these two life-enhancing books. Basil Boothroyd had just returned from holiday. Kington bumped into him. 'Hallo, Basil. Have a good holiday?' 'Awful,' replied Boothroyd. 'Nothing went wrong at all.'

THE RISE OF THE OFFICE CLERK IN LITERARY CULTURE 1880–1939
by Jonathan Wild

Lecturer in Victorian Literature at the University of Edinburgh

The following is an edited extract from The Rise of the Office Clerk in Literary Culture 1880–1939, *p.p. 224 illustr., hardback, £45, Pub. Palgrave Macmillan. Dr Wild has written an innovative study investigating the emergence and impact of the lower middle class on British print culture through the figure of the office clerk. Using a variety of source materials – including novels, magazines, newspapers, letters and life writing – the author traces the literary profile of the white collar worker during a time of unprecedented change in class and culture. This interdisciplinary work offers important insights into a previously – and undeservedly – neglected area of social and book history. Chapter 4 is devoted almost entirely to Jerome.*

In spite of routinely hostile criticism, Jerome and his fellow clerks-turned-writers (including W W Jacobs and W Pett Ridge) enjoyed considerable commercial success in the period before the Great War. This success was in large part due to the opportunities opened up by publications such as Robinson's *Home Chimes* which provided numerous outlets for the work of a new generation of late Victorian professional writers.

Taking into account the close attention Jerome gave to selecting his publisher and in anticipating the prospective readership for *Three Men in a Boat*, it is unsurprising that he had already taken considerable pains with the characterisation and setting of his literary 'product'. Rather than providing his anticipated clerkly readership with a straightforward mirror of themselves and their lives, Jerome decided to offer to his audience characters and scenes which reflected social aspirations within their sphere. To put it another way, Jerome constructed in *Three Men* the sort of lifestyle that, say, Lupin Pooter begins to live only after he assumes his £200-a-year position with Gylterson. A pre-promotion Lupin Pooter might indeed have provided Jerome with his likely target market; one can easily imagine the appeal to impoverished clerks of the self-confident demeanour and leisured indolence displayed by Jerome's 'Men'. Jerome helped to manufacture this atmosphere of indolence by consciously excising occupational work from the book. While work is mentioned as a comic concept – 'I like work; it fascinates me. I can sit and look at it for hours' (144) – only George's job as a bank clerk is defined in any detail. The lightly fictionalised Jerome, called 'J' in the novel, neglects any mention of his place in the solicitor's office, something that, given the anecdotal nature of the work, might appear a surprising omission. Only when we accept that this absence is a deliberately calculated decision on Jerome's part, does the lack of context here become explicable.

Where the banker's occupation was sufficiently prestigious to warrant incorporation in Jerome's scheme, casting a *mere* solicitor's clerk in the boat might bring into question the status of the seemingly urbane 'Men'.[i] Jerome's decision to 'forget' to give J an occupation was evidently designed to avoid the impression that his characters were in fact 'cockney' clerks aping their betters.

Jerome elaborated this relative embourgeoisement of his clerks in *Three Men* in a number of ways. Although he shows George and J living in furnished lodgings, he gives little impression in the story that they live on a modest income. During the time when Jerome himself was a Thames-rowing clerk he was earning about twenty-five shillings a week at the solicitor's, but his fictionalised counterpart offers few signs of these limited finances. Details casually dropped into the text imply a relaxed attitude to money: the 'Men', for example, routinely tip, thinking nothing of slipping half-a-crown into the hand of a railway engine driver to persuade him to change his timetable (48); they enjoy 'the odour of Burgundy, and the smell of French sauces'

(184); and whereas other contemporary fictional clerks meticulously record the extravagance of a rare cab journey, here there is an easy familiarity with this form of transport (47). Elsewhere J additionally gives the impression of being on equal terms with the professional classes, describing, in an early passage concerning hypochondria, a medical man as 'an old chum of mine' (9). It is, however, the presence of the dog that constitutes the most obvious affectation. Jerome admitted in his autobiography that Montmorency was an invention 'evolved out of my inner consciousness',[ii] and, all things considered, it could not have been otherwise. The type of lodging-house life and office routine known to Jerome would offer little scope for dog ownership. In the novel, however, the presence of the dog emphasises the general atmosphere of the leisured Englishman on holiday. The very name 'Montmorency' seems deliberately evocative of the established middle and upper classes.

Jerome's determination to control the social typing of his characters is also intriguingly revealed in a small but significant textual amendment that was made between the serialised and single volume versions of the tale. At the opening of the *Home Chimes* version, Jerome has his first person narrator J remarking:

> There was George, and Bill Harris, and me – I should say I – and Montmorency. It ought to be "were": there were George, and Bill Harris, and me – I, and Montmorency. It is very odd, but good grammar always sounds so stiff and strange to me. I suppose it is having been brought up in our family that is the cause of this. Well, there we were, sitting in my room ….[iii]

This self-conscious grammatical slip is excised by the time of the Arrowsmith's version of the tale: 'There were four of us – George, and William Samuel Harris, and Myself, and Montmorency' (7). Jerome made very few changes between published versions of the tale (indeed the 3/6 Arrowsmith's edition was published before the four-penny serialisation was completed in November 1889) and so this amendment to the introductory sentence appears to carry additional significance. Did Jerome decide between published versions of the tale that he wanted his narrator to appear a more cultured and a better educated guide? Did the weakness in grammar signalled in the original introduction place the speaker a little too close to the new breed of Cockney upstart clerk that was then becoming widely recognised? While Jerome and his friends were not men of independent means they would also have considered themselves as quite distinct from the Cockney 'Arrys much discussed in the contemporary press.[iv] In an apparent effort to establish this distinction conclusively, Jerome has his Three Men witnessing a separate boating 'party of provincial 'Arrys and 'Arriets, out for a moonlight sail' (88). The exchange between groups is notable for the way in which the Cockneys refer to J as 'sir' and as 'a gentleman'. Jerome clearly felt that this social disparity between the two parties on the Thames was, given the current social climate, a vital one to establish. The alteration of the tale's first lines, like this class marker, appears similarly designed to strengthen this distinction in readiness for its anticipated '3/6 public'.

Reading *Three Men in a Boat* over a century after its original publication, it would appear that Jerome was successful in achieving the above aims. Throughout the tale he manages to lend a bourgeois gloss to a narrative rooted in a distinctly autobiographical framework. The idyll he defines offers the impression of middle class ease, in a setting and form of transport familiar to, and within reach of, the majority of young clerks in London. Jerome was apparently so effective in creating the appearance of relative affluence for his characters that later dramatisations of the novel have tended to overlook the elements of the work that might suggest the 'Three Men's' more modest background. Instead, the characters in film and television versions of the work commonly affect the plummy accents and the carefree manners that imply a familiarity with an English Public School environment rather than a Board school one: in the 1957 film version, for example, the indisputably middle-class actors Jimmy Edwards and David Tomlinson were cast as Harris and J, whilst the 1976 Tom Stoppard television adaptation similarly employed Michael Palin and Tim Curry in these roles. This popular reinvention of the book seemingly inflates the social status of the Three Men to higher echelons of the middle class than those which Jerome had intended for his characters, indeed, one feels that this reconfiguration of the work in later twentieth century book illustrations and dramatisations risks making 'swells' out of the Three Men. While Jerome was careful in the text of *Three Men* to ensure that his characters were not mistaken for 'Arrys', he was equally determined that the men were distinguished from 'swells'. When they reach Maidenhead, for example, J records that the town is 'too snobby to be pleasant', adding that 'it is the haunt of the river swell and his overdressed female companion' (117).

It appears that Jerome was pronounced guilty of 'vulgarity' in the critical courtroom primarily because of the dialogue he chose for his 'Three Men'. The criticism of *The Saturday Review* was typical in basing its attack on Jerome's extensive use of slang. While *The Saturday Review's* critic does offer praise for Jerome's skill in recording the current clerk's argot, the compliment is heavily qualified:

> For the future student of late Victorian slang, Three Men in a Boat will be invaluable, if he is able to understand it …. In some of the sporting newspapers slang of this kind, and indeed of a much worse kind, may be discovered, but we do not recollect to have met any other book entirely written in it. In a sense, too, Three Men in a Boat, is a much truer specimen of lower middle-class English than are the paragraphs in the coloured newspapers, because they are exaggerated and non-natural, while Jerome is amazingly real. That it was worth doing, we do not say; indeed, we have a very decided opinion that it was not.[v]

The tone and angle of attack of this criticism was echoed in a *Punch* review, published in February 1890, by which time the tale had already proved a popular success. The *Punch* criticism usefully provides an index of the expressions which it considered particularly irksome: 'bally idiot', 'doing a mouch', 'boss the job', 'put a pipe in his mouth, and spread himself over a chair', 'land him with a frying pan', 'fat-headed chunk', and 'who the thunder'.[vi] These expressions, *Punch's* critic 'Baron de Book-Worms' scathingly suggested, were imported from 'Yankee-land, and patented here by the *Sporting Times* and its imitators', and had then trickled down into the parlance of the tale's characters. Jerome was later to recognise in this attack on his use of slang the existence of a double standard. In an article published in his own magazine, *The Idler*, in 1897, he argued that Kipling had contemporaneously used slang expressions such as 'bally' and 'rot', but had been more aware of the prejudice of the critics and had therefore 'taken the precaution to make his characters the younger sons of noblemen, so the language in that case was allowed to be perfectly correct'.[vii] Kipling's prestigious position as the established spokesman of Empire clearly rankled with Jerome when he considered his own critical reputation as a reviled Cockney upstart and 'new humorist'.

The public and critics seem to estimate the quality of literature according to the social quality of the characters. One book-reviewer, referring to Mr. Wells' *Wheels of Chance,* wrote, 'It does not need very great insight to analyse the feelings of a draper's assistant' ... . 'I was never favourably reviewed myself by the superior critic until I had gumption enough to make my hero marry the daughter of a peer.'[viii]

Jerome, although recognising the potentially limiting nature of this state of affairs, also realised the importance of conformity for a writer in his delicate financial position. To alienate his socially mobile readership with a succession of books labelled 'vulgar' by influential critics might prove disastrous in the long term. Although the extraordinary commercial success of *Three Men* had suggested that the general reading public were little influenced by 'superior' criticism, it would be far better to try to bring the critics on side as well as the readers. With this in mind, it was a logical move to elevate his characters into the established middle classes and to overlook those others whose social origins were closer to his own. This intention is seen in practice in *Three Men in a Boat's* sequel, *Three Men on the Bummel* (1900), in which J and his fellows lose any trace of slang from their language, and swap their London lodging house and double-skulled skiff for country house, Club, and yacht. While this move ultimately failed to convince the critics of the 'legitimate' nature of his comic prose, it at least closed off one avenue of their attack. As long as the modern clerk and the lower middle class at large remained literary pariahs, the professional English comic writer was, it seems, best placed simply to promote his characters into the adjoining class.

NOTES

i. Gregory Anderson notes that bank clerks were, during the Victorian period, considered to be 'the aristocracy of the clerical profession, [who] generally worked shorter hours than commercial clerks'. He adds that 'preference would be given in recruitment to those who were respectably connected'. This in effect meant that prospective bank clerks were 'known personally or were nominated by persons known to the employer'. Gregory Anderson, *Victorian Clerks,* op cit, pp. 12; 16. Jerome plays, to some extent, on the bank clerks' 'superior' reputation among other clerical workers in the following passage, in which J and

Harris discuss George's work: "'I never see him doing any work there," continued Harris, "whenever I go in. He sits behind a bit of glass all day, trying to look as if he was doing something. What's the good of a man behind a bit of glass? I have to work for my living. Why can't he work?'" (66).

ii. Jerome, *My Life and Times,* op cit, p. 104.

iii. *Home Chimes,* Vol VI, February 1889, p. 103.

iv. A recent article in the *The Pall Mall Gazette* had served to confirm the effect of the growth of this tribe with specific reference to the Thames:

'For the last few years it has been gradually dawning upon us, however sad and unwilling we might be to believe it, that the Thames was not the place for a holiday. 'Arry camping in rows of tents on the lock islands, house-boats anchored against every bank ... – all these were bad enough; but the bitterest part of all was perhaps the knowledge that every respectable person on the banks of the river who did not want to make money out of you regarded you as a pest and a nuisance. So we gave up the Thames once and for all, and, exiled by 'Arry, we tried the Seine instead.'

Unsigned article entitled 'A Boating Expedition on the Seine', *The Pall Mall Gazette,* 1 October 1886, p. 4.

v. *The Saturday Review,* op cit, pp. 387–8.

vi. *Punch,* 1 February 1890, p. 57.

vii. 'Letters to Clorinda', *The Idler,* Vol 9, Feb 1897, p. 134.

viii. *The Idler,* op cit, pp. 133–4.

THE FIRST EDITION OF
THREE MEN IN A BOAT
by Frank Rodgers, Bill Newsom and Andrew F Read

It can safely be assumed that any serious collector of Jerome K Jerome desires to have not merely a copy of the first edition of *Three Men in a Boat* (which would include all copies printed until 1908) but a copy of the first impression, published in August 1889. But how will you be able to determine whether the copy you are considering buying is a true first impression?

Any good bookseller will tell you that the publisher's address on the ti- tle-page must read 'QUAY STREET' rather than '11 QUAY STREET', and many will describe the latter as being 'second issue of the first edition'. This question was discussed in detail many years ago by Percy H Muir in *Points, 1874–1930* (London, Constable, 1931). But it is an over-simplification of the problem.

As long ago as November 1978, a brief article by Geoffrey Henderson (*Antiquarian Book*, vol. 5, no. 11, pp. 474–5) noted differences between two copies of the book with a 'QUAY STREET' address, and offered his opinion as to which of the two seemed to be a true first issue. We concur with his principal findings (front endpaper headed 'J W ARROWSMITH, BRISTOL', an unblemished ornamental initial 'T' on page 1, and inverted initial 'I' on pages 77 and 95), which are incorporated into this article. In 1982 Joseph Connolly, in the bibliography at the end of his biography of Jerome, agrees with Henderson on the heading of the font endpaper, but brushes aside the relevance of the inverted initials. Additional variables have come to light since the date of Henderson's article, and these, too are considered here. In the '3rd edition' of 1924, Arrowsmith gives a publishing history of the book which states that it was published in August 1889, reprinted in September, October and November, then twice in December. The firm's London agent, Simpkin, Marshall & Co., was incorporated as a limited company to 1889, a fact verified by Percy Muir in the files of the Public Record Office. The revised title – Simpkin, Marshall, Hamilton, Kent & Co., Limited – appears on the title-page at the same time as the change to '11 QUAY STREET' which we may therefore assume probably took place in one of the later 1889 printings.

The authors of this article have examined a dozen and a half copies of the 'QUAY STREET' title-page version, some with dated inscriptions, and including three important copies in libraries: Jerome's own copy of the book (now in the Bodleian Library) and the legal deposit copies at the British Library and the Cambridge University Library. These three copies must have been among the first off the press, and so their characteristics – assuming they were all in agreement – would have to be considered vital evidence of what constitutes a true first issue. The British Library copy has been rebound, and so lacks its front endpaper, but otherwise the three all display the same essential points. We have been able to identify four distinct states of the book with the 'QUAY STREET' title-page and can list with some confidence the sequence of the changes.

The first issue points are:

1. The heading on the front endpaper is 'J W ARROWSMITH, BRISTOL'.
2. The ornamental initial 'T' on page 1 is clear, without faults.
3. There is no moon in the sky of the illustration on page 20.
4. The ornamental initial 'I' on pages 77 and 95 is inverted (the dragons' heads point up).
5. The word "stream" is present at the end of page 271.

Second state:

1. The heading on the front endpaper is 'J W ARROWSMITH, BRISTOL'
2. The ornamental initial 'T' on page 1 is clear, without faults.
3. There is now what appears to be a moon in the centre of the page 20 illustration. We suspect that this is the result of a flaw that developed in the plate, rather than a deliberate change of the illustration. If that is so, although we have not seen any examples, there could theoretically be late printings of the first issue that show signs of the flaw developing.
4. The inverted initials on pages 77 and 95 have been corrected.
5. The word 'stream' is present at the end of page 271.

One of the examples that we have seen of this state has an owner's inscription dated 26 September, 1889.

'T' without faults

Inverted 'I'

Illustration without "moon"

Illustration with "moon"

Third state:

1. The heading on the front endpaper is changed to '11 QUAY STREET, BRISTOL'.
2. The ornamental initial 'T' on page 1 is clear, without faults.
3. There appears to be a moon in the page 20 illustration.
4. The inverted initials on pages 77 and 95 are correct.
5. The word 'stream' is present at the end of page 271.

Fourth state:

1. The heading on the front endpaper is '11 QUAY STREET, BRISTOL'.
2. The ornamental initial 'T' on page 1 is flawed: there is a large blemish below the mouth of the dragon on the left side of the initial.
3. There appears to be a moon in the page 20 illustration.
4. The inverted initials on pages 77 and 95 are correct.
5. The word 'stream' is missing from the end of page 271.

The message from the above descriptions is quite clear: the inverted initials on pages 77 and 95 are the essential requirement for a true first issue, and the correction of this error must have taken effect with the September 1889 printing.

With the change of the title-page address to '11 QUAY STREET' the illustration on page 20 is restored to its original state, and the word 'stream' is once more in place on page 271. However, the flawed initial 'T' on page 1 is not corrected until 1891 or later.

We must also comment on another point that is often cited as evidence of an early printing: the listing on the rear endpaper of *Prince Prigio* as 'READY IN OCTOBER'. Although the book was indeed published in October 1889, the announcement is in fact a false lead, since Arrowsmith apparently forgot about it and did not change it until 1891!

Faulty 'T'

We shall probably never know just how many copies were printed of the first impression, though we may hazard a guess. In the 'Publisher's Advertisement' to the 1909 edition, Arrowsmith stated that 5,000 copies of it were printed and noted that prior to that date, there had been a total of 202,000 copies printed. There had been 52 printings until then, which gives us an average of almost 4,000 copies per printing. It is unlikely that the first printings would have consisted of more than 1,000 copies, and they may have been as few as 500 copies. When Arrowsmith realized how steady was the popularity of the book, it is likely that he gradually increased the size of each printing to 5,000.

The findings of this article will be strengthened if more copies with 1889 owners' inscriptions come to light; so if any of our readers possess such copies, we should be eager to learn the details.

* * *

Reference in Three Men in a Boat *to The Great Coram Street Murder and the inclusion of the episode of the drowned woman at Goring reminds us of the real world amid the larks and laughter on the river. Here, two writers uncover the real stories behind the events.*

THE GREAT CORAM STREET MURDER

by Ian Wood

In *Three Men in a Boat*, when George, Harris and J are waiting with all their luggage for a cab to take them to Waterloo Station, Jerome makes reference to 'the Great Coram Street murder'. What was this murder? Was it real?

It certainly was, and although long-forgotten, it throws an interesting light on a corner of mid-Victorian London.

At three in the afternoon of Christmas Day, 1872, in a lodging-house at 12 Great Coram Street (near Russell Square), Clara Bruton, aged twenty-five, was found dead in her bed with her throat cut. She was found by her landlady, Mrs. Wright, who during the subsequent investigations went to great pains to assure everybody that hers was a respectable house.

This was possibly not entirely true. Clara, whose real name was Harriet Buswell, had claimed to make her living as a member of the corps de ballet, appearing, for instance, at the Alhambra, the vast music-hall that until 1937 stood in Leicester Square where the Odeon Cinema now stands. Certainly she spent many evenings at the Alhambra, often in one of its nine bars (she liked the odd glass of whisky, but was not a heavy drinker) and from time to time would bring home a gentleman from there to spend the night with her. Mrs. Wright, once meeting her with one of these men (a red-bearded vet called George) swore she 'thought they were man and wife, or I would have stopped it'.

The house was a full one. Fifteen people lived there. Mrs. Wright occupied the front parlour and kitchen with her husband, George, who was a goldsmith and jeweller, and the four of her seven children who still lived at home. In the ground floor back parlour slept Mrs. Alice Nelson, who had become a friend of Clara's from often meeting her at the Alhambra (and other similar places). She shared her room with a Mr. John Hooper, author and journalist, living as husband and wife, and they used another room, built over part of the back garden, as a living-room.

On the first floor was a drawing-room, on whose floor slept a Spanish merchant, Mr. Martini, and his English wife. In the second floor front bedroom lived Mr. Fernandez, an English-born professor of music. The second floor back bedroom was Clara's. Another professor of music, Mr. Hall, slept in the front attic on the third floor, and his two sons, aged seventeen and fourteen slept in the back attic.

Not at all the usual picture of a mid-Victorian household, it was cheerful and Bohemian, with many of its members involved in the arts and crafts. None of them had been there long. Even Mrs. Wright and her husband had had the house for only three-and-a-half years. Mr. Fernandez, who assumed that Clara was 'a gay woman' and didn't particularly mind, had been there for thirteen months. Mr. Hall and his sons had been there only three weeks, and Clara herself had lived there for only four. When she'd arrived, she had with here an eight-year-old daughter, Katie, but Katie was fostered out nearby. Her father, according to Clara, was one Major Brown.

Although seriously depressed (indeed suicidal) about the way her life was going, Clara was a good-looking, ladylike woman, and when she went out on the evening of Christmas Eve (at about twenty to ten) she was dressed to attract the eye, wearing a black silk dress, a black velvet jacket, and a dark green 'brigand' hat with a red feather. Her only jewellery was a pair of jet earrings borrowed from a friend.

Just before leaving the house she borrowed a shilling from her old friend Alice Nelson. This was all the money she had (earlier that day she'd pawned some underclothing for five shillings to pay for her daughter's keep), so she set off to walk the mile or so to the Alhambra. Passing through Russell Square she stopped for a moment to listen to the waits singing there, and fell into conversation with a foreign-sounding man who said he knew one or two of the men who had 'visited' her in the past.

Dark-haired and unshaven, he was stockily built, about five foot eight, in his mid to late twenties, and had the manner of someone who had once been a manual labourer. He told Clara he had just spent most of his money at the Argyle Rooms (another raffish music-hall), treating 'the ladies', but he had enough left to accompany her to the Alhambra and buy them both a meal in a restaurant near it, called the Hotel Cavour. They ate cold fowl and ham, and left at about ten to midnight (the restaurant closed at midnight).

At twenty-five-past twelve, at Piccadilly Circus (then called Regent Circus), they caught the last horse-bus on the Brompton-Islington route. Arriving home at about quarter to one, she took him up to her room and he gave her ten separate shillings. Immediately she went down to

Mrs. Wright on the ground floor and gave here nine of them for rent, keeping one for herself. She told Mrs. Wright that she'd got the money from a gentleman she'd bought home with her, and Mrs. Wright seemed neither surprised nor outraged. Later in court, she would deny that she had any idea the money might have been 'immoral earnings'.

In fact the Wrights, celebrating Christmas, were feeling merry. They offered Clara a drink, and she took a bottle of stout. But she stayed with them for only a couple of minutes before leaving. The door to her friend Alice's room (the ground floor back parlour) was ajar, and she went in. Alice drank some of her bottle of stout, and in return gave Clara a little brandy. Clara told her of the man she had bought home, then, having left him alone for some half an hour, went back upstairs.

Next day the man was gone, and Clara was lying under the bedclothes in a position of peaceful sleep, but with her throat cut savagely twice. When she was found, Mr. and Mrs. Martini moved out of the house at once, saying they wouldn't have boarded there at all if they'd known it was such an immoral place, but the rest of the inhabitants took the situation in their stride.

The police never tracked down Clara's killer, although a foreign-accented doctor named Hessel was arrested, tried for her murder, acquitted, and given a large compensation. No doubt it is this lack of successful resolution that caused the case to be forgotten, although it stuck in Jerome's mind strongly enough for him to remember it sixteen years later. And one can see why. As well as the Bohemian nature of the household, in some ways reminiscent of his early life in the lower reaches of the theatre, there is the character of the victim.

There was something in the sentimental moralising side of his nature that would have been attracted to the idea of a good-looking girl, with theatrical aspirations, falling into a life of sin and eventually paying the consequences. Not in a way unlike the women George discovered floating in the Thames ten miles above Reading.

THE DROWNED WOMAN

by R R Bolland

from In the Wake of Three Men in a Boat by R R Bolland, Oast Books, 1995

Jerome's story of the girl found drowned in the Thames near The Grotto, Basildon, has all the ingredients of Victorian melodrama – the girl who was seduced, rejected by her family, and who in desperation ended her life in the river. I confess that for a long time I assumed it was fiction, invented by Jerome to give balance to his book: a little tragedy as a counterpoise to the abundant 'humorous relief'. It seemed unlikely that a story that fitted so conveniently into a book of that period could be true. But even if it were, how could I unearth the long-forgotten facts?

A perusal of the local newspapers seemed to offer the only chance of finding the story. If the tragedy had occurred at the place and in the circumstances described by Jerome, the facts would have been reported in the local papers. All I had to do was to find them.

One Saturday early in 1966 I travelled to Reading, and in the Reference Library asked for the *Berkshire Chronicle* for the years 1885 to 1890. Several enormous volumes were produced, and opening the first I started on my lengthy task. In those days they believed in detailed reporting – every small incident was set out faithfully and fully. But they were sparing of headlines, and in order not to miss the vital story I had to run my eye down every column. Someone ought one day to write a book about all the human events – many of them tragic – that were reported in the local papers in the 1880s. Although I was looking for one particular story, a kaleidoscope of long-forgotten incidents passed in front of my mind's eye.

At last, after four hours, I saw a heading – it could not be called a headline, for it was little larger than the normal type – 'Extraordinary and Melancholy Case of Suicide at Goring'. A quick perusal of the report confirmed that my quest was over, and I started to copy the lengthy account into my notebook. This took 90 minutes. Now, for the first time since the incident was told in *Three Men in a Boat*, I knew the full story of the last few days in the life of Alice Sarah Douglass, and of her tragic death, as revealed at the inquest. So far as I knew nobody else had unearthed the story and connected the true tragedy with Jerome's account; this gave me pleasure, though perhaps that is scarcely the right word, for, to tell the truth, I was much saddened by the tale. Here, then, is the story.

Alice Sarah Douglass, or to give her stage name, Alicia Douglas, was described at the inquest as a 'tall and good-looking young woman connected with the Gaiety Theatre'. The Gaiety Theatre in the Strand was noted in those days for the Gaiety Girls, created by its manager, Mr. John Hollingshead. These girls were chosen for the beauty of their faces and figures: even today the words 'Gaiety Girl' are synonymous with glamour and beauty. We can be sure, therefore, that Miss Douglass was indeed a good-looking young woman, and this may account, in part, for the sympathetic way in which Jerome tells her story.

I know little about Alice's early life. At the inquest the Coroner was concerned only with the events leading to her death. Her home was in Brighton, but she had lived in London for some years. It is plain that the temptations of city life proved too strong for her, and it was stated that she had for four years 'been under the protection of a gentleman who was killed in the last Egyptian campaign'. To add to her troubles she had had an accident to her foot and there was a possibility she might lose a toe. These twin worries, the loss of her lover and the threat to her livelihood – for a Gaiety Girl had to be able to dance – probably account for her actions, culminating in her tragic death.

On Saturday 25 June 1887 Alice Sarah Douglass travelled by train from Paddington to Goring with a Mr. Charles Jewell, whom she had met some weeks previously in a London Park. She had confided her troubles to Mr. Jewell, including the fact that she lived in a 'wretched hole in Soho'.

Mr. Jewell suggested that they should go to Goring for a time, and Alice jumped at the proposal.

It may be that the contrast between the peace, the quiet and the beauty of Goring and the noise, bustle and squalor of Soho, and the thought of ultimately having to return to the latter, combined with her other troubles, proved too much for Alice. We can guess that she had probably never before seen the upper Thames in its summer glory. Goring, nestling under the heights of Streatley and flanked by the placid, tree-lined river, must have been a glimpse of heaven. After this, how could she settle again in the 'wretched hole in Soho'? It is possible, indeed, that by taking her to Goring Mr. Charles Jewell was inadvertently responsible for the girl's death. If he had chosen a less lovely spot, the thought of returning to her dismal existence in London might have been more bearable.

At Goring the couple took apartments for a month at Hill Cottage, owned by a Mr. Towerton, and appeared to live happily together as man and wife. After a few days Mr. Jewell had to return to London; he arrived back at Goring on 2 July, and three days later they travelled together to London, where he took her to some lodgings in Osnaburgh Street. On the following Friday, 8 July, he called for her at her lodgings and was told by the landlady that Miss Douglass had gone to the country for a few days. Mr. Jewell did not see her alive again.

Back at Goring, Miss Douglass had called on Thursday 7 July at Gatehampton Farm, a group of buildings about two hundred yards from Gatehampton ferry, which crossed the river just upstream of Hartslock Woods. Mrs Jane Gillam, who lived at the farm with her family, had several visits from Miss Douglass between the Thursday and the Saturday. She usually asked for food and drink, which she paid for, and she appeared to be desperate for company, for she asked and was granted permission to go for walks with the Gillam children. She also asked if she could stay there, and offered to pay six shillings a week. Mrs Gillam was unable to agree to this.

The amount of money mentioned is of interest, for Jerome in his account states that the drowned woman had six shillings a week to keep body and soul together. He also states that she had wandered about the woods and by the river's brink all day. He was wrong here, but only in the matter of time, for one of the puzzling features of this sad affair was that Miss Douglass wandered in Hartslock Woods and along the river bank for three days and nights. We know something about her thoughts and feelings during this time, for she left the following notes:

> Had I been able I should have done the deed last night, but meeting with a young Oxford man who so kindly talked to me [sic]. How can I forget his sweet manners? I am glad I met with him, for he unknowingly prolonged my stay on earth. I only wish I had met him before perhaps this would never have befallen me. I die so young.

A.D.

July 8 1887. Have been in the woods all day with nothing to eat. Am tired and weary tonight. It will soon be over, and after all what have I to make me stay here? Nothing much.

Sunday afternoon. Still here. Cannot bring myself to die in the river. I am not mad, and so therefore being quite sane I am backward in destroying my life. Wood and river full – boats and people. Must remain close, am so untidy and so ashamed to be seen.

July 8th, 9th and 10th.

Sunday morning in the 'Lockheart' woods. Two nights wet through and no food since I left town last Thursday. For me so carefully brought up this is so fearfully hard to bear. The fearful pain of my heart, the dark and lonely woods, all add to my wretchedness. Yet, alas I would rather be there miserable than return to town where deep and unknown sorrow will be my fate.

It is too hard to die young. I try to struggle against this unhappy death, and I think if some kind friend were only here now I would listen to advice. But, too late, I must die.

Another note said:

Never shall I gain the love I have lost, and like the poet Tennyson, I will say–

"'Tis better to have loved and lost
Than never to have loved at all."
The woods to-day (Sunday) are full of happy folk; some are singing. They little know that one so miserable is quite near. But I dare not show myself.

The last entry, perhaps written just before her death, is as follows:

Mother, my dearest Mother, forgive your child. I have been much sorrow and trouble to you, Dearest, forgive me now. I am thinking my dearest of you. Father I also ask your forgiveness, and my brother's. I ask God's mercy and forgiveness, for I am a sinner. May He grant me a little mercy. If I cannot receive it, Oh Heavenly Father, let my soul rest in peace. Father, forgive me. I am so unworthy and am not fit to ask even this mercy.

Reading these poignant words after sitting for several hours in the quiet library brought a mist to my eyes. I had to stop taking notes, for the print was blurred. I regretted my inability to do justice to this story: but, upon consideration, these tragic sentences need no embellishment. Indeed, I do not think that any writer could improve on that last entry. The words were hewn out of the girl's very soul. The story is all there: the girl from a decent family, obviously an educated girl, who left home in disgrace and who, in the last moments of her life had thoughts only of her parents and her God. I feel sure that he granted her mercy and forgiveness in abundance.

On Monday evening, 11 July, two women called at the Gatehampton ferryman's cottage and told the ferryman's son, Thomas Bossom, that they had seen a bag and a hat beside the river a short distance upstream. He went to the spot and saw a body in the water. The body was recovered and taken to the Miller of Mansfield, the largest inn in Goring, which was owned by Thoam Bower. There the body was identified as that of Alice Douglass.

The inquest was held on Wednesday, 13 July, in the Temperance Hall, Goring, after the jury had viewed the body at the Miller of Mansfield. During the inquest the story was told of Alice Douglass's unhappy wanderings for three days and nights. The verdict recorded was, 'Found drowned'.

As I have previously stated, I have assumed that the trip described by Jerome in *Three Men in a Boat* was an amalgam of the various holidays that he and his friends had spent on the Thames. But it is possible that he had in mind one particular trip as a kind of backbone to the story. If this were true, and supposing that they started from Kingston on Saturday, 9 July, according to the itinerary they would have arrived at Goring and Streatley on Tuesday, 12 July, the day after the finding of Alice Douglass's body.

They stayed two days at Streatley, where they had their clothes washed after their own disastrous attempts to wash them in the river, so they would have been in the area on Wednesday, the day of the inquest. It appears likely, from Jerome's obvious knowledge of the details of the tragedy, that they attended it. There are, for instance, the significant similarities between Jerome's story and the newspaper accounts of the girl's death: apart from the mention of the six shillings a week to which I have already referred, it will be noted that he stresses that she had sinned – as she herself said in her letters – and he finished his account by asking God to help her, which is what she asked in her last message. No doubt Goring and Streatley – two small villages joined by the bridge over the Thames, were seething with news of the tragedy, and the tiny Temperance Hall would have been crowded with inquisitive spectators. Jerome, being a journalist and a writer, would never have missed such an opportunity for gathering the raw material of his profession.

THE FIRST REVIEW

The first review of Three Men in a Boat *appeared in the* Saturday Review *of the 5 October, 1889. It is reproduced below.*

THREE MEN IN A BOAT

Twenty years ago many young persons, who are no longer very young, used to be fond of a swashbuckler lyric of Mr. Swinburne's which has for refrain the lines:

While three men hold together
The kingdoms are less by three.

These were certainly 'three in a boat', for they were instructed to 'push, for the wind holds stiff, and the gunwale dips and rakes'. Mr. Jerome's three men, however, are of a less exacting order. They have no wish to master the Devil's riddle, and, happily, show no inclination towards those 'kisses that sting', a commodity which seems to have gone out of fashion since 1866. They are without any other mission than that of enjoying themselves innocently, vaguely, lazily, ignorantly, like other clerks from banks and lawyer's offices.

To tell the truth, we hardly know what to make of *Three Men in a Boat*, of which we have no desire to make much, either good or ill. It is not a piece of fiction, as might be supposed, since the author goes out of his way to say in a preface that 'its pages form a record of events that really happened'. Again, George and Harris and Montmorency' – that is the dog, a fox terrier – 'are not poetic ideals, but things of flesh and blood'. There can be no meaning in these words unless we are intended to understand that the book is a more or less realistic account of what it professes to describe – a week's trip, in early summer, on the Thames. The events are, obviously, exaggerated for purposes of humour, but they seem to be real events. 'Other works,' says Mr. Jerome, 'may excel this in depth of thought and knowledge of human nature; other books may rival it in originality and size; but for hopeless and incurable veracity nothing yet discovered can surpass it.' On the whole, after reading *Three Men in a Boat* we come to the conclusion that this is not intended for irony. These are what French novelists call 'documents'; this is the genuine relation of a passage in the lives of actual people. We are face to face with a British species of the genus which has produced Amiel and Marie Bashkirtseff. Let not Mr. Jerome think us unkind in making a few reflections on his volume from this point of view. It is the only point of view from which it appears to us to be interesting; and if we do not consider it as 'documents' we shall not consider it at all.

The whole chronicle is an account of how the author and two young friends went up the Thames from Kingston to Oxford, and back so far as Pangbourne, in a double-sculling skiff. It reproduces all the minute adventures of such a summer outing, mildly describes, for the thousandth time, but in a novel spirit, the objects on the shore, and is written entirely in colloquial clerk's English of the year 1889, of which this is an example taken at random:-

'She was nuts on public-houses, was England's Virgin Queen. There's scarcely a pub, of any attractions within ten miles of London that she does not seem to have looked in at, or stopped at, or slept at, sometime or other. I wonder now, supposing Harris, say, turned over a new leaf, and became a great and good man, and got to be Prime Minister, and died, if they would put signs over the public-houses that he had patronized. "Harris had a glass of bitter in this house"; "Harris had two of Scotch cold here in the sum of '88"; "Harris was chucked from here in December 1886".'

This is not funny, of course; to do Mr. Jerome justice it is not intended to be particularly funny; but it is intensely colloquial, and, as an attempt to reproduce, without any kind of literary admixture, the ordinary talk of ordinary young people today, it seems to us remarkable, especially as the whole book is kept at the same simple and yet abnormal level of style. It will be observed that in this short passage just quoted there are no less than six phrases which would be wholly unintelligible to a foreigner thoroughly conversant with the English of books, and yet not one of the six is the least strained, or, though vulgar, would offer the least difficulty to a Londoner. For the future student of late Victorian slang *Three Men in a Boat* will be invaluable, if he is able to understand it, and if, by the time he flourishes, the world of idle youth has not entirely forgotten what a 'bally tent' and 'Sunday-school slops' and 'a man of about number one size' are. In some of the sporting newspapers slang of this kind, and indeed of much worse kind, may be discovered, but we do not recollect to have met any other book entirely written in it. In a sense, too, *Three Men in a Boat* is a much truer specimen of lower middle-class English than are the paragraphs in the coloured newspapers, because they are exaggerated and non-natural, while Mr. Jerome is amazingly real. That it was worth doing, we do not say: indeed, we have a very decided opinion that it was not. But the book's only serious fault is that the life it describes and the humour that it records are poor and limited, and decidedly vulgar. It is strange that a book like *Three Men in a Boat*, which is a *tour de force* in fun of a certain kind, should leave us with a sigh on our lips at the narrowness and poverty of the life it only too faithfully reflects. The illustrations, which are reproduced in some ineffectual modern process, go very well with the text, and are not less modern or faithful or incongruous. The figures in the really clever design on p. 71 give with complete accuracy, and without the least caricature the outward appearance in the present year of grace of the sort of young men who figure in the pages of *Three Men in a Boat*. How droll and old-fashioned both will seem before the twentieth century opens!

ON GETTING THREE MEN INTO PRINT
by Frank Rodgers

It is just one hundred [2000] years since the appearance of *Three Men on the Bummel*. So it seems appropriate to review some aspects of its publication and to compare the circumstances with those that prevailed eleven years earlier, when Jerome surprised the reading public with *Three Men in a Boat*. In those years, Jerome had become internationally famous. He had published six more books, several of his plays had had successful runs on the London stage, and for four years he had been the editor of both a monthly and a weekly journal. So the situation was very different from the conditions in 1889, when the earlier classic came out.

Before appearing in book form, *Three Men in a Boat* was serialised in Home Chimes, a rather obscure magazine edited by the novelist F W Robinson. It began as a weekly in January, 1884, and the first of Jerome's 'Idle Thoughts' essays appeared in the issue for October 4 of that year. In February 1886 it changed to a monthly, with Jerome contributing a 'Gossips' Corner' to each issue. *Three Men in a Boat* was serialised in the spring and summer months of 1889. The magazine was not a financial success – Jerome recalled receiving only a guinea for each of his 'Idle Thoughts'– and it ceased publication at the end of 1893.

Jerome's choice of J W Arrowsmith of Bristol rather than a London publisher for the book may have seemed strange, but in one of his letters to Arrowsmith (preserved in Walsall), Jerome wrote 'I am anxious to bring it out through you as I know yours is for energy and push, I suppose the leading firm, now.' Arrowsmith liked the work at once, and Jerome had no difficulty negotiating good terms with him. The authorised publisher in the United States was Henry Holt, who brought the work out in 1890 and paid royalties on it. But Jerome ruefully commented in *My Life and Times*, 'I reckon my first and worst misfortune in life was being born six years too soon: or, to put it the other way round, that America's conscience, on the subject of literary copyright, awoke in her bosom six years too late for me.' As happened earlier, with *The Idle Thoughts of an Idle Fellow*, *Three Men in a Boat* was pirated by at least a dozen American publishers, some of them issuing it at several different prices, with varying bindings and quality of paper.

How different was the situation in 1900! *Three Men on the Bummel* was published simultaneously in both England and the United States, both in serial and in book form. It is fair to assume that all the typesetters were working from copies of the same typescript, probably prepared by Mrs. Marshall's Typewriting Office in London, whose services Jerome used frequently. In England, it was serialized in *To-Day*, from the issue of January 4 to that of April 5. The American version appeared in the *Saturday Evening Post*, probably the best known of all American magazines, which claimed proudly on its masthead that it was founded by Benjamin Franklin in 1728. The title was changed, perhaps because of fears that the German term 'bummel' might be unfamiliar. The front cover of the January 6 issue was devoted entirely to an illustration of the three men engaged in a dinner table conference, and the title *Three Men on Four Wheels*. On the following two pages, the first chapter is printed in full. As in *To-Day*, it ran for fourteen weeks, ending on April 7. Some of the later chapters were edited slightly, to make them fit into the available space.

Publication in book form came in the first week of May, with Arrowsmith as the English publisher. Dodd, Mead published the American edition. With the title now shortened to *Three Men on Wheels*, it has fewer pages than the Arrowsmith version – 299 text pages versus 318 – but it is much more impressive. It is printed on thicker paper, and the lime green cover with a silhouette of the three men riding through the forest is very striking. It bears an American copyright statement. An edition was also published in Toronto by the Copp, Clark Company, probably simultaneously, using the plates of the Dodd, Mead edition, but bearing a Canadian copyright statement

Impressive as was the Dodd, Mead edition, it was not without problems. At some date within the next eighteen months, without any announcement being made, the book was reissued, this time with 301 pages of text. What could be the reason for this difference? To answer the question, one must compare the texts of the two Dodd, Mead Versions with that of *Three Men on the Bummel*. For the most part, they are identical. But the major difference between the Dodd, Mead versions occurs on page 60, near the end of the third chapter. In the earlier version, the text breaks off in mid-conversation and the chapter ends inconclusively. In the later rendition, the conversation is brought to a conclusion. One must assume that the typesetter for the May

1900 impression either received a typescript lacking a couple of pages or lost them in the course of his work.

The conversation that was cut off, however, is significant in the chronology of what follows. The three friends had already made all their travel arrangements to go by boat from London to Hamburg. In *Three Men on the Bummel* on the evening before their Wednesday departure, George comes to the author's house, with an idea to occupy the morning hours before their boat's noon departure from Tilbury, in the East End of London. He produces a very antiquated guide to English conversation for the use of German travellers, and suggests that they go up to town early the next morning and spend a couple of hours shopping with its assistance to see what effect it might have.

In the reissued version, the restored text is quite different, and although it is a fair copy of Jerome's style, it was certainly not written by him. Now George comments '... our boat does not leave Harwich till Thursday evening'. So he proposes that they spend two days 'doing' London as tourists, with the aid of the old phrase book. This, of course, is quite inconsistent with the chronology of what follows. For in the next chapter – as planned in the original Chapter III text – they spent the morning shopping and then take a cab to Fenchurch Street Station, where their luggage and bicycles are already waiting for the journey to Tilbury. And Chapter VI finds them arriving in Hamburg on Friday, which would not have been possible with a Thursday evening departure from Harwich.

Dodd, Mead reprinted this version a number of times, and also authorised the issuing of cheap editions by Grosset & Dunlap and the New Amsterdam Book Company, all using the Dodd, Mead plates. But the erroneous text on pages 60–62 was never corrected.

Jerome with his wife, 'Ettie', c. late 1890s

Elsie and Rowena Jerome with dogs Punch and Jim

MESSING ABOUT WITH JEROME K JEROME
by Derek O' Connor

Without a doubt, two of the most oft-quoted phrases about the river are 'simply messing about in boats', Ratty's refrain from Kenneth Grahame's classic *The Wind in the Willows* (1908) and 'Three Men in a ...' (something or other).

Although separated by almost twenty years, both works are set in an age when bachelorhood was a cherished interlude between leaving school or university and, after a schematic courtship, taking on the heavy responsibilities of husband and father. Yet, whereas the bachelor heroes of *The Wind in the Willows* were clearly fictional – not to mention anthropomorphic – those of *Three Men in a Boat* were, to borrow Jerome's words, 'not poetic ideals, but things of flesh and blood – especially George who weighs about twelve stone'. Which is to say nothing of Montmorency, their combative fox terrier.

Not a few people surmise that the eponymous three must have been the feckless sons of upper class families, dilettantes with time on their hands to skylark about on the river. In truth, Walsall-born Jerome was a railway clerk and failed actor turned journalist, George a bank clerk and Harris a photographer. They were three very ordinary pipe-smoking, beer-drinking young men who took regular advantage of the South Western Railway's cheap excursions to Thameside towns, where double-skulling skiffs equipped for camping could be hired to explore the river.

The three men loved everything about the river – save perhaps the periodic soakings from the unpredictable weather (no change there). They loved its clean air, the gentle scenery, the riparian pubs (especially the pubs), the dressing up in candy-striped blazers, the strumming on banjos and, in Harris's case, the interesting tombs to be found in graveyards along the way.

Three Men in a Boat is still one of the best travel guides to the Thames Valley. Maidenhead is described by Jerome, with rare petulance, as 'too snobby to be pleasant ... the haunt of the river swell and his overdressed female companion'; Cliveden Woods as 'perhaps the sweetest stretch of the river; Marlow as 'one of the pleasantest river centres I know of' (they put up at The Crown); and Bisham Abbey as 'rich in melodramatic properties'. They had trouble with the lock-keeper at Hambledon, passed quickly through Henley in pre-regatta week and rowed on to Wargrave 'which makes a sweet picture as you pass it' and which they evidently took their time over because there is a detailed description of the pub sign at the George and Dragon. Sonning is 'the most fairy-like nook on the whole river' with The Bull as the place to stay. Reading gets the thumbs down because 'the river is dirty and dismal here', but the stretch between Mapledurham and Streatley is 'glorious', and at Pangbourne stands the 'quaint little Swan Inn'. Enough said.

During a recent [1999] walk by the river at Henley we called in at the tourist information centre near the town's new and splendiferous River and Rowing Museum. Amongst the many leaflets was one from Tom Balm of Richmond-upon-Thames advertising 'Camping Skiff Holidays'. The blurb promised a 'complete escape from the twentieth century', with the chance 'to be part of an age-old boating tradition as described by Jerome K Jerome in *Three Men in a Boat*'. Age-old? Well, three men in a coracle might be stretching things a bit. But at least as far back as those halcyon days when three impecunious young Victorians – and a dog – could savour friendship and the simple pleasures on our most beautiful of waterways.

* * *

Frank Forbes-Robertson (?1879–?) was the actor-manager nephew of Sir Johnston Forbes-Robertson, see letter opposite. His daughter Meriel married Sir Ralph Richardson. Frank's father, Norman, also an actor, was a prominent member of the Garrick Club. It was he who was responsible for the introduction of the Club's famous salmon-and-cucumber tie in the 1920s.

41. BELSIZE PARK,
N.W. 3.

Jan; 1st 1925

Dear Mr Frank Forbes-Robertson,

I agree to your performing my play, "The Passing of the Third Floor Back," during Your forthcoming Provincial Tour (including the London suburban theatres) commencing Feb; 2nd & terminating about the end of June on terms of my receiving five per. cent of the gross takings.

Yours sincerely,

J. K. Jerome.

Please confirm ? x ?

Letter to Frank Forbes-Robertson

A FAVOURITE BOOK IS A SOLACE, A BALM AND A CONSOLATION
by Robert McCrum

Literary Editor, The Observer Review

This article first appeared in The Observer *on the 24 September, 2000.* © *Guardian News & Media Ltd 2000.*

If you believe that spin doctors and focus groups have taken all the fun out of electioneering, the news that Democratic presidential hopeful Al Gore's favourite reading, as revealed to Oprah Winfrey and millions of American voters, is Stendhal's *Le rouge et le noir* seems rather thrilling.

Gore's choice is unblemished by any suggestion of political correctness; it also offers a witty, covert commentary on the Clinton presidency. Why? Because Stendhal's Bourbon restoration hero, Julien Sorel, is greedy, hypo critical and devious. Apart from his insane ambition, he is utterly lacking in the qualities the American people might look for in a presidential hopeful.

A pretty odd choice, then as a 'favourite' and an implausible candidate for the book to which you return for psychological reassurance. Many people, I remember, had a similar reaction when Tony Blair chose Sir Walter Scott's *Ivanhoe* as his preferred desert island reading.

A favourite book is the one you curl up with again and again, the familiar, dog-eared copy you take to bed with you, huddle over in the hospital waiting room, settle down with at the end of a hard day. This is the book from which you derive succour during life's darker moments and in which you happily lose yourself in search of renewal and reassurance.

Such a book is a solace, a balm and a consolation. It probably evokes childhood or teenage sensations and, almost certainly, it is freighted with nostalgia. In his essay *The Lost Childhood*, Graham Greene wrote: 'What do we ever get nowadays from reading to equal the excitement and the revelation in those first 14 years?'

A favourite book may be an acknowledged classic, but it doesn't have to be. Often, it's a personal touchstone that has become forgotten or overlooked by the unfathomable vicissitudes of literary fashion. It can have many qualities, but, above all, it must be comforting.

So what, exactly, makes a comfort book?

We can argue about this indefinitely, but examples are helpful. To this end, a straw poll conducted by Gallup-like scrupulousness around *The Observer* office reveals three things; first, many people have more than one comfort book; second, sophisticated readers often find relaxation in quite lowbrow reading pleasures and third, contemporary writing does not give as much deep comfort as a magazine like *Vogue* or the *New Yorker*.

Leaving aside magazines, we are talking about books that were probably published at least 20 years ago. Crime seems to be popular. 'Anything by P D James,' says my neighbour in *Review*. 'Inspector Morse,' says *Home News*. 'P G Wodehouse' cries a sub-editor.

Some journalists idolise Michael Frayn's *Towards the End of the Morning*; others return to *The Secret Garden* or *The Lion, the Witch and the Wardrobe*. Comic classics such as Evelyn Waugh's *Scoop* or Nancy Mitford's *The Pursuit of Love* are always popular. There was one vote for Yukio Mishima's *Sea of Fertility* and Nabokov's Ada or *Ardour*.

In the end, my survey produced an all-purpose English comfort book list that looked like this:

Dodie Smith: *I Capture the Castle*
P G Wodehouse: *The Code of the Woosters* or *Joy in the Morning*
J R R Tolkein: *Lord of the Rings*
T H White: *The Once and Future King*
Jane Austen: *Pride and Prejudice* or *Emma*
E B White: *Charlotte's Web*

Jerome K Jerome: *Three Men in a Boat*
Lewis Carroll: *Alice's Adventures in Wonderland* or *Through the Looking Glass*
Mary Wesley: *Harnessing Peacocks*

Comfort reading, then, is not about literary greatness. You won't find many calls for *Portrait of a Lady*, *Heart of Darkness*, *Ulysses* or *To the Lighthouse*, although all of these books, and a number of others, will routinely get nominated as great books of the twentieth century.

Comfort reading confirms the essential truth that reading is a solitary and private occupation. It offers a moment in which we can be free from the pressures of everyday life and yet be still in the receipt of wisdom and consolation.

As J D Salinger's Holden Caulfield famously put it: 'What really knocks me out is a book that, when you're all done reading it, you wish the author that wrote it was a terrific friend of yours and you could call him up on the phone whenever you felt like it.'

Sadly, if Al Gore had chosen *Catcher in the Rye*, he would probably have been psychoanalysed from here to eternity – and lost the presidential election into the bargain.

6

JEROME THE DRAMATIST

THE MANY FACES OF *THE PASSING*
by Alan R Whitby

Even if one subscribes to Benny Green's put-down ('really is an awful play') one must acknowledge that the story of *The Passing of the Third Floor Back* remained popular for over forty years. It appeared in all manner of formats: a short story, a three act play, a full-length novel, two feature films, and three known radio versions for the BBC. The purpose of this article is to provide some background to these various guises.

THE SHORT STORY

The story was first collected in the volume of six stories published by Hurst and Blackett in 1907. In the short story we have Mrs Pennycherry rather than Mrs Sharpe and the character of Stasia does not exist. It is nonetheless an effective story in this original form.

While the collector may want to obtain a first edition of this work, it is well worth seeking out a later edition as well. By the year 1929 (the date of my copy) Hurst and Blackett had added three extra stories to the volume, increasing the pages from 160 to 232. The extra stories are *His Time Over Again, The House Of The Two Cedars,* and *House Hunting.* In style they could fit into either the *Passing* collection or the *Malvina of Brittany* collection. Interestingly these three extra stories are not included in either the Logan or Connolly bibliographies of Jerome. Can any reader advise where these extra stories originated?

THE PLAY

Jerome of course turned the title story from 1907 into his most famous play, premiered in 1908, and then published as a play script by Hurst and Blackett in 1910.

Although later editions by French are very easy to obtain, the early edition by Hurst and Blackett is worth obtaining for the 16 plates of the original cast led by Johnston Forbes-Robertson as the Stranger. The pictures are rather over posed in the fashion of the day, but give some idea how the play first looked. Some of these photographs were produced as postcards, and were also featured in popular magazines of the day like *The Play Pictorial.*

The French's Acting Edition of the play remained in print for over seventy years, only disappearing from *Books In Print* in 1985.

FILMS

1917

The first film version was produced by an independent American company in 1917, directed by Herbert Brenon (1880–1958) who later went on to make respectable versions of *Peter Pan*, *Beau Geste* and *Oliver Twist*. Johnston Forbes-Robertson had recently been knighted and officially retired from the stage, but was prevailed upon to repeat his famous stage role as the Stranger on film.

Sadly no known copy of this film exists, although there have been rumours of a couple of reels in private hands in the United States a few years ago. Discovering and obtaining a copy have long been priorities of the National Film Archive I have been advised. Unfortunately, 1917 is just too early for the substandard gauges like 9.5 mm on which so many 'lost' films have been discovered.

The film would obviously have been true to Jerome's play. With a bit of imagination one can get the flavour of Forbes-Robertson's acting style from his 1915 film of *Hamlet* which has survived; also his Shakespearean recitals on 12 inch 78 rpm records in the Columbia Lecture Series of 1928.

1935

The second film version was produced by Gaumont British in 1935 as a ten reeler. It was re-issued by Rank in 1940 now cut to eight reels, a loss of about twenty minutes. The Gaumont British titles appear on the version shown occasionally on Channel 4.

Professional opinions on this film differ considerably. The book *The Great British Films* by Jerry Vermilye (published by Citadel Press in 1978) includes it as one of the 75 *best* British films of the period 1933–1971. The review praised its ensemble playing, including that of Conrad Veidt as the Stranger and Rene Ray as Stasia. Also featured were a host of familiar faces from British cinema including Frank Cellier, Mary Clare, Beatrix Lehmann and Cathleen Nesbitt. The more recent *Radio Times* review on its TV revival was less kind, stating that it had not dated too well, and giving it just two stars out of five.

The cast for the film is slimmed down from the play – noticeably the Jew, Jape Samuels, disappears from the story. And as often happens in filmed versions of plays, the action is opened out. So we leave the boarding house for a trip on a steam launch on the Thames in an episode captioned 'Bank Holiday'. Here, Miss Kite starts to redeem herself by leaping into the water to save Stasia who has fallen in!

Perhaps the biggest shift from the play is the character of Joey Wright. Wright, the play's bookmaker, now becomes Wright, the property developer, and is virtually portrayed as the force of evil trying to undo the Stranger's work. So we have a running Gabriel v. Lucifer scenario over the fate of the boarders, particularly Stasia. However, in the episode captioned 'The Night of Darkness' she is saved from 'a fate worse than death' at the hands of Wright, when he is attacked by the Organ Grinder (who?). Wright drops dead, and the organ grinder conveniently falls to his doom, but is still allowed to make one of the most dreadful deathbed speeches (actually death-pavement) in the history of the movies! Stasia, about to be accused of murder, is protected and defended by the Stranger who has witnessed the whole thing! (It is all rather like a bad episode from *Highway to Heaven*.)

Before complaining too loudly it must be noted that the film never claims to be based on the play, but rather is 'From the story by Jerome K Jerome'. Even if a long way from! The extra emphasis on murder and mayhem can perhaps be understood when one notes that the screenplay was co-written by Alma Reville. In real life she was Mrs Alfred Hitchcock.

THE NOVEL

In 1935, likely to tie in with the new film version, a 316-page novel of *The Passing Of The Third Floor Back* was published by Queensway Press. The author was Claude Houghton, a pseudonym for Claude Houghton Oldfield (1889–1961). Houghton was a reasonably popular author in his day; the British Library contains 35 of his books and plays, but none are in print to-day.

Houghton's *Passing* claimed the official approval of Jerome's widow, and contained the following explanation on its title page:

> Under this title many years ago, Jerome K Jerome, the world famous novelist, wrote a short story and his most successful play. With the consent and approval of his widow, Mr. Claude Houghton handles the same theme, but deals with it from the standpoint of today.

In spite of the ominous suggestion of updating, unlike the 1935 film, Houghton's book is generally faithful to the play. There are some 1930s references to Greta Garbo, Adolf Hitler, talking pictures, etc., but the play's flow is reasonably intact. Apart from the opening scene, where a policeman and a factory girl see the Stranger in the street, and see him as two different people, the action all takes place in Mrs Sharpe's establishment. While the characters remain there in the play, at the end of the novel they decide to start a better boarding house further down the road, and a reformed Jape Samuels will handle the details for them. The Stranger, on leaving, is met by the factory girl who needs him.

Houghton's novelisation was popular enough to go into paperback in the *Reader's Library* in 1937. In a typical marketing ploy, the paperback reissue in 1949 gained a dramatic cover picture of a frightened man and woman hiding under the stairs as the ominous shadow of feet descend ... This was somewhat at odds with the sedately spiritual subject matter inside.

RADIO

The BBC archives have no record of ever producing *The Passing* on TV. (By the time the ITV companies came on the scene the play had passed its sell-by date and was not really their kind of material anyway.) However, BBC Radio did broadcast the play on three occasions.

The first was a Home Service broadcast on December 1st 1939, and Jerome is the only one credited. The play ran for just one hour so must have been abridged in some form.

In 1947 an adaptation by Beatrice Gilbert was used for *Saturday Night Theatre*. This was broadcast nationally on the Home Service on April 12.

In 1951 a new production of the Beatrice Gilbert adaptation was recorded. It was broadcast on March 10 on the Midland Home Service only, again in the *Saturday Night Theatre* slot. Whether other BBC regions repeated it later is not known. The script and cast list from this recording (actually made on February 28) survive in the BBC archives. In the 1951 recording the Stranger was played by Edgar Lane and Stasia by Pamela Mant. The only famous name in the cast is Theodore Bikel who played Jape Samuels. In 1951 Bikel had his first film part (in *The African Queen*) and embarked on a long film career as a character actor and sometime folk singer!

Sadly, as is all too often the case, no recordings of any of the above productions survive in the BBC archives.

In 1977, the year Jerome's work came out of copyright, the Beatrice Gilbert script was again considered, but was now rejected by the BBC as being 'not what they wanted'. 'Modern' morality plays had now gone out of fashion.

The number of mediums taking on Jerome's story testify to its appeal and longevity this century. As to the future – that is more doubtful. Perhaps the only hope for a revival in our secular world would be for an Andrew Lloyd Somebody to rediscover it. Are there any takers out there? How about – *Passing – The Musical*.?

THE MOST VERSATILE LIVING NOVELIST

This article appeared in the Penny Magazine No. 547, 17 April 1909, pages 10/11

It is fairly common knowledge that the man who has risen to be one of our greatest living authors, one Jerome K Jerome, started his career on the stage, and it was the insight into stage craft he derived thereby that enabled him to write such charming comedies as *Miss Hobbs*, *The Passing of the Third Floor Back*, and, incidentally, helped him produce his book *On the Stage and Off*, with which he made his debut as an author. Perchance, too, it was his stage life that brought him in touch with the many quaint characters one meets in his books, men and women we see everyday around us but pass by unnoticed till the clever pen of such a master writer as Mr. Jerome points them out to us.

HIS FIRST PLAY

Very early in life Mr. Jerome became a candidate for honours as a dramatist, for his first play, a one-act piece entitled *Barbara*, was produced

7438 A ROTARY PHOTO E.C.
"THE PASSING OF THE THIRD FLOOR BACK"
MISS GERTRUDE ELLIOTT   MR FORBES ROBERTSON
AS 'STASIA'   AS "THE THIRD FLOOR BACK"

when he was about twenty-seven. It was his third dramatic effort, and was hawked around, he tells us, for four years before it was eventually produced, and ran for eighteen months. Managers were just as hard to convince as to the merits of the play of a promising young author then as now, it would seem, for Mr. Jerome had his play refused by every manager in London. One manager who had the play to read he hunted round at restaurants and clubs,

THE PASSING OF THE THIRD FLOOR BACK
MISS AGNES THOMAS   MR FORBES ROBERTSON   MISS GERTRUDE ELLIOTT
AS MRS SHARPE   AS THE THIRD FLOOR BACK   AS STASIA

but failed to find him and get him to accept it. The piece was afterwards accepted by the actress, Miss Norreys, and in due course the little fledgling appeared at the Globe Theatre and started its author on his road to success. Since then Mr. Jerome has produced several plays, but his favourite is, I believe, *The Third Floor Back*. At least, I judge so, for he told me a few weeks ago that the story on which he based the play was his favourite. And in referring to Mr. Jerome's connection with the stage I may mention that it was he who introduced Mr. J M Barrie to the lady who is now his wife. Mr. Barrie was just about to produce his first play, *Walker, London*, and he wrote to his friend Jerome to ask him if he could recommend a lady to play the leading part. Mr. Jerome at once thought of Miss Mary Ansell, one of the cleverest actresses of her day, and she it was who in a very great measure was responsible for the success of the piece. Not very long afterwards she married the young author who had written it.

A DAUGHTER ON THE STAGE
by Dr. Richard G Wilson FRCP DCH

Before the Second World War the literary and theatrical world of London (and therefore of England) seemed exceedingly small. It is not surprising that the paths of individuals crisscrossed.

Lady Winifred Fortescue was a country rector's daughter who went on the stage. In 1914 she married Sir John Fortescue, the historian of the British army. He had previously written *The Story of a Red Deer* which encouraged Henry Williamson to contact him. Sir John wrote the introduction to *Tarka the Otter* and received the first copy printed.

Lady Fortescue began to write after she and Sir John settled in the South of France. *Perfume from Provence* was published in the early thirties and had delightful illustrations by A H Shepherd. Incidentally numerous anecdotes of local life appeared almost unchanged when Peter Mayle wrote more recently about Provence – how slowly life changes!

In a subsequent book *There's Rosemary … there's Rue*, Lady Fortescue describes performing in plays by Ansley and then how she met Jerome K Jerome. She played Vivian in *The Third Floor Back* and then appeared in a Jerome farce which was less successful. I enclose those passages from her book but would encourage members to read her delightful series of memoirs in full.

EXTRACTS FROM *THERE'S ROSEMARY … THERE'S RUE*

I think that I must have become very difficult during my convalescence, for, with returning strength, came the longing to get back to London. There I could see John Fortescue again. He wrote to me now and then, surprising me by the confidential tone of his letters. Surely so reserved a man would never talk of his life and work, his hopes and his fears, so intimately to one who meant nothing to him?

In any case I realised that in work lay my salvation, and quite evidently I must have fretted myself into a fever on hearing that Jerome K Jerome had seen me act and wished to cast me for the part of Vivian in his wonderful play *The Passing of the Third Floor Back*. Rehearsals were soon to begin in London. He wished me to visit him in his home near Marlow and to read the part to him, as he was already fixing up dates for the tour.

It was a part that I longed to play, but poor Mummie, having so nearly lost me, was terrified that if allowed to go back to London after so short a convalescence I should catch cold and develop pneumonia.

At last I got my own way and returned to London, and I travelled down to Marlow and found Mr. Jerome living in a modern baronial hall with pitch-pine galleries and staircases and large stained-glass windows. The man himself was a delightful surprise in these rather pretentious surroundings, for he was modest, simple and kindness itself.

He took me into his study where I read the part of Vivian, he reading the part of The Stranger. The play always touches me deeply. I know that as a play it has glaring faults of construction, that it has been said that the series of 'conversions' coming swiftly one after another are inartistic and some think ridiculous. But there is a wonderful spirit irradiating the whole, and the person who can witness that play and come out of the theatre unmoved must, in my opinion, be in some way wanting.

Feeling my scene with The Stranger so sincerely, I suppose I read my lines sympathetically, for Mr. Jerome told me that I was 'exactly what he had been looking for', and gave me the part, asking me always to wait quietly in the wings, apart from everyone, before my big scene with The Stranger so as to get into the spirit of it.

Then he led me into the hall and introduced me to his family, who were just going to have tea.

Mrs. Jerome was a tiny gentle little woman with dark hair and wistful blue eyes always full of enthusiastic admiration for her husband and adoration for her family, two daughters, one married and very delicate, the other, Rowena, in those days a healthy fair-haired tom-boy.

I was introduced as the new 'Vivian' and Rowena, rushing up to me, told me impulsively that she was to play 'Stasia' the little maid-of-all-work in her father's play, so that we should be touring together, and 'what fun it would be'. Remembering Miss Gertrude Elliott's pale-faced, hollow-eyed representation of the poor little drudge, I found it hard to picture this plump, flaxen-haired rosy girl in the same part. But make-up can do wonders, and perhaps a coat of pale greasepaint, shadowed eyes, and a smut or two artistically smeared upon that laughing round face might give it the necessary mask of pathos. Certainly her father's child ought to be able to interpret one of his best characters.

The Jerome family were all charming to me, and I travelled back to London well pleased with my afternoon.

In nearly every town *The Passing of the Third Floor Back* had had a tremendous success, and there can be nothing much more delightful than acting in a popular play. My scene with The Stranger closed the most important Act, and it was always our ambition completely to silence the audience. If the curtain dropped upon utter stillness, which was maintained for several seconds after it had fallen, we knew that we had conveyed our message and caught up our audience into the true spirit of the play.

It was the most difficult entrance I have ever had to make, coming into that quiet fire-lit room with bare feet, hair unloosed, and groping hands, as though sleep-walking and drawn from my bed by something – or Someone – stronger than I; to walk noiselessly down to the fireplace, sink down upon my knees, and plead with a Presence felt, but not seen.

Mr. Jerome did not travel with the company, but constantly visited us and often rehearsed my big scene quietly with me, when he thought that the provincial audiences were sucking the spirituality from my performance. It is so terribly easy to broaden one's style, and everyone has a tendency to rant in the provinces. I don't know quite why; but Mr. Jerome's kindness and interest in my work saved me from that pitfall.

We had such fun together, the Jeromes and I, going for expeditions into the surrounding country, and having cosy tea-parties in the dressing-room which I shared with Rowena.

Little Mrs. Jerome was tremendously proud of her daughter's performance and obsessed by the idea that Rowena was delicate and must be fortified and nourished continually between the Acts. Personally I never saw a healthier specimen, and was vastly amused by the egg-drink, glasses of port, and other stimulants poured down the throat of my rosy little friend.

She was her father's darling and their relationship was a very pretty thing to watch; they were such perfect companions, laughing and teasing each other and always so happy to be together.

During the tour we began to rehearse a farce of Mr. Jerome's which he hoped to produce in London when *The Passing of the Third Floor Back* finished its run.

I shall never forget my depression during the first reading of the play by the author to the assembled company. Personally I think that the day of farcical comedy is over. Our humour now is far more subtle, conveyed by suggestion – a lifted eyebrow, the twist of a mouth, or ever an eloquent silence; and I have long since found it difficult to laugh at the blatantly obvious. I had hoped to find this farce of Mr. Jerome's so excruciatingly funny that it would even wrench laughs out of me, but as he read it my smile became more and more like stretched elastic for I found the situations forced and not funny. His little family, who were present at the reading laughed loyally at all the expected places, and their mirth prevented the play from falling entirely flat; for to my consternation, I saw that the rest of the company (all seasoned actors and actresses) were likewise failing to find it amusing.

I was all the more disappointed, because I had been cast for a really delightful part, straight and sincere – the one foil to all the farcical characters in the play.

I did not see how it could succeed in London, even if it survived the provinces. We were going to try it out in Brighton, and my entire family decided to come down for the opening night – a great event for me. It was thrilling to welcome them all in my lodgings and to present them proudly to the company and the Jerome family, who promptly got up a gala evening in their honour at one of the hotels.

But they did not find the play very funny and were as doubtful of its success as I, although we didn't do so badly in Brighton.

When we reached London the play was put on at the Vaudeville Theatre, preceded by Bernard Shaw's *Great Catherine*, in which Gertrude Kingston starred, under the direction of Mr. Norman MacKinnel.

We had a trial performance before him, and the deep gloom with which he witnessed the play damned it forever in my eyes, as I had a great respect for his judgment. To play our scenes to that frowning face and never once see it relax into a smile was, to say the least of it, depressing.

He had taken us on the recommendation of Miss Kingston, who had seen us play at Brighton, and thought that an amusing farce might successfully replace the tragedy which was then being played before *Great Catherine*, and, as she imagined, was killing it. We killed it just as surely, and after a very short run both plays were taken off.

My personal notices in the newspapers were good, and I was not sorry to have a rest after touring the provinces for so many weeks. But all the same it was very sad to be disappointed of a run in London.

Rowena Jerome as Stasia in
The Passing of the Third Floor Back

Rowena Jerome

7
A JEROMIAN MISCELLANY

JEROME IN ESPERANTO
by W H Simcock

from a letter to The Editor, Idle Thoughts, 29 April 1994

Why not submit a piece on your first encounter with JKJ, asks the secretary.

Well, I was very young, for my father (born in the year of Queen Victoria's Golden Jubilee) was a Jerome enthusiast, and an elocutionist, and I followed him. The reciter before the war was still an essential element in the church or chapel weekday concert, and, in my youth, I must have recited 'How Uncle Podger hung the Picture' in almost every such place in North Staffordshire. The story of 'The Plaster of Paris Fish' was also in my repertoire.

In my retirement I spend a good deal of time teaching Esperanto and working as one of the Midlands Representatives of the British Esperanto Association. I have recently collected together pieces, mainly humorous, which I have, over the years, written or translated into the international language. The booklet has been printed by the Esperanto Society of North Wales.

Here are the opening lines of Podger in Esperanto:

Vi neniam vidis tian tumulton en domo en via tuta vivo kiel kiam onklo Podger entreprenis taskon.

Unufoje la enkardigisto sendis al nia hejmo bildon, kaj ĝi staris en la man ĝo ĉambro atendante, ke iu pendigu ĝin. Kaj Onklino Maria demandis, kion oni faru pri ĝi, kaj Onklo Podger diris, "Ho, vi lasu tion al mi; ne vin ĝenu pri tio. Mi faros la tuton."

Tiam li deprenis sian jakon kaj komencis. Li forsendis la servistinon por alporti najlojn kontraŭ ses pencoj, kaj unu el la knaboj post ŝi por diri al ŝi precize kiajn. Kaj, post tio, li laborigis la tutan familion! and the opening lines of the 'Fiŝa Rakonto' go like this:

Ce wallingford, georgo kaj mi vizitis malgrandan riverbordan trinkejon, por ripozo – kaj aliaj aferoj.

Ni eniris en la salonon kaj sidiĝis. Estis tie maljunulo, fumanta sian pipon, kaj ni nature komencis babili.

Li diris al ni, ke la vetero estis bela hodiaŭ, kaj ni diris al li, ke estis bela tago hieraŭ; kaj, poste, ni ĉiuj informis unu la alian, ke ni opinias, ke estos bela tago morgaŭ.

Post tio, evidentiĝis, iamaniere, ke ni estas fremduloj en la regiono, kaj ke ni foriros venontan matenon.

Tiam paüzo sekvis en la konversacio, dum kiu ni ĉirkaŭrigardis la ĉambron. Fine ni rigardis polvkovritan, malnovan vitrujon, fiksitan tre alte super la kamenkadro kaj enhavanta truton. Ĝi iom ĉarmis min, tiu truto, ĝi estis tiel grandega fiŝo. Fakte, je la unua rigardo, mi opiniis, ke ĝi estas moruo.

BIOGRAPHICAL CONUNDRUMS
by Maurice W White

Having read through JKJ's *My Life and Times* and Joseph Connolly's *JKJ A Critical Biography* I was interested to find numerous statements which are conflicting. It is about these that I write.

I will use ML&T and ACrB as my references, throughout.

Commencing with Jerome père's marriage:

ACrB – page 8: '... married in 1838 and early in 1840 moved to Appledore .... Built a fine house on the land ... named it Milton'.

However, on page 18: ML&T refers to his mother's diary entry:

'... June 7th 1867, our wedding day... Twenty Five years have passed.'

Also: page 15: '... we might get back possession of the farm in Devonshire, to which my father had brought her home after their honeymoon ...'

This of course made for marriage in 1842.

On page 14 ACrB there is another statement which has to be a publisher's error: '... the holiday in Appledore was quite an event ...' The family had not been there for nearly twelve years. Mrs. Jerome, her daughters and JKJ stayed in the old house 'Milton' where her first son had died.

I must admit that this threw me, because I could not tie this up with Milton's short life. Indeed initially I was of the impression that Milton was born at Appledore, whence the name. However his birth date made this impossible, as the Jeromes had moved to Walsall in 1854 – page 9 ACrB –... It was then 1858, and the Jeromes had been in Walsall for four years. ... 2nd May 1859 Marguerite gave birth to a son (JKJ).

It is interesting to note that there is no mention at all of the place of birth of Milton, which must have been at Walsall, or that he died at Stourbridge. Page 229 ML&T' ... I had a little brother who died when I was a baby.'

There is another comment, re Milton's death, referring to his mother's diary: page 11 ML&T ... On each anniversary of his death, she confides to her diary that she is a year nearer to finding him again. The last entry, sixteen years afterwards, and just ten days before she died herself, run: 'Dear Milton's birthday ...' Since her death was in 1874 this is inaccurate.

By the way, I understand that his gravestone lies somewhere at the rear of Belsize House. The name Belsize raised another question. When was it given to the Bradford Street house? I feel that it was possibly tied up with JKJ's 1927 visit, and that it came from his living at Belsize Park, London.

Aunt Fan appears to have two guises, on page 12: ML&T ... she is 'my mother's sister'. Whilst page 10; ACrB' ... Jerome's sister had moved in with the family ...'

Regarding the Cannock Chase mines, both books talk of the 'Conduit Colliery' and 'Jerome Pit'. (I was interested in trying to identify the sites, having done my 'square bashing' during my National Service at RAF Hednesford in 1955.) I refer first to the JKJ Museum references to Jerome senior being 'A partner in the Birchills Iron-works' he having a 'coal mining venture at Norton Canes'.

Re the Birchills Iron-works, I have an 19th century map showing it, at the site of what appears to be the Birchills Canal Museum to-day. An unexpected source of information, the Birmingham A to Z, shows a 'Jerome Road', 'Jerome Drive' and 'Belsize Close' at Norton Canes. Now I am assuming that since the Conduit Colliery closed only fifty-one years ago, that perhaps these roads were given as a record of the former sites (purely a guess). At least 'Jerome' remains but no record of the 'Conduit pit'. It is certainly '... on land over-looking Cannock Chase' (page 9 ACrB).

Joseph Connolly did of course have access to 'previously unpublished letters, diaries and memoirs', which means that it is not possible to correctly question differences from *My Life and Times*, and I certainly am not intending criticism in my comments. A number of points, however, come with Connolly's statements referring his step-daughter Elsie:

Page 50: '... neither does she seem to have accompanied them at any other time ... or her presence was not mentioned.'

Page 129: '... nowhere in Jerome's *My Life and Times* ... is even her existence recorded, save Jerome's single allusion to his eldest girl ... It is strange ... Jerome seems to have gone to such lengths to keep Elsie so firmly in the background ...'

Page 130 '... despite his apparently callous attitude towards Elsie ....'

On pages 159/160 in *My Life and Times* there is the hilarious 'outside Munich far-famed brewery' episode. Surely a description worthy of George, Harris and J (and of course the dog). Throughout the tale Jerome mentions only Elsie by name. '... you my dear Elsie will take this gentleman's arm – or rather arms ...', all other references being 'the girls', 'my girls', 'my eldest girl'. Indeed he refers to his youngest (Rowena) as 'the child'.

It is of course very difficult to follow Jerome's *My Life and Times* in terms of a chronology of dates and events. He even, almost as an afterthought, mentioned '... I had just married.'

I do hope, that the above observations might provide some information for discussion and/or comment.

ANSWERS TO CONUNDRUMS – AND SOME NEW CONUNDRUMS
by Frank Rodgers

Maurice W White raises some fascinating questions about conflicting statements in Jerome's *My Life and Times* and Joseph Connolly's *Jerome K Jerome: a Critical Biography*, and makes very pertinent observations on them. To be fair, one should also compare references made in *Jerome K Jerome: His Life and Work*, by Alfred Moss. Let me begin with a brief review of their usefulness as sources of information, before examining the specific topics raised by Mr. White.

The primary source is, of course, Jerome's own work, published in 1926. It is a delightful memoir, full of wonderful observations about the society of his time, about his friends and acquaintances, and about the highlights of his own life. But, as Mr. White observes, it does not provide a chronology of dates and events. Jerome had no interest in providing such a well-organised history of his career, and when he does refer to events that could be dated, his memory is often at fault. And, of course, he could never resist the temptation to add humorous touches … Do you really believe that Mrs. Jerome mistook the Pittsburgh rats for kittens?

The biography by Alfred Moss, published a year after Jerome's death, must be viewed primarily as a tribute by a friend and admirer. Joseph Connolly (pp.195–6) dismisses it with the comment that it 'contained no information that is not in Jerome's own memoirs'. This is not only untrue but unkind, since Connolly himself used information obtainable only from Moss's work. Moss described Jerome as 'an old friend' (they were of the same age), and some of his material probably came from conversations with Jerome. He also, in his Preface, thanks Mrs. Kernahan Harris, Frank Shorland, Mr. and Mrs. Harry Shorland (the Shorlands were nephews of Jerome), George Wingrave and Carl Hentschel for biographical material, as well as a number of others for permission to use letters. Moreover, he was a native of Walsall, and thus able to provide reliable information about the circumstances of Jerome's earliest years – he states (p. 50) that he had been 'fortunate enough to discover two or three aged persons who knew Jerome's parents personally'. Finally, Moss gives full coverage of the Freedom of the Borough conferred on Jerome in 1927.

Connolly's work does not deserve its subtitle *A Critical Biography*. Although it is well written and handsomely produced, most of its information is taken directly from Jerome's *My Life and Times*. When Connolly ventures beyond Jerome as a source, he is frequently in error. Although both Jerome and Moss state that he made three visits to America, Connolly not only transforms them into four visits but gives incorrect dates for all of them! Yet he could easily have obtained the correct information from the indexes to *The Times* and the *New York Times*.

Many years ago (long before Connolly's work appeared), I had contemplated writing a biography of Jerome myself. I visited the collection at the Walsall Public Library, and researched a number of original sources, including those at the General Register Office. I had several very pleasant meetings with Rowena Jerome, who very graciously loaned me her grandmother's diary, from which Jerome quotes a number of excerpts in the first chapters of *My Life and Times*. But I eventually concluded that, being employed full-time on the wrong side of the Atlantic, I could not do justice to the project. However, I still have the notes that I made at that time, which are helpful in addressing the questions raised by Mr. White.

First of all, there is the question of the date of Jerome Clapp's marriage to Marguerite Jones. One should surely trust a wife's awareness of her silver wedding anniversary! The marriage was registered on June 7, 1842. Sadly, her diary does not suggest that the couple did anything to celebrate the occasion.

Jerome (p. 12) places his father at Cirencester in 1833, and then states, 'On his marriage, my father settled down in Devonshire, where he farmed land at Appledore …' Moss (pp. 42–43), mentions his ministry at Cirencester and then his marriage to Marguerite Jones before saying 'In 1840 he moved to Appledore'. He also states that he built a house and called it 'Milton'. Since *My Life and Times* does not mention the building or naming of a house, we can only guess at the source of Moss's information. Connolly adds an 1838 date of marriage and a move to Appledore early in 1840. He also takes from Moss the building and naming of the house and embellishes the account by claiming that Jerome had predetermined it should be named after some famous literary figure.

But the chronology in all three cases is wrong. Jerome Clapp was still single when he moved to Appledore. An undated letter from him, addressed to Miss Jones and headed 'Appledore', discusses a Sabbath School party and promises to send her a copy of the music to be sung by the children. Since Marguerite saved this letter for the rest of her life, it must have had a special significance for her. Is it too fanciful to suppose that his proposal of marriage to her occurred on his next visit?

Now to deal with Jerome's elder brother Milton. He must indeed have been born at Appledore for Mrs. Jerome records in her diary on September 23, 1867 '12 years ago we came to Walsall'. His father, who had left to work in London some time in 1861, came home for the funeral. Moss (p. 52) states: 'His remains were interred in the burial-ground behind the High Street Congregational Church, Stourbridge. A tombstone there has the following inscription on it:

MILTON MELANCTHON JEROME
He increased in wisdom and stature, in favour
With God and man.
Born June 11th, 1855. Died January 26th, 1862.

Notes that I made in Walsall in 1962 indicate that, after 100 years of neglect, it had been excavated and photographed. Perhaps one of the Society's members from the Walsall area could ascertain whether the grave is still to be found.

Turning now to Mrs. Jerome, the reference on page 14 of *My Life and Times* should, of course, refer to the last entry in her diary as being twelve years after Milton's death. And the entry simply reads 'Dear Milton's birthday'. The remaining words, 'It can be now but a little while longer. I wonder if he will have changed,' were added by Jerome. Nor was the entry written just ten days before her death. After the death of her husband, Marguerite's diary entries became infrequent and very brief. She wrote no more after June 11, 1874, but her death was not certified until July 20, 1875, the cause being given as 'Strangulation of the Bowels Exhaustion'.

I come now to some biographical conundrums that have frustrated me for a long time. First of all, there is the question of the middle name of Jerome's father. In *My Life and Times*, Jerome claims that relics found near his father's house near Bideford proved that 'one Clapa, a Dane' had been the founder of the Jerome house about the year 1,000 AD. But he does nothing to suggest that his father's family had its roots in Devonshire, stating only that he attended the Merchant Taylors' School in London. Moss adds that he was born in London and Connolly describes him as a Londoner. So what evidence is there for a connection with Clapa? Since Jerome Clapp Jerome was born before the establishment of the General Register Office in 1836, we lack a readily accessible record of his parentage. And if, as we presume, his family background was Nonconformist rather than Church of England, research into his antecedents is not easy to pursue. Perhaps this history is just another 'idle fancy' on the part of Jerome!

Next, there is the unusual middle name of Klapka, which is not mentioned in *My Life and Times*. The earliest explanation of it appeared in a letter to *The Times* from a Professor Michal M Bálint of Budapest shortly after Jerome's death. He states that Klapka, a hero of the Hungarian Revolution, had come to London as an exile, and received a contract to write his memoirs. 'It was a question now of finding a quiet retreat, as the book had to be finished in two months. Klapka gladly accepted the invitation of the Rev. Jerome Jerome. In Walsall he found a home, and even in later years, whenever tired of restless wandering, he always returned to his kind host. When, in 1859, a son was born to the Rev. J Jerome, in honour of his famous guest he named him Jerome Klapka.' Since the memoirs were published in 1850, if the story is at all accurate, Klapka must have written them in Devonshire rather than in Walsall. Moss repeats Bálint's story, suggesting that in all probability Klapka was staying with the family at the time of Jerome's birth. Connolly misinterprets the chronology, and has Klapka writing his memoirs while staying with the family at the time of Jerome's birth.

One might well wonder why the name was not given to the older son, Milton, which would have been a more timely recognition of the hero. Also, Jerome's birth certificate shows him to have exactly the same name as his father. Connolly notes that fact, and adds that the name Klapka was an afterthought, 'decided upon months after the birth of little Jerome'. How Connolly could know the timing of the deed is not apparent. What is even more puzzling is that the 1875 certificate of his mother's death – when he was sixteen years old – notes 'J C Jerome/ Son/ present at death'.

Finally, let me address the mystery of Jerome's father-in-law, George Nesza. At the time of Georgina's first marriage in 1881, his profession is described as 'Gentleman'. When she married Jerome in 1888, the certificate notes that her father is deceased and gives his profession as 'Soldier'.

Moss (p.85) describes Georgina as 'daughter of Lieutenant Nesza of the Spanish Army'. Connolly (p.50) repeats this statement, with a slight variation: '... daughter of a Spaniard, one George Nesza, a lieutenant in the army ...'. However, in response to an inquiry made in 1997, I have a letter from the head of the Archivo General Militar in Segovia, Spain, indicating that they have no record of a George Nesza. Moreover, his surname is certainly not Spanish – if anything, it looks as though it might be of Eastern European origin. It is also very rare. You will not find it in the telephone directories of the United States, despite the millions of immigrants who came there from Europe. Nor does it appear in the directories for London, Paris, Madrid and a number of other European capitals! When and where he died is also unknown, but there is no record of his death occurring in England or Wales.

JEROME THE PARTY POLITICIAN
by Peter Wilson

Membership Secretary of the Jerome K Jerome Society

On 17 February 1927 Jerome was granted the Freedom of the Borough of Walsall in recognition of his birth at Belsize House, Bradford Street on 2 May 1859. The town's factories and mines closed on what was advertised as 'Jerome Day' and a large crowd turned out to hear his acceptance speech. He described his political views in a rather dismissive manner:

'Now that I am one of you, and that you may know about me, and that nothing may be hid, I ought perhaps to confess to you my politics – not an unimportant matter in a fellow citizen. I am happy to say that I have been at various times in complete agreement with the political opinions of every one of you.

'I commenced as a Radical. It was your Radical who was then the bogey of respectable society. The comic paper generally represented him as something between a half starved Guy Fawkes and an extraordinary gorilla.

'I reformed. I became a true-blue Conservative. I forget what converted me. It may have been the Liberal press. From Toryism I passed on naturally to Socialism, and joined the Fabians in company with Wells and Shaw. With them, I grew tired of Fabianism ... I might have joined the Labour Party, but that with the years there has come to the reflection that the future of mankind does not depend upon any party, but upon natural laws, shaping us to their ends quite independently of governments and politics.'

Had he genuinely rejected politics or was he merely pleasing a crowd? Jerome was a man of strong views, but was he someone who would have surrendered his independence to the dogma of one political party for long? Joseph Connolly, in his biography of Jerome, came to the conclusion that although he was not glib about politics in the widest sense, he had kept clear of party politics so that he could concentrate on single issues that really moved him such as abolition of cruelty to animals.

He was often asked to lend his support to the issues of the day and in a letter of reply written by Jerome in 1904 to someone trying to obtain his support he apologised '... I should much like to assist the cause and indeed feel somewhat ashamed of myself for not doing so – but some of my spare time of late has been taken up with political work ...'. Joseph Connolly was unsure what political work so engrossed him but I believe that there is evidence that in 1903 and 1904 he was actively involved in conventional party politics.

The discovery that the National Portrait Gallery holds a 1923 photograph taken by Lady Ottoline Morrell of Jerome in the company of Virginia Woolf at Garsington Manor perplexed me. As one vaguely interested in the Bloomsbury Set, I knew that Lady Ottoline and Mrs Woolf had been leading members and Garsington was their most famous playground, but I had never heard of any connection between Jerome and the 'Bloomsberries'.

Lady Ottoline Morrell was an inspiration to many of the finest literary and artistic minds of the first quarter of the twentieth century. Whilst not talented herself, she was intensely charismatic and could spot genius in young artists and writers. She was a muse to some and mistress to others. She was caricatured by Aldous Huxley as Priscilla Wimbush in *Crome Yellow* and as 'Mrs Dalloway' by Virginia Woolf. D H Lawrence used one aspect of her character for Hermione Roddice in *Women in Love* and another for Constance Chatterley in *Lady Chatterley's Lover*. During her reign at Garsington Manor between 1915 and 1928 it was the most important literary meeting place in the English speaking world. In 1923 Jerome was still an important writer but I still find it strange that Jerome had anything in common with the exotic Lady Ottoline.

A search of the internet revealed that The Harry Ransom Center of Austin, Texas, holds many of Lady Ottoline's personal papers including three letters to her from Jerome. Two were written in the summer of 1923 and so tie in with the photograph but the first was written on 29 June 1903:

> Dear Lady Ottoline,
>
> Mr. Foster tells me that you have not received my answer to your letter. I wrote the same day to 23 Grosvenor Road to say that I would support you on the 21st & bring Mrs Jerome with me. I presume that you will be going back to Clifton Hampden on that night. If it will be any convenience to you for us to put you up I need hardly say we should both be delighted.
>
> Sincerely yours,
>
> J K Jerome

This letter is interesting because it was written well before she had become a famous celebrity. On 8 February 1902 she married Philip Morrell, an Oxford solicitor with neither ambition nor means. She was the rich daughter of an aristocrat, well connected and very determined. Photographs of Ottoline prove that she was not photogenic and so we must accept contemporary reports that men considered her to have incredible sexual appeal. Asquith, then leader of the Liberal Opposition, had pursued Ottoline in the hope of making her his mistress and only ceased when she met Philip. She knew that Asquith still held strong feelings for her and so easily persuaded him to adopt Philip as a prospective parliamentary candidate for the next election. In 1903 he was accepted as the Liberal candidate for the South Oxfordshire Constituency which included Jerome's home in Ewelme. Ottoline then devoted all her considerable energies into organising public meetings to canvass support for Philip so that eventually he unseated the sitting Tory MP at the 1906 election. It is clear from his letter that Jerome was very happy to support Ottoline at a political meeting she had organised in the summer of 1903 in the Wallingford area. It would not be fanciful to assume that when he wrote in 1904 'my spare time has been taken up with political work' that he was working for a Liberal victory in his constituency. That part of Oxfordshire was then, as now, a Conservative stronghold and Philip Morrell could not hold the seat in the 1910 election but the fact that he won it in 1906 was, without doubt, due to the determination of his wife, helped, it appears, by Jerome.

Garsington is not far from Ewelme and although between 1915 and 1923 (when the photograph was taken) many writers did visit the Morrells, there is no record that Jerome was one of them. It is a pity because it would have been interesting to know his opinions on Yeats, Sassoon, Eliot and the others. There can be no doubt that Jerome and Ottoline became friends because of politics at a time before she was a famous literary hostess. She considered their friendship important and had kept his letters to her.

It is clear that when in 1927 he addressed the people of Walsall he was being truthful. He had become disillusioned by party politics but twenty four years earlier he had been an active and enthusiastic supporter of the Liberal cause.

JEROME AT THE AUTHORS' CLUB

The following report appeared in The Times *newspaper on the 22 February 1905*

MR. JEROME AT THE AUTHORS' CLUB – Mr. Jerome K Jerome was the principal guest on Monday night at a dinner of the Authors' Club, held at the club premises in Whitehall-court. Mr. F Gribble presided; and the company included Sir A Conan Doyle, Major P Trevor, Mr. C A Kelly, Mr. Walter Emanuel, the Rev. H N Hutchinson, Mr. John Todhunter, Mr. W V Greener, Mr. Lacon Watson, Mr. T Higgins, Mr. R Higgins and Mr. G H Thring, hon secretary.

The chairman proposed Mr. Jerome's health and Mr. Jerome, responding, said that he had been accused, among other things, of belonging to the middle classes. The superior critic had apparently heard of the middle classes, but he had determined that, if he could prevent it, the reading public should not be insulted by much reference to them. Formerly, provided that a writer had imagination, knew something of human nature, and could write, he was generally accepted; but the social strata from which George Eliot and Dickens drew their characters were no longer interested. The modern novel carefully avoided anything suburban. All its characters were to be found within the tragic circle bordered by the Park and Bond Street, which would appear to be an overcrowded neighbourhood. The British drama, too, had advanced beyond recognition. What, in these circumstances, were the middle-class dramatists and novelists to do? They were told on excellent authority that drama did not evolve itself in the parlour. They knew of no nobler apartment. Year by year his friends gained access to the charmed circle of the nobility, and he was left in a minority. But, seriously, the author always was, and always would be, of the middle class. He could never hope to be really great unless he wrote about things of which he knew.

1984 – GEORGE ORWELL: 2900 – JEROME K JEROME
by Tony Gray

Hon. Sec. of the Jerome K Jerome Society

'He took little part in the day-to-day struggle for political power in the country but his attitude was clearly and consistently anti-communist and anti-fascist. He believed in the freedom of the individual and his concern with the state of the poor, the under privileged and the destitute was a deeply felt realisation that their lot was, to a large extent, the negation of this fundamental right to individual freedom.'

The above could have been written about Jerome K Jerome but is in fact a comment by H M Burton MA(Cantab.) in the introduction to George Orwell's *1984*. Orwell hated both extremes of the political spectrum feeling that the Right tended to shade off into Fascism, the Left into Communism. The same could be said of Jerome K Jerome as is illustrated by his satirical essay on socialism, *The New Utopia*.

There are some striking similarities between Jerome's essay and *1984*.

The populace are, in both cases, required to wear uniforms to ensure uniformity. 'Everyone was dressed ... in a pair of grey trousers, and a grey tunic, buttoning tight round the neck and fastened round the waist by a belt.' (*The New Utopia*). This is reminiscent of the overalls worn by everyone in Orwell's dystopia.

JKJ's guide in *The New Utopia* says: 'We don't need houses – not houses such as you are thinking of. We are socialistic now; we live together in fraternity and equality. We live in these blocks that you see. Each block accommodates 1,000 citizens. It contains 1,000 beds – 1,000 in each room and bathrooms and dressing rooms in proportion, a dining hall and kitchens.' Orwell's Winston Smith lived in a flat on the seventh floor of Victory Mansions.

'Love, we saw, was our enemy at every turn. It made equality impossible. It bought joy and pain, and peace and suffering in his train. He disturbed men's beliefs and imperilled the Destiny of Humanity; so we abolished him and all his works.' This is JKJ but it could be Orwell – part of Julia and Winston's rebellion in *1984* as their love for each other which was not acceptable to the State and Big Brother.

"'Smith!' yelled a voice from the telly-screen. "6079 Smith W! Hands out of pockets in the cells!'" (*1984*). In Jerome's *The New Utopia* J. discovers that all citizens are known by the number allocated to them by the State. They don't have names because '… there was so much inequality in names. Some people were called Montmorency, and they looked down on the Smiths; and the Smythes did not like mixing with the Joneses: so, to save further bother it was decided to abolish names altogether, and to give everybody a number.'

That Jerome had a social conscience is well known to us but there is a doubt whether he was indeed a committed Socialist. His social conscience emanated from his observation at first hand of the poverty in the East End of London during his boyhood; the influence of his deeply religious mother; and of his father who was, it will be remembered, a lay preacher. There is, perhaps, even doubt about whether he remained a committed Christian towards the end of his life after his experiences on the Western Front in the First World War.

* * *

Tony Benson was also much taken with The New Utopia, '*J's satirical look at Socialist ideals of the time'.*

I had admired this piece as a remarkable forerunner of Aldous Huxley's *Brave New World* but had not given it much thought except to wonder how far it reflected his own politics:

'I was a die-hard Tory at twenty-five, later I was asked to accept a safe Liberal seat but declined. Now I am vice-president, I believe, of the Oxford University Labour Party.'

On a trip to Kelmscott Manor, the country home of William Morris, I chanced to pick up a copy of Morris's *News from Nowhere*. It took very little reading to see that here was the source of J's inspiration. He is clearly writing a tongue-in-cheek riposte to the idealism of the founder of the Arts and Craft Movement. Discovering that J's short story was published in the year following Morris's book strengthened my opinion.

I can't recall other examples of J writing deliberate parody in this way, though there might be many more.

THE NEW UTOPIA
by Jerome K Jerome

I had spent an extremely interesting evening. I had dined with some very 'advanced' friends of mine at the 'National Socialist Club'. We had had an excellent dinner: the pheasant, stuffed with truffles, was a poem; and when I say that the '49 Chateau Lafitte was worth the price we had to pay for it, I do not see what more I can add in its favour.

After dinner, and over the cigars (I must say they do know how to stock good cigars at the National Socialist Club), we had a very instructive discussion about the coming equality of man and the nationalisation of capital.

I was not able to take much part in the argument myself, because, having been left when a boy in a position which rendered it necessary for me to earn my own living, I have never enjoyed the time and opportunity to study these questions.

But I listened very attentively while my friends explained how, for the thousands of centuries during which it had existed before they came, the world had been going on all wrong, and how, in the course of the next few years or so, they meant to put it right.

Equality of all mankind was their watchword – perhaps equality in all things – equality in possessions, and equality in position and influence, and equality in duties, resulting in equality in happiness and contentment.

The world belonged to all alike, and must be equally divided. Each man's labour was the property, not of himself, but of the State which fed and clothed him, and must be applied, not to his own aggrandisement, but in the enrichment of the race.

Individual wealth – the social chain with which the few had bound the many, the bandit's pistol by which a small gang of robbers had thieved from the whole community the fruits of its labours – must be taken from the hands that too long had held it.

Social distinctions – the barriers by which the rising tide of humanity had hitherto been fretted and restrained – must be for ever swept aside. The human race must press onward to its destiny (whatever that might be), not as at present, a scattered horde, scrambling, each man for himself, over the broken ground of unequal birth and fortune – the soft sward reserved for the feet of the pampered, the cruel stones left for the feet of the cursed, but an ordered army, marching side by side over the level plain of equality.

The great bosom of our Mother Earth should nourish all her children, like and like; none should be heavy, none should be too much. The strong man should not grasp more than the weak; the clever should not scheme to seize more than the simple. The earth was man's and the fullness thereof; and among all mankind it should be portioned out in even shares. All men were equal by the laws of Nature, and must be made equal by the laws of man.

With inequality comes misery, crime, sin, selfishness, arrogance, hypocrisy. In a world in which all men were equal, there would exist no temptations to evil, and our natural nobility would assert itself.

When all men were equal, the world would be Heaven-freed from the degrading despotism of God.

We raised our glasses and drank to EQUALITY, sacred EQUALITY; and then ordered the waiter to bring us green Chartreuse and more cigars.

I went home very thoughtful. I did not go to sleep for a long while; I lay awake; thinking over this vision of a new world that had been presented to me.

How delightful life would be, if only the schemes of my socialistic friends could be carried out. There would be no more of this struggling and striving against each other, no more jealousy, no more disappointment, no more fear of poverty! The State would take charge of us from the hour we were born until we died, and provide for all our wants from the cradle to the coffin, both inclusive, and we should need to give no thought even to the matter. There would be no more hard work (three hours' labour a day would be the limit, according to our calculations, that the State would require from each adult citizen, and nobody would be allowed to do more – I should not be allowed to do more) – no poor to pity, no rich to envy – no one to look down upon us, no one for us to look down upon (not quite so pleasant this latter reflection) – all our life ordered and arranged for us – nothing to think about except the glorious destiny (whatever that might be) of Humanity!

Then thought crept away to sport in chaos, and I slept.

When I awoke, I found myself lying under a glass case, in a high, cheerless room. There was a label over my head; I turned and read it. It ran as follows:

'MAN–ASLEEP
PERIOD – 19TH CENTURY

This man was found asleep in a house in London, after the great social revolution of 1899. From the account given by the landlady of the house, it would appear that he had already, when discovered, been asleep for over ten years (she having forgotten to call him). It was decided, for scientific purposes, not to awaken him but to just see how long he would sleep on, and he was accordingly brought and deposited in the "Museum of Curiosities", on February 11, 1900.'

'Visitors are requested not to squirt water through the air-hole.'

An intelligent-looking old gentleman, who had been arranging some stuffed lizards in an adjoining case, came over and took the cover off me.

'What's the matter?' he asked, 'anything disturbed you?'

'No,' I said; 'I always wake up like this when I feel I've had enough sleep. What century is this?'

'This,' he said, 'is the twenty-ninth century. You have been asleep just one thousand years.'

'Ah! Well, I feel all the better for it,' I replied, getting down off the table. 'There's nothing like having one's sleep out.'

'I take it you are going to do the usual thing,' said the old gentleman to me, as I proceeded to put on my clothes, which had been lying beside me in the case. 'You'll want me to walk round the city with you, and explain all the changes to you, while you ask questions and make silly remarks?'

'Yes,' I replied, 'I suppose that's what I ought to do.'

'I suppose so,' he muttered. 'Come on, and let's get it over,' and he led the way from the room.

As we went downstairs, I said: 'Well, is it all right, now?'

'Is what all right?' he replied.

'Why, the world,' I answered. 'A few friends of mine were arranging, just before I went to bed to take it to pieces and fix it up again properly. Have they got it all right by this time? Is everybody equal now, and sin and sorrow and all that sort of thing done away with?'

'Oh, yes,' replied my guide; 'you'll find everything all right now. We've been working away pretty hard at things while you've been asleep. We've just got this earth about perfect now, I should say. Nobody is allowed to do anything wrong or silly and as for equality, tadpoles ain't in it with us.'

(He talked in rather a vulgar manner, I thought; but I did not like to reprove him.)

We walked out into the city. It was very clean and very quiet. The streets, which were designated by numbers, ran out from each other at right angles, and all presented exactly the same appearance. There were no horses or carriages about; all the traffic was conducted by electric cars. All the people that we met wore a quiet, grave expression, and were so much like each other as to give one the idea that they were all members of the same family. Everyone was dressed, as was also my guide, in a pair of grey trousers, and a grey tunic, buttoning tight round the neck and fastened round the waist by a belt. Each man was clean shaven, and each man had black hair.

I said: 'Are all these men twins?'

'Twins! Good gracious no!' answered my guide 'Whatever made you fancy that?'

'Why, they all look so much alike, 'I replied; 'and they've all got black hair!'

'Oh, that's the regulation colour for hair,' explained my companion: 'we've all got black hair. If a man's hair is not black naturally he had to have it dyed black'.

'Why?' I asked.

'Why!' retorted the old gentleman, somewhat irritably. 'Why, I thought you understood that all men were now equal. What would become of our equality if one man or woman were allowed to swagger about in golden hair, while another had to put up with carrots. Men have not only got to be equal in these happy days but to look it, as far as can be. By causing all men to be clean shaven, and all men and women to have black hair cut the same length, we obviate, to a certain extent, the errors of Nature.'

I said: 'Why black?'

He said he did not know, but that was the colour which had been decided upon.

'Who by?' I asked.

'By THE MAJORITY,' he replied, raising his hat and lowering his eyes, as if in prayer. We walked further, and passed more men. I said: 'Are there no women in this city?' 'Women!' exclaimed my guide. 'Of course there are. We've passed hundreds of them!'

'I thought I knew a woman when I saw one,' I observed; 'but I can't remember noticing any.'

'Why, there go two, now,' he said, drawing my attention to a couple of persons near to us, both dressed in the regulation grey trousers and tunics.

'How do you know they are women?' I asked.

'Why, you see the metal numbers that everybody wears on their collar?'

'Yes: I was just thinking what a number of policemen you had and wondering where the other people were!'

'Well, the even numbers are women; the odd numbers are men.'

'How very simple,' I remarked. 'I suppose after a little practice you can tell one sex from the other almost at a glance?'

'Oh yes,' he replied, 'if you want to.'

We walked on in silence for a while. And then I said: 'Why does everybody have a number?'

'To distinguish him by,' answered my companion.

'Don't people have names, then?'

'No.'

'Why?'

'Oh! there was so much inequality in names. Some people were called Montmorency, and they looked down on the Smiths; and the Smythes did not like mixing with the Joneses: so, to save further bother, it was decided to abolish names altogether, and to give everybody a number.'

'Did not the Montmorencys and the Smythes object?'

'Yes; but the Smiths and Joneses were THE MAJORITY.'

'And did not the Ones and Twos look down upon the Threes and Fours, and so on?'

'At first, yes. But, with the abolition of wealth numbers lost their value, except for industrial purposes and for double acrostics, and now No. 100 does not consider himself in any way superior to No. 1,000,000.'

I had not washed when I got up, there being no conveniences for doing so in the Museum, and I was beginning to feel somewhat hot and dirty. I said: 'Can I wash myself anywhere?'

He said: 'No; we are not allowed to wash ourselves. You must wait until half-past four, and then you will be washed for tea.'

'*Be* washed!' I cried. 'Who by?'

'The State.'

He said that they had found they could not maintain their equality when people were allowed to wash themselves. Some people washed three or four times a day, while others never touched soap and water from one year's end to the other, and in consequence there got to be two distinct classes, the Clean and the Dirty. All the old class prejudices began to be revived. The clean despised the dirty, and the dirty hated the clean. So, to end dissension, the State decided to do the washing itself, and each citizen was now washed twice a day by government-appointed officials; and private washing was prohibited.

I noticed that we passed no houses as we went along only block after block of huge, barrack-like buildings, all of the same size and shape. Occasionally, at a corner, we came across a smaller building, labelled 'Museum', 'Hospital', 'Debating Hall', 'Bath', 'Gymnasium', 'Academy of Sciences', 'Exhibition of Industries', 'School of Talk', &c., &c; but never a house.

I said: 'Doesn't anybody live in this town!'

He said: 'You do ask silly questions; upon my word, you do. Where do you think they live?'

I said: 'That's just what I've been trying to think. I don't see any houses anywhere!'

He said: 'We don't need houses – not houses such as you are thinking of. We are socialistic now; we live together in fraternity and equality. We live in these blocks that you see. Each block accommodates one thousand citizens. It contains one thousand beds – one thousand in each room and bath-rooms and dressing-rooms in proportion, a dining-hall and kitchens. At seven o'clock every morning a bell is rung, and every one rises and tidies up his bed. At seven-thirty they go into the dressing-rooms, and are washed and shaved and have their hair done. At eight o'clock breakfast is served in the dining-hall. It comprises a pint of oatmeal porridge and half-a-pint of warm milk for each adult citizen. We are all strict vegetarians now. The vegetarian vote increased enormously during the last century, and their organisation being very perfect, they have been able to dictate every election for the past fifty years. At one o'clock another bell is rung, and the people return to dinner, which consists of beans and stewed fruits, with rolly-polly pudding twice a week, and plum-duff on Saturdays. At five o'clock there is tea, and at ten the lights are put out and everybody goes to bed. We are all equal, and we all live alike – clerk and scavenger, tinker and apothecary – all together in fraternity and liberty. The men live in blocks on this side of the town and the women are at the other end of the city.'

'Where are the married people kept?' I asked.

'Oh, there are no married couples,' he replied; 'we abolished marriage two hundred years ago. You see, married life did not work at all well with our system. Domestic life, we found, was thoroughly anti-socialist in its tendencies. Men thought more of their wives and families than they did of the State. They wished to labour for the benefit of their little circle of beloved ones rather than for the good of the community. They cared more for the future of their children than for the Destiny of Humanity. The ties of love and blood bound them together fast in little groups instead of in one great whole. Before considering the advancement of the human race, men considered the advancement of their kith and kin. Before striving for the greatest happiness of the greatest number, men strove for the happiness of the few who were near and dear to them. In secret, men and women hoarded up and laboured and denied themselves, so as, in secret, to give some little extra joy to their beloved. Love stirred the vice of ambition in men's hearts. To win the smiles of the women they loved, to leave a name behind them that their children might be proud to bear, men sought to raise themselves above the general level, to do some deed that should make the world look up to them and honour them above their fellow-men, to press a deeper footprint than another's upon the dusty highway of the age. The fundamental principles of Socialism were being daily thwarted and contemned. Each house was a revolutionary centre for the propagation of individualism and personality. From the warmth of each domestic hearth grew up the vipers, Comradeship and Independence, to sting the State and poison the minds of men.

'The doctrines of equality were openly disputed. Men, when they loved a woman, thought her superior to every other woman, and hardly took any pains to disguise their opinion. Loving wives believed their husbands to be wiser and braver and better than all other men. Mothers laughed at the idea of their children being in no way superior to other children. Children imbibed the hideous heresy that their father and mother were the best father and mother in the world.

'From whatever point you looked at it, the Family stood forth as our foe. One man had a charming wife and two sweet-tempered children; his neighbour was married to a shrew and was the father of eleven noisy, ill-dispositioned brats – where was the equality?

'Again, wherever the Family existed, there hovered, ever contending, the angels of Joy and Sorrow; and in a world where joy and sorrow are known, Equality cannot live. One man and woman, in the night, stand weeping beside a little cot. On the other side of the lath-and-plaster, a fair young couple, hand in hand, are laughing at the silly antics of a grave-faced, gurgling baby. What is poor Equality doing?

'Such things could not be allowed. Love, we saw, was our enemy at every turn. He made equality impossible. He brought joy and pain, and peace and suffering in his train. He disturbed men's beliefs, and imperilled the Destiny of Humanity; so we abolished him and all his works.

'Now there are no marriages, and, therefore, no domestic troubles; no wooing; therefore, no heartaching; no loving, therefore no sorrowing; no kisses and no tears.

'We all live together in equality, free from the troubling of joy or pain.'

I said: 'It must be very peaceful; but tell me – I ask the question from a scientific standpoint – how do you keep up the supply of men and women?'

He said: 'Oh, that's simple enough. How did you, in your day, keep up the supply of horses and cows? In the spring, so many children, according as the State requires, are arranged for, and carefully bred, under medical supervision. When they are born, they are taken away from their mothers (who, else, might grow to love them) and brought up in public nurseries and schools until they are fourteen. They are then examined by State-approved inspectors, who decide what calling they shall be brought up to, and to such calling they are thereupon apprenticed. At twenty they take their rank as citizens, and are entitled to a vote. No difference whatever is made between men and women. Both sexes enjoy equal privileges.'

I said: 'What are the privileges?'

He said: 'Why, all that I've been telling you.'

We wandered on for a few more miles, but passed nothing but street after street of these huge blocks. I said: 'Are there no shops nor stores in this town?'

'No,' he replied. 'What do we want with shops and stores? The State feeds us, clothes us, houses us, doctors us, washes and dresses us, cuts our corns, and buries us. What could we do with shops?'

I began to feel tired with our walk. I said: 'Can we go in anywhere and have a drink?'

He said: 'A drink! What's a drink? We have half-a-pint of cocoa with our dinner. Do you mean that?'

I did not feel equal to explaining the matter to him, and he evidently would not have understood me if I had; so I said: 'Yes, I meant that.'

We passed a very fine-looking man a little further on, and I noticed that he only had one arm. I had noticed two or three rather big-looking men with only one arm in the course of the morning, and it struck me as curious. I remarked about it to my guide.

He said: 'Yes, when a man is much above the average size and strength, we cut one of his legs or arms off, so as to make things more equal; we lop him down a bit, as it were. Nature, you see, is somewhat behind the times but we do what we can to put her straight.'

I said: 'I suppose you can't abolish her?'

'Well, not altogether' he replied. 'We only wish we could. But,' he added afterwards, with pardonable pride, 'we've done a good deal.'

I said: 'How about an exceptionally clever man. What do you do with him?'

'Well, we are not much troubled in that way now,' he answered. 'We have not come across anything dangerous in the shape of brain-power for some very considerable time now. When we do, we perform a surgical operation upon the head, which softens the brain down to the average level.'

'I have sometimes thought,' mused the old gentleman, 'that it was a pity we could not level up some times instead of always levelling down; but, of course, that is impossible.'

I said: 'Do you think it right of you to cut these people up and tone them down, in this manner?'

He said: 'Of course, it is right.'

'You seem very cock-sure about the matter,' I retorted. 'Why is it "of course" right?' 'Because it is done by THE MAJORITY.'

'How does that make it right?' I asked.

'A MAJORITY can do no wrong,' he answered.

'Oh! is that what the people who are lopped think?'

'They!' he replied, evidently astonished at the question. 'Oh, they are in the minority, you know.'

'Yes; but even the minority has a right to its arms and legs and heads, hasn't it?'

'A minority has NO rights,' he answered.

I said: 'It's just as well to belong to the Majority, if you're thinking of living here isn't it?'

He said: 'Yes; most of our people do. They seem to think it more convenient.'

I was finding the town somewhat uninteresting, and I asked if we could not go out into the country for a change.

My guide said: 'Oh, yes, certainly;' but did not think I should care much for it.

'Oh! but it used to be so beautiful in the country,' I urged, 'before I went to bed. There were great green trees, and grassy, wind-waved meadows, and little rose-decked cottages and —'

'Oh, we've changed all that,' interrupted the old gentleman; 'it is all one huge market-garden now, divided by roads and canals cut at right angles to each other. There is no beauty in the country now whatever. We have abolished beauty; it interfered with our equality. It was not fair that some people should live among lovely scenery, and others upon barren moors. So we have made it all pretty much alike everywhere now, and no place can lord it over another.'

'Can a man emigrate into any other country?' I asked; 'it doesn't matter what country – *any* other country would do.'

'Oh, yes, if he likes,' replied my companion; 'but why should he? All lands are exactly the same. The whole world is all one people now – one language, one law, one life.'

'Is there no variety, no change anywhere?' I asked. 'What do you do for pleasure, for recreation? Are there any theatres?'

'No,' responded my guide. 'We had to abolish theatres. The histrionic temperament seemed utterly unable to accept the principles of equality. Each actor thought himself the best actor in the world, and superior, in fact, to most other people altogether. I don't know whether it was the same in your day?'

'Exactly the same,' I answered, 'but we did not take any notice of it.'

'Ah, we did,' he replied, 'and, in consequence, shut the theatres up. Besides, our White Ribbon Vigilance Society said that all places of amusement were vicious and degrading; and being an energetic and stout-winded band, they soon won THE MAJORITY over to their views; and so all amusements are prohibited now.'

I said: 'Are you allowed to read books?'

'Well,' he answered, 'there are not many writers. You see, owing to our all living such perfect lives, and there being no wrong, no sorrow, or joy or hope, or love or grief in the world, and everything being so regular and so proper, there is really nothing much to write about except, of course, the Destiny of Humanity.'

'True!' I said, 'I see that. But what of the old works, the classics? You had Shakespeare, and Scott, and Thackeray, and there were one or two little things of my own that were not half-bad. What have you done with all those?'

'Oh, we have burned all those old works,' he said. 'They were full of the old, wrong notions of the old, wrong, wicked times, when men were merely slaves and beasts of burden.'

He said all the old paintings and sculptures had been likewise destroyed, partly for that same reason, and partly because they were considered improper by the White Ribbon Vigilance Society, which was a great power now; while all new art and literature were forbidden, as such things tended to undermine the principles of equality. They made men think, and the men that thought grew cleverer than those that did not want to think; and those that did not want to think naturally objected to this, and being in THE MAJORITY, objected to some purpose.

He said that, from like considerations, there were no sports or games permitted.

Sports and games caused competition, and competition led to inequality.

I said: 'How long do your citizens work each day?'

'Three hours,' he answered; 'after that, all the remainder of the day belongs to ourselves.'

'Ah! that is just what I was coming to' I remarked. 'Now, what do you do with yourselves during those other twenty-one hours?'

'Oh, we rest.'

'What! for the whole twenty-one hours?'

'Well, rest and think and talk.'

'What do you think and talk about?'

'Oh! Oh, about how wretched life must have been in the old times, and about how happy we are now, and – and – oh, and the Destiny of Humanity.'

'Don't you ever get sick of the Destiny of Humanity?'

'No, not much.'

'And what do you understand by it? What *is* the Destiny of Humanity, do you think?'

'Oh! – why to – to go on being like we are now, only more so – everybody more equal and more things done by electricity, and everybody to have two votes instead of one and—'

'Thank you. That will do. Is there anything else that you think of? Have you got a religion?'

'Oh, yes.'

'And you worship a God?'

'Oh yes.'

'What do you call him?'

'THE MAJORITY.'

'One question more – You don't mind my asking you all these questions, by-the-by, do you?'

'Oh, no. This is all part of my three hours' labour for the State.'

'Oh, I'm glad of that. I should not like to feel that I was encroaching on your time for rest; but what I wanted to ask was, do many of the people here commit suicide?'

'No; such a thing never occurs to them.'

I looked at the faces of the men and women that were passing. There was a patient, almost pathetic, expression upon them all. I wondered where I had seen this look before; it seemed familiar to me.

All at once I remembered. It was just the quiet troubled, wondering expression that I had always noticed upon the faces of the horses and oxen that we used to breed and keep in the old world.

No. These people would *not* think of suicide.

Strange! how very dim and indistinct all the faces are growing around me! And where is my guide? and why am I sitting on the pavement? and – hark! surely that is the voice of Mrs. Briggs, my old landlady. Had *she* been asleep a thousand years, too? She says it is twelve o'clock – only twelve? and I'm not to be washed till half-past four; and I do feel so stuffy and hot, and my head is aching. Hulloa! why, I'm in bed! Has it all been a dream? And am I back in the nineteenth century?

Through the open window I hear the rush and roar of old life's battle. Men are fighting, striving, working, carving out each man his own life with the sword of strength and will. Men are laughing, grieving, loving, doing wrong deeds, doing great deeds, – falling, struggling, helping one another – living!

And I have a good deal more than three hours' work to do to-day, and I meant to be up at seven; and, oh dear! I do wish I had not smoked so many strong cigars last night!

LETTERS TO *THE TIMES*

The Jerome K Jerome Society is most greatful to Times Newspaper Ltd for their kind permission to reproduce the following correspondence.

'Writing letters to *The Times*,' according to Barrie, is – or was in our young days – 'the legitimate ambition of every Englishman.' Barrie was lodging in a turning out of Cavendish Square, and I was in Newman Street nearby. I confided to him one evening that the idea had occurred to me to write a letter to *The Times*. It seemed to me a handy way of keeping one's name before the public.

'They won't insert it,' said Barrie.

'Why not?' I demanded.

'Because you're not a married man,' he answered.

'I've been studying this matter. I've noticed that *The Times* make a speciality of parents. You are not a parent. You can't sign yourself "Pater-familias", or "Father of Seven" – not yet. You're not even "An Anxious Mother". You're not fit to write to *The Times*. Go away. Go away and get married. Beget children. Then come and see me again, and I'll advise you.'

But I was not to be disheartened. I waited for the Academy to open. As I expected, a letter immediately appeared on the subject of 'The Nude in Art'. It was a perennial topic in the 'eighties. It was signed 'British Matron'. I forget precisely what I said. (*My Life and Times*)

What Jerome in fact said was printed in *The Times* of May 23rd of 1885 as follows:

TO THE EDITOR OF THE TIMES

Sir, – I quite agree with your correspondent, 'A British Matron', that the human form is a disgrace to decency, and that it ought never to be seen in its natural state.

But 'A British Matron' does not go far enough, in my humble judgement. She censures the painters, who merely copy Nature. It is God Almighty who is to blame in this matter for having created such an indelicate object.

I am, Sir, your obedient servant.

Jerome K Jerome

To subsequent letters of mine *The Times* was equally kind. I wrote upon the dangers of the streets – dogs connected to old ladies by a string; the use of the perambulator in dispersing crowds; the rich man's carpet stretched across the dark pavement and the contemplative pedestrian. I advised 'Paterfamilias' what to do with his daughters. I discussed the possibility of living on seven hundred a year. *The Times*, in an editorial, referred to me as a 'Humorist'. (*My Life and Times*)

The following letter appeared in *The Times* of 21 April 1885:

MAT TRAPS

TO THE EDITOR OF THE TIMES

Sir – Your article in *The Times* of to-day upon the case 'De Teyron Waring', in which the plaintiff recovered damages for injuries sustained by tripping over a piece of matting laid across the pavement by the defendant, would seem to imply a sympathy with the latter. The writer has evidently never fallen a victim to this system of Belgravian atrocity. I have; and am, as a consequence, strongly in favour of any step taken to put a stop to it. What between peg-tops and tip-cats, coals being taken in and dust being taken out, beer barrels being let down public house cellars, shop-boys' brooms, scavengers' carts, perambulators, poodles, and idiots who carry their umbrellas under their arms, &c., the London streets are quite lively enough. At night we who love to walk and ponder look for a little happiness. We choose a quiet street or square, and, lighting a cigar, anticipate the luxury of a contemplative dawdle. Before we have gone 20 yards we find ourselves on our noses, with a grinning flunkey standing over us, wanting to know why the – we cannot look where we are going. Walking along a West-End street on an evening in the season is like picking one's way over an Irish bog and one has to go along lifting up one's legs like a circus horse. Surely the most dainty-footed can step from the kerb to the door on a dry night without this absurd paraphernalia.

I am, Sir you obedient servant.

Jerome K Jerome

And on 31 December 1885 *The Times* published the following letter:

CRUELTY TO HORSES

Sir – Can no one be made responsible for the gross cruelty that is daily inflicted upon London horses? I suppose a vestry (which, like a corporation, has no soul to be damned and nobody to be kicked) cannot be punished for its brutal supineness; but is there no official whose humanity and sense of duty might be quickened by a week's hard labour or a fine? In this damp, foggy weather the oily slime known as London mud lies an inch deep on every thoroughfare, and over its slippery, treacherous surface the tortured horses have to fight and struggle with their heavy loads. The sight of these brave, patient, willing creatures panting and staining at their traces, their muscles stretched to the utmost tension, their every nerve twitching with terror and pain, and their gentle eyes so full of trouble, is a disgrace to a Christian people.

A few cartloads of gravel sprinkled over the streets would remove the daily horror from our midst. I do not ask that this should be done for the sake of humanity. That would be idle to expect. But the injury caused to valuable animals must be considerable, and, in the sacred name of property, I plead that their sufferings may be relieved.

I am, Sir, your obedient servant.

Jerome K Jerome

* * *

'To have a letter published in *The Times* is the duty of the distinguished and the ambition of the obscure' (Bernard Levin). The Hon. Sec. thought he would fulfil his ambition and follow Jerome's lead. His letter appeared in *The Times* on 15 March 1997.

Surname usage
From Mr. Tony Gray

Sir, Persons who corresponded with Jerome K Jerome (or for that matter Ford Madox Ford) were relieved of the problem of having to decide whether to use Christian name or surname (letters. March 8. etc.), as the following verse of unknown origin neatly illustrates.

Said Jerome K Jerome to Ford Madox Ford.

'There is something, old boy, that I've always abhorred:

When people address me and call me Jerome

Are they being standoffish, or too much at home?'

Said Ford, 'I agree: It's the same thing with me.'

Yours faithfully,

A A GRAY (Honorary Secretary),

Jerome K Jerome Society

Four years later, there was some correspondence in *The Times* about rats. The letter that started off the subject came from a reader who felt that a Channel 4 series *Survivor* did not give due credit to the food value of the rat. His prompted various other letters on the same subject, including another winner from the Hon. Sec.

Roast rat and veg
From Mr. John Selley

Sir, According to the *Larousse Gastronomique*, rats nourished in the wine stores of the Gironde were at some time in the 19th century highly esteemed by the coopers (letters, May 18 and 19), who grilled them on a fire of broken barrels and seasoned them with a little oil and plenty of shallots. This dish was known as 'Cooper's Entrecote' it is not clear whether copious drafts of wine were drunk either before or after eating this dish.

The next entry but one is another recipe (for a couple of vegetarians) under the title 'Ratatouille'.

Yours faithfully,
JOHN W SELLEY
May 20

From Mr. T R Norcross

Sir, I recall a meal some years ago at an hotel in Belize City. A menu item which caught my eye was 'Gibnut'. On inquiry, I was told that this was Game Rat. I found it commendably edible.

Yours faithfully,
T R NORCROSS
May 20.

From the Honorary Secretary of the Jerome K Jerome Society

Sir, In Jerome K Jerome's *Three Men in a Boat* the three men produced a very successful Irish stew. The dog Montmorency's contribution to the dish was a dead water rat (letters, May 18, 19 and 23).

George objected, but Harris said 'If you never try a new thing, how can you tell what it is like? It's men such as you that hamper the world's progress. Think of the man who first tried German sausage!'

We are told that there is an over-plus of rats in this country. If one or more of the ubiquitous television chefs could popularise the rat as a chic dish, two birds (or rats) could be killed with one stone.

Yours faithfully,
TONY GRAY,
Honorary Secretary,
Jerome K Jerome Society
May 24.

From Mr. Peter Presence

Sir, Tony Gray (letter, May 25) may be an expert on Jerome K Jerome, but not one when it comes to zoology.

Montmorency's contribution to the Irish stew was, in my view, the near-extinct water vole, whose attempted salvation is the subject of your report and photograph (May 25); and, as the text makes clear, it is not a rat at all.

Yours constructively,
PETER PRESENCE,
May 25.

From Consul General Terence Fuery

Sir, Mr. T R Norcross (letter, May 23) mentions the Gibnut. Delicious as it is, it was served to Her Majesty the Queen on a visit to Belize some years ago and it is now popularly known as the Royal Rat.

Yours faithfully,
TERENCE FUREY
(Honorary Consul General of Belize)
May 29.

From Mr. Ross Robertson

Sir, The culinary delights of curried rat (letters, May 30) were well known to the tea-estate workers in the Dooars, West Bengal, where I was a tea planter in the early 1960s.

Field rats, as they were called, had the annoying habit of burrowing beneath young tea plants and severing the tap root. A squad of older men was employed to catch these creatures. This was a job much sought after, where curried rat for *khana* (dinner) was a bonus to pay received.

Yours faithfully
ROSS ROBERTSON,
May 31

From Professor Emeritus Brian G Palmer

Sir, I was lunching with French-speaking friends who have a farm in Quebec province. Part way through the meal the husband exclaimed to his wife that they should have served what I heard as ramusquet'. As soon as he explained that he caught them and had one in the freezer, I realized that it was *rat musque* – muskrat. It is a delicacy and we would certainly have it next time.

I haven't been back.

Yours faithfully,
BRIAN PALMER,
May 30

A CHAT ABOUT HOME-MADE FURNITURE
by Jerome K Jerome

Adapted from the chapter entitled 'On the Exceptional Merit attaching to Things we Meant to Do', in The Second Thoughts of an Idle Fellow.

I can remember a long time ago when there was in great demand a certain periodical called *The Amateur*. Its aim was noble. It sought to teach the beautiful, lesson of independence, to inculcate the fine doctrine of self-help. One chapter explained to a man how he might make flower-pots out of Australian meat-cans; another how he might turn butter-tubs into music-stools; a third how he might utilise old bonnet-boxes for Venetian-blinds: that was the principle of the whole scheme – you made everything from something not intended for it, and as ill suited to the purpose as possible.

The thing that *The Amateur* put in the front and foremost of its propaganda was the manufacture of household furniture out of egg boxes. With a sufficient supply of egg-boxes, no young couple need hesitate to face the furnishing problem. Three egg-boxes made a writing-table; on another egg-box you sat to write; your books were ranged in egg-boxes around you and there was your study complete.

For the dining-room two egg-boxes made an overmantel; four egg-boxes and a piece of looking-glass a sideboard; while six egg boxes, with some wadding and a yard or so of cretonne, constituted a so-called 'cosy-corner'. About the 'corner' there could no possible doubt. You sat on a corner, you leant against a corner; whichever way you moved you struck a fresh corner.

I have from Saturday to Monday, as honoured guest, hung my clothes in egg-boxes. I have sat on an egg-box at an egg-box to take my dish of tea; I have made love on egg-boxes. I have spent many an evening on an egg-box: I have gone to bed in egg-boxes. They have their points – I intend no pun – but to claim cosiness from them would be but to deceive.

Picture-frames you fashioned out of gingerbeer corks. You saved your gingerbeer corks, you found a picture – and the thing was complete. How much gingerbeer it would be necessary to drink, preparatory to the making of each frame, and the effect of it upon the frame-maker's physical, mental and moral, well-being, did not concern *The Amateur*. For a fair-sized frame sixteen dozen bottles might suffice. Whether, after sixteen dozen of gingerbeer, a man would take any interest in framing a picture – whether he would retain any pride in the picture itself – is doubtful. But this, of course, was not the point.

One young gentleman of my acquaintance – the son of the gardener of my sister, as friend Ollendorff would have described him – did succeed in getting through sufficient gingerbeer to frame his grandfather, but the result was not encouraging. Indeed, the gardener's wife herself was but ill satisfied.

'What's all them corks round father,' was her first question.

'Can't you see that's the frame!'

'Oh! but why corks?'

'Well, the book said corks'.

Still the old lady remained unimpressed.

'Somehow it don't look like father now,' she sighed.

'What does it look like, then?' he growled.

'Well, I dunno. Seems to me to look like nothing but corks.'

Another young gentleman friend of mine made a rocking-chair, according to the instructions of the book, out of a couple of beer-barrels.

From every practical point of view it was a bad rocking-chair. It rocked too much, and it rocked in too many directions at one and the same time ....

I had called and had been shown into the empty drawing-room. The rocking-chair nodded invitingly at me. I never guessed it was an amateur rocking-chair. I threw myself into it lightly and carelessly. I immediately noticed the ceiling. I made an instinctive movement forward. The window and a momentary glimpse of the wooded hills beyond shot upwards and disappeared. The carpet flashed across my eyes, and I caught sight of my own boots vanishing beneath me at the rate of about two hundred miles an hour. I made a convulsive effort to recover them. I suppose I overdid it. I saw the whole of the room at once, the four walls, the ceiling, and the floor at the same moment. Something hit me violently in the small of my back. Reason, when recovered, suggested that my assailant must be the rocking-chair. Investigation proved the surmise correct. Fortunately I was still alone, and in consequence was able, a few minutes later, to meet my hostess with calm and dignity, I said nothing about the rocking-chair. As a matter of fact, I was hoping to have the pleasure, before I went, of seeing some other guest arrive and sample it. I had purposely placed it in the most prominent and convenient position. But though I felt capable of schooling myself to silence, I found myself unable to agree with my hostess when she called for my admiration of the thing. My recent experience had too greatly embittered me.

'Willie made it himself,' explained the fond mother. 'Don't you think it was very clever of him?'

'Oh yes, it was clever,' I replied; 'I am willing to admit that.'

'He made it out of some old beer-barrels,' she continued; she seemed proud of it.

My resentment, though I tried to keep it under control, was mounting higher.

'Oh, did he?' I said. 'I should have thought he might have found something better to do with them.'

'What?' she asked.

'Oh, well, many things,' I retorted. 'He might have filled them again with beer.'

My hostess looked at me astonished. I felt some reason for my tone was expected.

'You see,' I explained, 'it is not a well-made chair. These rockers are too short – and they are too curved, and one of them, if you notice, is higher than the other and of a small radius; the back is at too obtuse an angle when it is occupied – the centre of gravity becomes' – My hostess interrupted me.

'Why, you have been sitting on it!' she said.

'Not for long,' I assured her.

8
THE IDLER AND *TO-DAY*

The July–August 1994 issue of the modern-day The Idler *profiled 'a seminal idler' with particular reference to Jerome's role as editor and businessman.*

JEROME K JEROME – IDLE IDOLS NO. 5
by Dan Glaister

You never know who you might bump into in a park. In his semi-autobiographical novel *Paul Kelver*, Jerome K Jerome claimed to have seen Dickens one evening taking the air in Victoria Park in Hackney, East London. 'Oh, damn Mr. Pickwick,' said the walking, talking legend, who had reached a wide public with *The Pickwick Papers*. For Jerome, this brush with greatness was enough. He and the master, if not one and the same, had at least suffered a similar plight.

Say Jerome K Jerome to anyone to-day and you will discover the name of the complaint: *Three Men In A Boat*. Jerome, to his consternation, was known exclusively as 'the author of *Three Men In A Boat*, his comic novel published in 1889 about a trip down the Thames taken by three friends and their dog.

Jerome had not expected to be branded a master of whimsy. 'Like most men who have the reputation of being funny,' he was to write in his autobiography *My Life and Times*, 'I am somewhat a gloomy personage.' He felt, quite justifiably, that his other talents had been overlooked.

For six years, from 1892 to 1898, Jerome edited *The Idler*, a monthly blend of fiction, essays, cartoons, interviews and poems, a 19 century gentleman's club in magazine form (ladies admitted).

The turn-of-the-century-idler, with Jerome as his prophet, took his pursuits seriously. Jerome records how he had to force himself to learn how to drink alcohol, graduating from the horrors of cheap claret, which he used to sip with his eyes shut, to the more acceptable pleasures of whisky, which he was eventually able to drink 'without a shudder'.

The idle fellow was usually to be found sitting in an arm-chair before an open fire, sipping a glass of whisky while smoking his pipe. With a small group of friends gathered around him, sometimes including a benefactor or distant relation, the idler would while away the hours swapping tales. An apparently inexhaustible supply of anecdotes was an essential part of the idler armoury, as was the ability to be sidetracked, to lose one's train of thought, or to nod off in the middle of telling a story. The idler could feign firsthand experience or expertise of virtually any subject, while affecting a disdain for earthly matters. Prevarication and deviation were a must, oneupmanship to be admired. The idler, in short, knew where his slippers were.

Cover of *The Idler*, 1893

Jerome was expert at portraying his ideal idler. His *Idle Thoughts Of An Idle Fellow*, published in 1886 and dedicated to his pipe, opens with the words: 'It is a most remarkable thing. I sat down with the full intention of writing something clever and original; but for the life of me I can't think of anything clever or original – at least, not at this moment. The only thing I can think of is being hard up.'

Costing sixpence, the first issue of *The Idler* ranged from the juvenile to the sophisticated. 'Detective Stories Gone Wrong – The Adventures Of Sherlaw Kombs' by Luke Sharp, and 'Enchanted Cigarettes', a paean to the pleasures of smoking, ran alongside 'Famous Idling Places – Hyeres' in the first issue, followed by Orvieto and Madeira in later numbers – and the Idler's Club, a joint manifesto for the idle way of life.

Yet if he embraced idleness with enthusiasm, Jerome was no slouch, as businessman or editor. For the first number of *The Idler*, he ran a new story by Mark Twain. The magazine was an immediate success, and as it developed, so new items were introduced. 'My First Book' had authors ruminating on their early successes, a gimmick that still appeals to newspaper editors to-day, while the archetype for *Idler* articles had the title 'People I Have Never Met'.

The magazine breathed idleness. Newcomers to the *Idler* offices off the Strand were soon taken over by 'the idling influence of the place', seduced by *Idler* 'at homes' – Friday afternoon tea parties. Jerome assembled an impressive collection of idle friends to help him with his work, including Arthur Conan Doyle, George Bernard Shaw and Rudyard Kipling, who Jerome beat to the editorship of the magazine, Jerome being deemed easier to 'manage' by co-founder Robert Barr. Some, like H G Wells, didn't fit the idle bill: 'How Wells carries all his electricity without wearing out the casing and causing a short circuit in his brain is a scientific mystery,' wrote Jerome.

But *The Idler* did attract one man who fitted Jerome's vision of the productive yet contemplative figure. W W Jacobs, a regular contributor, was the antidote to the 'industry and steadfastness' of other, more well-known figures. 'Often he will spend … an entire morning constructing a single sentence,' Jerome gushed. 'If he writes a four-thousand word story in a month, he feels he has earned a holiday; and the reason that he does not always take it is that he is generally too tired.'

There is, of course, a conceit at work. For Jerome, idleness had little in common with laziness. His notion of idleness in the world beyond his fiction was one of contemplative productivity with the minimum of fuss. While Jerome praised idleness to the full, his own life, at least in his early years, was a busy affair.

Jerome was born in Walsall in 1859. His family, having lost its former wealth, moved to London when he was young and by his late teens Jerome was out on his own, leading a life of Dickensian deprivation in the East End of London. The young Jerome pursued a variety of careers: clerk, actor, journalist, with varying degrees of success. His writing began at an early age, a mysterious lady on a train telling him, aged six, that 'there is only one person you will ever know … Always write about him.' Jerome took the advice to heart, and many of his later writings were semi-autobiographical. It was, after all, easier that way.

His first paid writing was thanks to a journalist friend who introduced him to 'penny-a-lining'. Jerome was once more treading in the footsteps of Dickens, perfecting shorthand and filing court reports to newspapers. Journalism's competitive nature provided him with a grounding in comic writing. 'I found out how to make "flimsy" more saleable by grafting humour on to it,' he wrote, 'so sub-editors would give to mine a preference over more sober and possibly more truthful records.' The idler's penchant for labour-saving adornment was already evident.

Despite having several books and plays, as well as stories and essays published, Jerome did not have the courage to devote himself entirely to writing until the publication of *Three Men In A Boat* in 1889. The uncertainty of his youth had left its mark, and the constant striving for financial security that had obsessed his parents was to express itself in Jerome's reluctance to place himself at risk, intellectually or financially.

After the success of *Three Men In A Boat*, Jerome was recognised as one of the foremost humorists of his day. He mixed with the great and the good, and went to all the right clubs. He was able to settle down to a more leisurely way of life: travel, sport, good food and literature. Even with his new-found success, however, he was denied the recognition by the critics that he felt he had earned.

One reviewer of his best-known play, *The Passing Of The Third Floor Back*, wrote that 'it seems the work of a man of great cleverness, some fancy, and a shrewd humour, but one who has never tried his hardest to find out what is in him'. This is perhaps the main criticism to be had of Jerome. Shy and retiring, he preferred to cloak his writings in humour and avoid challenging his readers. Although his idleness was productive, it provided him with a security which was eventually to stifle his talents.

Occasionally a book or play would receive a favourable review, but it was the exception not the rule. *Punch* referred to him as Arry K Arry, lecturing him on 'the sin of mistaking vulgarity for humour and impertinence for wit'. Jerome saw himself as 'the best abused author in England'.

Jerome wrote a sequel to *Three Men In A Boat* – *Three Men On The Bummel* – as well as, among other works, *The Second Thoughts Of An Idle Fellow*, *Told After Supper*, a collection of ghost stories, and *Idle Ideas In 1905*. None of them was to reproduce the success of *Three Men In A Boat*. The only book by Jerome that approaches it is his autobiography, published in 1926, the year before he died.

Cover of *To-Day*, 1893

His involvement with *The Idler* was curtailed in 1898 by a libel action: in true Dickensian style the lawyers were the only victors. Jerome and the aggrieved company promoter who had brought the action against him being left to pay their own costs, in Jerome's case £9,000. He was later to write, 'I have the satisfaction of boasting that it was the longest case, and one of the most expensive, ever heard in the Court of Queen's Bench.'

In 1904 Jerome decided to put an end to his journalistic career to concentrate on writing and cultivate an interest in politics. He developed his taste for travel, becoming 'an habitué of the Continent'. On a lecture tour of the States (again following in the footsteps of Dickens) Jerome publicly condemned a lynching, a rare and brave act of defiance at the time.

One event was to shape Jerome in his later years. The outbreak of the First World War had produced mixed feelings in him. He had lived for several years in Germany and had a great affection for its people. The jingoism whipped up by the war made him extremely uncomfortable, souring relations with several old friends, notably Kipling and Wells.

In 1916, at the age of 55, Jerome decided to enlist. He managed to get a commission as an ambulance driver with the French army, serving on the Western Front near Verdun. The experience was to prove traumatic, perhaps breaking his health and prompting the emergence of a hitherto latent spirituality. Whatever else, his wartime experiences, movingly recorded in his autobiography, cured him of his fascination with war and confirmed his mistrust of politicians. Jerome returned to England to continue writing plays and settle increasingly into the Jeromeian mode. He died in Northampton in 1927 after suffering a heart attack while returning from holiday in Devon.

Despite enjoying the good things in life, he was to write shortly before his death that 'Happiness is not our goal, either in this world or the next. The joy of labour, the joy of giving are the wages of God.' A long way from the young man who had determined to 'learn the vices.' 'My study of literature had impressed it upon me,' he wrote, 'that without them one was a milksop, to be despised of all true men, and more especially of all fair women.'

JKJ AND OSCAR

by Jeremy Nicholas

Jerome condemned in his own publication, *To-day*, the contents of a new magazine, *The Chameleon*, which, in the words of Wilde's biographer Richard Ellmann, was 'an attempt to win acquiescence at Oxford for homosexuality'. In his play *The Invention of Love*, Tom Stoppard further added to speculation surrounding Jerome's connection with Wilde's subsequent arrest and incarceration. But what had Jerome written exactly? What had he said or done that might have had any bearing whatever on Wilde's disgrace?

The definitive answer arrived in the shape of the biography of Wilde by Neil McKenna. *The Secret Life of Oscar Wilde* (Arrow Books, 2004) is a brilliantly-written and -researched piece of work, 'whisky to Ellmann's water' as one reviewer described it, which goes into some prurient detail over Wilde's sex life.

In the first (and, as it transpired, only) edition of *The Chameleon* there appeared the unsigned story 'The Priest and the Acolyte'. It was written by an undergraduate, Jack Bloxam, one of the founders of the magazine and who later, incidentally, followed his fictional hero's footsteps into the priesthood. It concerned the sexual relationship between a man and a boy. Shockingly, the boy was portrayed not as seduced but as a willing partner. Further, the story made it quite clear that the love between the man and the boy was 'divinely ordained'. Not the sort of thing to appeal to genteel Victorian sensibilities.

Mc Kenna makes it abundantly clear that Wilde had an obsession with rent boys and engaged in a long series of relationships with several of them. It was first thought amongst his circle that Wilde was the author of this Uranian romance, but he himself, while approving of its sentiments, thought the story 'too direct … There is no nuance … still it has interesting qualities, and is at moments poisonous: which is something'.

Here is Jerome's reaction, in part, thundered in an editorial in *To-day* on 29 December 1894. He thought that *The Chameleon* was 'certainly a case for the police' and that 'the publication appears to be nothing more nor less than an advocacy for indulgence in the cravings of an unnatural disease'. *The Chameleon* was bound to absolutely corrupt and ruin any boys and young men attracted to members of their own sex. 'That young men are here and there cursed with these unnatural cravings, no one acquainted with our public school life can deny. It is for such to wrestle with the devil within them; and many a long and agonised struggle is fought, unseen and unknown, within the heart of a young man. A publication of this kind, falling into his hands before victory is complete, would, unless the poor fellow were of an exceptionally strong nature, utterly ruin him for all eternity.' Jerome described *The Chameleon* as 'is an insult to the animal creation … an outrage to literature … unbridled licence … garbage and offal'.

It was not long before *The Chameleon* found its way into the hands of the Marquis of Queensberry. There is absolutely nothing to link Jerome with this particular event beyond what he had written in *To-day,* and nothing, as Stoppard suggests in his play, to connect Jerome to Wilde's arrest, trial or imprisonment in Reading Gaol. We must remember that Queensberry was already a self-confessed hater of 'snob queers' and 'Jew nancy boys' having discovered that his elder son, Viscount Drumlanrig, had been the secret lover of Lord Roseberry (Foreign Secretary and future Prime Minister). Drumlanrig committed suicide in 1894. One can imagine Queensberry's state of mind so soon after losing a son, and already knowing not only that his younger son, Lord Alfred Douglas ('Bosie'), was associated with Oscar Wilde but that both of them were connected with the publication of *The Chameleon*.

This sorry tale does not, on the face of it, cast Jerome in the best of lights. But his views would not have differed substantially from those of the average member of the public at that time, one with very different attitudes to our own more tolerant and enlightened age. His strictly-observed Bible-based religious upbringing too would have made it impossible for him to countenance the idea of homosexuality. Its practice would have horrified him.

Nevertheless, the pompous moraliser we read in the *To-day* editorial could hardly be more different from the genial riverside companion describing Harris's attempts to make scrambled eggs. Jerome makes but one reference to Wilde in *My Life and Times,* a chilly dismissal and one that tactfully obscures his unfettered condemnation of thirty-two years earlier: 'The Florence [restaurant in Rupert Street]…was a cosy little place where one lunched for 1/3d and dined for 2/-. One frequently saw Oscar Wilde there. He and friends would come in late and take the table in the further corner. Rumours were already going about, and his company did not tend to dispel them. One pretended not to see him.'

UNCOLLECTED MATERIAL IN *THE IDLER* AND *TO-DAY*

by Alan R Whitby

It is well-known that Jerome K Jerome was editor of two magazines, the monthly *The Idler* between 1892–1898, and a weekly magazine-journal *To-day* between 1893–1898. These were used for the first publication of a number of his works. Also within these journals were many miscellaneous writings that were never reprinted. The collector who wants all of Jerome's works faces the daunting task of completing a set of both magazines.

In *The Idler* Jerome first serialised his own *Novel Notes*, and then contributed to the series later published as *My First Book.* (His preface called 'Echoes' was, however, first published in *To-day.*) Various short stories from *The Idler* and *To-day* later appeared in the volumes *John Ingerfield and Other Stories* and *Sketches in Lavender, Blue and Green.* Even though one may have these books, the original magazine publication can still be of interest for the illustrations. Additionally, Jerome often revised his work before book publication. As one example, the version of 'Silhouettes' in *The Idler* (February 1892) had a different opening to that found later in *John Ingerfield.*

In this article we are particularly concerned with magazine contributions that were never republished. Taking *The Idler* first: throughout Jerome's tenure there was a regular feature at the end of each magazine called 'The Idler's Club'. This was a series of rambling views from various hands on a featured topic in each issue, and often featured some humorous paragraphs from Jerome. W W Jacobs was a later contributor to this feature. Then there were the oddities like 'The Mystery of Black Rock Creek' (*Idler*: October 1894). This was a story in five chapters. Jerome wrote the first chapter, the remaining four being written by Eden Phillpotts, E F Benson, F Frankfort Moore and Barry Pain. A more substantial work in *The Idler* came in 1896 with the series 'Letters to Clorinda'. Old popular encyclopedias like *Harmsworth's* and *Nelson's* mention this as a book Jerome published in 1898.

However, Joseph Connolly's bibliography omits it, and no copy is in the British Library. Whether or not it ever appeared in book form, it was serialised in *The Idler* throughout 1896. 'Letters to Clorinda' is a series of letters to one Clorinda who lives in a Himalayan village, and therefore is completely out of touch with 1890's Britain. Jerome writes to her to comment on the current literary scene, much in *Idle Thoughts* style. His anecdotes are well up to standard, and one extract from this series is printed at the end of this article to illustrate this.

For some reason, Jerome's other magazine, the weekly *To-day* does not appear so collectable, and yet there is far more material from Jerome's pen in this than in *The Idler*. To start with, Jerome wrote the editorials each week. These were often in the form of crusading journalism, with current targets in politics, religion and the temperance movement. The style of the paper would eventually lead to the famous libel action of 1897. Although not written in the *Three Men in a Boat* style, there are little turns of phrase we can still enjoy to-day. From the December 30, 1893, editorial, under the heading 'The Ideal Club':

> They have opened an Ideal Club at 185, Tottenham Court Road, and to make sure that nobody shall misunderstand it they call it The Ideal Club. Drinking and smoking are prohibited. The president is the president of the London Vegetarian Society, so I presume it is a vegetarian club, and that meat is also prohibited. It was opened by Sir Julian Goldsmid, and maybe he will look in now and then. Every lady over seventeen and every gentleman over nineteen is eligible for membership. Whether they will all join is another matter. Altogether as a place to send one's enemies to, pending purgatory, the institution seems to supply a distinct want, but I would not call it an ideal club. At least it is not my ideal club ...

A news item on a centenarian prompted this comment on January 13, 1894:

> The reporter finds them out and asks them how it is that they have managed to live so long. The secret of longevity has been assigned by different long-lived people to indulgence in tobacco, and abstinence from tobacco; to indulgence in drink, and abstinence from drink; to daily exercise, and to a sedentary occupation; to fresh air, to every advertised drug, almost to everything. Miss Eliza Worth, of Henrietta NY USA, has been recently explaining her great age. She never drank tea or coffee, and she never married. Her brother only lived to the age of one hundred and one. She explains his premature decease by the fact that he was married ...

The editorial for January 20, 1894, had a personal note:

> Keenly do I regret the death of *Home Chimes*, a magazine edited by that kindliest of men and best of friends to young authors, Mr. F W Robinson, the novelist. *Home Chimes* was a little too sober and literary to catch on with the great public, but there are few of us younger writers who do not owe to it grateful remembrance. I recollect J M Barrie telling me that London was, at one time, chiefly remarkable to him as being the town in which *Home Chimes* was published. I think it was the first periodical in London that accepted anything from his pen, and it was in its pages that I first began to annoy the critics.

Home Chimes had of course first serialised *Idle Thoughts of an Idle Fellow* and then *Three Men in a Boat*, insisting on the editing that would turn the latter into a classic.

Jerome relinquished editorial control of *The Idler* and *To-Day* in 1898, and collectors may be inclined to dismiss later copies of these journals. This would be a big mistake. Although Joseph Connolly's biography suggests that Jerome lost contact after the break, this was certainly not the case with *To-Day*. He continued to feature prominently in its pages right up to the magazine's demise in 1905. *To-Day* serialised *Three Men on the Bummel* throughout 1900. Each episode was copiously illustrated by L Raven Hill, and many of these illustrations were omitted when the book appeared. *To-Day's* main serial though 1902–03 was *Paul Kelver*. In 1905, perhaps in an attempt to rectify flagging circulation, Jerome was invited to write 3–4 pages every week, with two series running at the same time. One was called 'Idle Thoughts' and started on February 1st, 1905. After a surprisingly long three year delay this eventually appeared as *The Angel and the Author – and Others*. (This book was not, as Connolly suggests, a rewrite of *Idle Ideas in 1905*.) There were a few small revisions in the text, and sadly the illustrations from *To-day* were absent.

Jerome was interviewed in the January 25, 1905 issue on how he had founded *To-Day*. He lamented the loss of authors from the old days and gave his views on mixing humour and seriousness. It was announced that from the next issue he would have a weekly column (in addition to 'Idle Thoughts') called 'Answers to Correspondents'. This series was to be exclusively Jerome's own, with his name in the title. It was almost back to Jerome's days as editor, except that 'Answers' was more entertaining. Immediately correspondents wrote in. From the first column (February 1, 1905):

> ROB ROY. I should like to answer you, because you ask me to do so, and evidently you are such a good fellow. But there is nothing to your letter to answer. It is filled with such pleasant compliments. How can I argue with you? I agree so entirely with all you say. I cannot answer you. Your kindness leaves me speechless!

> WILL BOOTH sends me an indefinite sort of article headed 'The New Potato'. He has evidently spent some pains writing about these potatoes, but I cannot help feeling he would have used his time to more advantage hoeing them. I find some difficulty in saying what I think concerning his effort, in spite of the fact that he urges me to be frank with him. He is either an exceedingly foolish young man who thinks himself clever, or else an exceptionally clever young man who is trying to palm himself off on his friends as an ass, and succeeding to perfection. Maybe he knows; personally I have not the time to work it out for him.

The riposte to the luckless Will Booth suggested to many readers that Jerome was editor again, and he was deluged with unwanted manuscripts. On February 22, 1905, he was forced to write a fairly lengthy piece under the heading 'To All Whom it May Concern'. He wrote (in part):

> I am not the editor of *To-Day*, nor of any other periodical. MSS. should not be addressed to me. I do not read MSS., and I do not advise ladies and

gentlemen as to whether they possess literary ability or not... There is no easy road to success in any branch of life. Interest and connection make the path smoother for the few. Prime Ministers, never intended by nature to be Prime Ministers, have gained the position without an effort owing to their having had uncles in the business... Some of my correspondents wish me to tell them whether they possess the literary aptitude or not. There is no one that can tell them that but the reading public. So many men, so many opinions. For one thing, my taste is not that of the majority. There are ladies and gentlemen at the present day in the literary profession earning fine incomes who, if they had come to me for my advice, and had followed it, would have been bank clerks, or board school teachers. Had I myself followed the advice of able critics tendered to me for my good I should long since have abandoned the pen and taken my stand at some busy corner with a shoe box. Each man's business is his own, and nobody else on earth can do it for him.

One K N (from Lisieux) Ignored this advice at his peril. Jerome commented (March 8, 1905):

I am not the editor, to whom all MSS. should be sent. If an impracticable mind were proof of capability, there should be hope for you. You carefully send me an envelope for return, stamped with a 25 cent. French stamp. The envelope is not big enough to contain the MS. under any circumstances; a French stamp does not run in England, and if you wish, as apparently you do, that the MS. shall be returned to you in an enclosed envelope, it will cost much more than 21/2d. I am keeping your MS. by me, waiting to hear from you.

Never one to back down from controversy, within a few weeks Jerome was in the thick of a raging debate of Catholicism and Papal Infallibility. Sadly, *To-Day* died in July 1905 and with it Jerome's weekly columns.

LETTERS TO CLORINDA

by Jerome K Jerome

An extract from The Idler *of June 1896*

I wonder sometimes if good temper might not be taught. In business we use no harsh language, say no unkind things to one another. The shopkeeper, leaning across the counter, is all smiles and affability; he might put up his shutters were he otherwise. The commercial gent no doubt thinks the ponderous shopwalker an ass, but he refrains from telling him so. Hasty tempers are banished from the city. Can we not see that it is just as much to our interest to banish them from Tooting and Hampstead?

The young man who sat in the chair next to me, how carefully he wrapped the cloak round the shoulders of the little milliner beside him. And when she said she was tired of sitting still, how readily he sprang from his chair to walk with her, though it was evident he was very comfortable where he was. And she! She had laughed at his jokes; they were not very clever jokes. The majority of them, I am inclined to think, had come out of *Tit-Bits*, where, possibly, she had read them herself, weeks before. Yet the little bit of humbug made him happy. I wonder if ten years hence she will laugh at such old humour, if ten years hence he will take such clumsy pains to put her cape about her. Experience shakes her head, and to both questions answers sadly, 'No.'

I would have evening classes for the teaching of temper to married couples, only I fear the institution would languish for lack of pupils. The husbands would recommend their wives to attend, generously offering to pay the fee as a birthday present. The wife would be indignant at the suggestion of good money being thus wasted. 'No, John, dear,' she would unselfishly reply, 'you need the lessons more than I do. It would be a shame for me to take them away from you.' And they would wrangle upon the subject for the rest of the day.

Once, cycling along a country road, I heard angry voices behind me, and turning my head, saw coming after me, a man and woman on a tandem. I eased down to allow them to pass me, and then followed a little way behind. They were quarrelling steadily. It seemed an odd place to choose for a quarrel; but I suppose they had to get it in. I found them established at the same inn where I put up for the night, and learnt in conversation with the man, that they had just commenced a cycling tour, which was to last a fortnight.

'Can you chat comfortably together, two people, on a tandem?' I asked. 'I have never tried a tandem myself.'

'Oh, yes,' he answered, cheerily, 'you don't think about the machine. The wife and I talk nearly all the while we ride, don't we, Bella?'

'Oh, yes,' was Bella's comment, 'that's the beauty of a tandem. We used to ride two machines, but then we were always getting away from one another. On a tandem, you can't, you see.'

'Oh, it's just the thing for a married couple,' said the man.

I suppose they knew their own business; I should have taken to an ordinary, had I been the man.

I saw them start off the next morning from my bedroom window; they were quarrelling as to who should sit in front.

'You steer so badly,' said the lady.

'I should steer all right if you didn't keep on talking,' retorted the man.

'There would be nothing to talk about, if you steered straight,' replied the lady.

It comes by nature to some folk to quarrel. They do not start to quarrel, but all roads of conversation lead to that. I remember a clever artist friend of mine telling me of one of the most bitter quarrels he ever had with his father, from whom he inherited a hasty temper. He came in one day late for lunch, and having an early afternoon appointment, was in a desperate hurry. His mother had just helped him, when the father arrived upon the scene.

'Ah, Tom, you here,' he cried, drawing, up his chair towards the table. 'Give me something to eat, Jane, I am famishing.'

'Take this, father,' said the son, dutifully, putting his plate in front of his father.

'No, no, my lad,' replied the other, returning it. 'You go on, you've got a train to catch.'

'No, no, dad, you take it,' and a second time he pushed the lunch across the table.

'Don't be silly,' said his father, pushing it back. 'You have only got ten minutes.'

'I can eat all I want to in five,' returned the other. 'You take that.'

'Don't get playing quoits with the thing,' cried his parent, beginning to get angry.

Jerome and a favourite dog, perhaps a descendant of Montmorency

'Well, why don't you eat it then?' was the answer. 'You say you're hungry.'

'Damn you, and your lunch!' roared the old gentleman. 'Eat if, I tell you, and don't be a blithering idiot.'

'I won't be called an idiot,' retorted the son hotly. 'What do you want to lose your temper about a little thing for?'

'Who's losing his temper?'

'Why, you are; you're always losing it.'

The subsequent dialogue grew confused; the incident terminating with the father's covering his affectionate son from head to foot with minced veal and gravy. The son jumped up and overturned the table, swore at his father and left the room. His mother burst into tears, while his male parent threw a potato after him which broke the clock.

'Yes, I remember your father,' I said, as my friend finished the anecdote, 'he was a bad-tempered man.'

'Not at all,' replied my friend quite hotly, 'he was the best fellow that ever lived.'

I did not argue the question. Had we done so, we should have quarrelled.

Ever sincerely yours,

Jerome K Jerome

9

JEROME IN AMERICA

MEMORIES OF MARTYRS
by Tony Benson

If Jerome has an image in popular imagination it is certainly far from the truth. The sensitive boy who was never sure that he was a humorist obviously thought and felt deeply and those who care about his works might welcome some insights into the roots of his imagination.

In his autobiography, J records that to comfort him when, as a child in the East End of London, he was bullied for his tidy appearance and Walsall accent, his mother gave him *Foxe's Book of Martyrs* to read. The result was:

'The suffering caused to an imaginative child can hardly be exaggerated. It caused me to hate God and, later on, when my growing intelligence rejected the conception as an absurdity, to despise the religion that had taught it.' Later, he was to soften this view.

I was curious and managed to find *Foxe* on the internet. Among many horrors I read:

The principal of these martyrs were Blandina, a Christian lady, of a weak constitution; Sanctus, a deacon of Vienna; red hot plates of brass were placed upon the tenderest parts of his body; and Pothinus, the venerable bishop of Lyons, who was ninety years of age. Blandina, on the day when she and the other champions were first brought into the amphitheater, was suspended on a piece of wood fixed in the ground, and exposed as food for the wild beasts; at which time, by her earnest prayers, she encouraged others. But none of the wild beasts would touch her, so that she was remanded to prison. When she was again produced for the third and last time, she was accompanied by a youth of fifteen, and the constancy of their faith so enraged the multitude that neither the sex of the one nor the youth of the other were respected, being exposed to all manner of punishments and tortures. Being strengthened by Blandina, he persevered unto death; and she, after enduring all the torments heretofore mentioned, was at length slain with the sword.

Bearing in mind that Blandina was the name of Jerome's favourite sister with whom he shared some recorded adventures and that St Jerome's sufferings are also described it is not too surprising that he experienced such horror.

It struck me, too, that his outrage at the treatment of Negroes in the Southern States of America, leading him to speak out to a large audience in Chattanooga, Tennessee, must owe something in its language to memories of *Foxe*:

Once only – at Chattanooga – did I meet with disagreement; and then I was asking for it. Two Negroes had been lynched a few days before my arrival on the usual charge of having assaulted a white woman: proved afterwards (as is generally the case) to have been a trumped-up lie. All through the South, this lynching horror had been following me: and after my reading I asked for permission to speak on a matter about which my conscience was troubling me. I didn't wait to get it, but went straight on. At home, on political platforms, I have often experienced the sensation of stirring up opposition. But this was something different... it seemed to me that I could actually visualise the anger of my audience. It looked like a dull, copper-coloured cloud, hovering just above their heads, and growing in size. I sat down amid silence. It was quite a time before anybody moved. And then they all got up at the same moment, and turned towards the door. On my way out, in the lobby, a few people came up to me and thanked me, in a hurried furtive manner. My wife was deadly pale. I had not told her of my intention. But nothing happened, and I cannot help thinking that if the tens of thousands of decent American men and women, to whom this thing must be their country's shame, would take their courage in both hands and speak their mind, America might be cleansed from this foul sin.

So what on earth provoked such hostility? In his autobiography he tells us exactly what he said:

I ask my American friends – and I have many, I know – to forgive me. Who am I to lecture the American nation? – I feel, myself, the absurdity of it – the impertinence. My plea is that I am growing old. And it comes to me that before long I may be called upon to stand before the Judge of all the earth, and to make answer, concerning the things that I have done and – perhaps of even more importance – the things that I have left undone. The thought I am about to set down keeps ringing in my brain. It will not go away. I am afraid any longer to keep silence. There are many of power and authority who could have spoken it better. I would it had not been left to me. If it make men angry, I am sorry.

The treatment of the Negro in America calls to Heaven for redress. I have sat with men who, amid vile jokes and laughter, told of "Buck Niggers" being slowly roasted alive; told how they screamed and writhed and prayed; how their eyes rolled inward as the flames crept up till nothing could be seen but two white balls. They burn mere boys alive and sometimes women. These things are organised by the town's "leading citizens". Well-dressed women crowd to the show, children are lifted up upon their fathers' shoulders. The Law, represented by grinning policemen, stands idly by. Preachers from their pulpits glorify these things, and tell their congregation that God approves. The Southern press roars its encouragement. Hangings, shootings would be terrible enough. These burnings; these slow grillings of living men, chained down to iron bedsteads; these tearings of live, quivering flesh with red-hot pinchers can be done only to glut some hideous lust of cruelty. The excuse generally given is an insult to human intelligence. Even if true, it would be no excuse. In the majority of cases, it is not even pretended. The history of the Spanish Inquisition unrolls no greater shame upon the human race. The Auto-da-fé at least, was not planned for the purpose of amusing a mob. In the face of this gigantic horror, the lesser sufferings of the Negro race in America may look insignificant. But there must be tens of thousands of educated, cultured men and women cursed with the touch of the tar-brush to whom life must be one long tragedy. Shunned, hated, despised, they have not the rights of a dog. From no white man dare they even defend the honour of their women. I have seen them waiting at the ticket offices, the gibe and butt of the crowd, not venturing to approach till the last white man was served. I have known a woman in the pains of childbirth made to travel in the cattle wagon. For no injury at the hands of any white man is there any redress. American justice is not colour blind. Will the wrong never end?

I think we can hear in that description that he was still haunted by *Foxe's Book of Martyrs*.

JEROME IN AMERICA: PROBLEMS OF A BIOGRAPHER
by Frank Rodgers

Jerome K Jerome devoted a chapter of *My Life and Times* to his three visits to America. He did not, however, give a chronological account of his journeys, but rather tried to convey his impressions of the young American nation, of the places he visited and the people he met. Writing many years after the events, his memory was sometimes at fault. Moreover, he sometimes indulged in a skilful embellishment or exaggeration of fact, in the manner that made him such a successful comic artist. His humorous comparisons of the British and American way of life should not be taken too literally; but there are other occasions – in his discussion of lynching, for example – when he was deadly serious. Since the journeys were significant events in his life, it seems worthwhile to try to learn more about them. When did they occur? Where did he go? What did he do? How did the American public receive him?

Joseph Connolly, in *Jerome K Jerome: a Critical Biography*, chose to assign dates to Jerome's visits, and to specify which of the events described by Jerome took place on which occasion. One should, however, be aware that Connolly's account is not to be trusted. He describes four visits rather than the three that occurred, and gives incorrect dates for all of them. It is obvious that Connolly did not undertake the elementary task of consulting the indexes to *The Times* and the *New York Times*, from which the broad parameters of the visits can easily be ascertained. He places the first journey early in 1908 and the second later in the same year. He describes 'a second lecturing tour' in 1911; but all of the events that he associates with it took place on the first visit. Jerome's wartime visit he assigns to 1915.

Jerome's first visit was by far the most ambitious, lasting from early October 1905 to the end of April 1906, and most of the events described in his memoirs belong to this journey. On 29 September 1905, the evening before he sailed, W W Jacobs and Pett Ridge held a dinner at the Garrick Club for a dozen and a half of his friends – 'to say au revoir'. Primarily authors and artists, most prominent among them were Arthur Conan Doyle, H G Wells and J M Barrie. Also present were Carl Hentschel and George Wingrave, the originals for Harris and George in *Three Men in a Boat*. The party was reported in the *Daily Chronicle* of October 2 and the British Weekly of October 5. The *Daily Chronicle* reporter wondered 'But what will America make of the accent that Jerome K Jerome cherishes – a Midland snarl with kindliness, humour – and a seriousness behind?' Whether or not the identification of the accent as a 'Midland snarl' was valid, many Americans did indeed find his accent difficult.

His arrival in New York a week later was greeted so enthusiastically by the American press that, according to the *New York Times*, he was glad to escape in a cab with the manager of his tour. His first reading there, on the afternoon of 17 October, was reviewed by the press the following day. There is no further report on his activities in the *New York Times* until 26 April 1906, the day after he sailed back to England. To find out what he did in between, we must look for clues elsewhere – mainly in his own writings, and in local papers where his memoirs indicate a probable date. There is no sense of chronology in his account: it is not until near the end of his chapter, for example, that he mentions giving a reading in Albany just a few days after his arrival. Since he says that, a fortnight after he arrived, he cabled an urgent request for his wife to join him one must assume that he was back in New York to meet her.

An undated letter in my possession, from a hotel in Port Hope, Ontario, a small town east of Toronto, mentioned his expecting to be in that city the next weekend It seemed likely that this would occur while he was still in the north-eastern part of the continent. A search of the Ottawa and Toronto papers revealed that he gave a reading in Ottawa on 1 November and readings in Toronto on 2 November and 3 November. And the Ottawa paper mentioned his already having given a reading in Boston.

We know that his wife was concerned about his heavy schedule and persuaded his manager to lighten the load by teaming him up with an American humorist, Charles Battell Loomis. But we do not know how soon this occurred. And where he travelled in the two months after the Toronto engagement remains undocumented. His claim that his tour 'took in every state in the Union together with Canada and British Columbia' is obviously suspect. But given the number of places he mentions, it was certainly extensive. After Toronto, a journey across the centre of the country seems likely, bringing him to Vancouver and the west coast in time to enjoy their milder winter climate.

Jerome makes a few references to events that could easily be dated, the most specific being 'I was in San Francisco the week before the earthquake. My wife and I were the guests of Bancroft the historian.' The great earthquake occurred on 18 April 1906. The fondness with which he describes the generous hospitality of Hubert Howe Bancroft and his wife leaves one unable to doubt that Jerome and his wife did indeed stay with them. But the *San Francisco Chronicle* in the period immediately preceding the earthquake not only had no mention of Jerome, but printed an article announcing that the Bancroft family was leaving on 14 April to spend the summer in Europe. It appears that Jerome's memory of the timing of his visit was at fault. In fact, a reading by Jerome and Loomis was given in San Francisco on 24 January. The following day's review noted that the couple would leave that afternoon for San Jose, return for an evening at Oakland, and then go to the southern part of California before returning to New York by way of Arizona, New Mexico and Texas.

'Strange birds at times fluttered into our seclusion,' wrote Fred Lewis Pattee, professor of American Literature at the Pennsylvania State College of the 9 March appearance there of Jerome and Loomis. Pattee found him a difficult guest, and considered his performance a failure. To the students both his accent and his style of humour were unfamiliar. 'But Loomis saved the day.' They had come to State College from Dayton, Ohio; and Jerome was reported as having to speak to the Beef-Steak Club of New York the following week.

On 22 March the pair gave a reading in Boston, and William Dana Orcutt gave a dinner in Jerome's honour. Since Mark Twain was visiting Boston at the time, he thought he had done well to include Twain among the guests. But Jerome, on hearing of this, was indignant, insisting that he be the guest of honour and saying that he had no intention of playing second fiddle to Twain. When Twain arrived, Orcutt took him aside and explained the situation, at which Twain discreetly withdrew.

When Jerome began thinking of turning his story *The Passing of the Third Floor Back* into a play, he wanted to write it for the American actor David Warfield and tells us that he discussed his ideas with Warfield's manager, David Belasco, in a train between Washington and New York. The result was a contract signed in New York on 28 March.

Jerome gave a reading in Chattanooga on 9 April and it was on this occasion that he spoke out against lynching, in the light of a highly publicised lynching that had occurred there shortly beforehand. He vividly describes the ominous atmosphere and then the silent departure of his audience. However, the *Chattanooga Times* the following day reported that he was 'roundly applauded' by his mainly female audience at the conclusion of his comments.

Jerome recalled being at a press luncheon in Chicago with a man who had that morning published an angry leader about Maxim Gorky, who was in New York accompanied by a woman who turned out not to be his wife. Although Gorky arrived on 11 April, it was not until 15 April that the press revealed the scandal. Since Jerome was in Atlanta to visit Joel Chandler Harris on 20 April, it seems a little unlikely that he would have made the long journey back to Chicago between his Chattanooga reading and the Atlanta visit, those two cities being little more than a hundred miles apart. If he did, his manager had planned a very awkward itinerary! So perhaps he was in some other city at the time of the Gorky event (there is no reference to him in the *Chicago Tribune* during this period).

Jerome's memoirs name many other places that he presumably visited during this tour, but without mentioning any events that would enable one to date them. He mentions a meeting with President Theodore Roosevelt, but there was no press coverage of this occasion. So we shall have to be satisfied with the few events and dates that I have given above.

Jerome's second visit, in October 1907, was brief and clearly focused. His purpose was to produce *Sylvia of the Letters*, which he had written for Grace George. In an interview that appeared in the *New York Times* of 20 October, he reported having rehearsed Grace George and her company all day in a theatre in Waterbury, Connecticut. He gives us no explanation for the fact that the play never enjoyed a normal London or New York run. It had a single daytime performance (perhaps just a reading) in London on 15 October for the purpose of establishing copyright; and Grace George appeared in it in Atlanta in November 1907.

It was on this journey, too, that Jerome read *The Passing of the Third Floor Back* to David Belasco and David Warfield. He tells us that they liked it and asked him to have sketches made for the characters on his return to England. While he was engaged on this task, he reports that, at more or less the same time, Forbes-Robertson expressed an interest in it and Belasco asked to be released from his contract. Belasco's version of the story differs greatly. He claims that the 1906 contract called for the play to be finished in time for the opening of his new theatre in 1907, but that Jerome kept on asking for extensions of time. By the time Jerome brought the play in 1907, Belasco had been forced to disband the company assembled to play it, and to make plans to open his theatre with another play. He suggested deferring the opening of Jerome's play until 1908, and they apparently parted with this understanding. But, clearly, negotiations broke down not long afterwards.

The 1914 visit was from 9 October to 14 November, and the apparent purpose was to ascertain the views of Americans on the war and attempt to influence them in favour of Britain. He gave a reading at the Cort Theatre the day before his return to England. No other details of this journey have emerged, though the press when he arrived indicated that his tour was to include St. Louis and a visit to Canada. But the highpoint of the journey was his meeting on 29 October with President Wilson, who gave a very reasoned statement on America's neutral position. And it is interesting to note, given that *My Life and Times* was published in 1926, long before Hitler's rise to power, Jerome's perceptive comment: 'But for America, the war would have ended in stalemate. All Europe would have been convinced of the futility of war. "Peace without victory" – the only peace containing any possibility of permanence – would have resulted.'

10
JEROME AT HOME

THE HAPPY FAMILY MAN
by Celia Lamont-Jones, OBE

Mrs Lamont Jones was not only a founder-patron of the Jerome Society but a gener-ous benefactor of the Jerome K Jerome Birthplace Museum. Celia Lamont-Jones was a close friend of Jerome's daughter Rowena and inherited many of the family's be-longings. She writes here about Jerome's family life – aspects of which are only briefly mentioned in his autobiography.

Readers of Jerome K Jerome's autobiography, *My Life and Times*, often express disappointment that it contains so few details about Jerome's wife and daughters, while considerable insight is given into his early family life with his parents. Even Alfred Moss in his biography gives little information about the family, explaining that 'both Mr. and Mrs. Jerome shrank from the "limelight"' and he hesitated, therefore, 'to draw aside the curtain of purely domestic affairs'. Moss does speak, however, of the great affection the Jeromes had for each other – an affection which kept them 'free from the deplorable quarrels' experienced in 'the married life of so many literary men'. He writes of Jerome's marriage, in 1888, to 'the lady who henceforth was to be the gracious companion of his life'. Her father was a Lieutenant Nesza of the Spanish Army and her mother was Irish. Jerome himself alluded to his wife's Irish ancestry in his memoirs when he wrote of her encouragement to him to burn his boats and devote all his time to writing, adding in his whimsical way – 'She is half Irish and has a strain of recklessness.'

There is no doubt that his wife was held in affection by all who knew her. So when and where did he meet the 'gracious companion'? Jerome was still a bachelor in his late twenties, showing little or no interest, it seems, in women and marriage. But his life changed suddenly when he was introduced to a woman who has been described to me as pretty, petite, charming and vivacious – Jerome was completely captivated. The woman's name was Georgina Elizabeth Henrietta Stanley Nesza, known to Jerome and his friends as 'Ettie'. Indeed the initials 'E J' are embroidered on the household linen which I inherited and use to this day.

It would appear that Ettie spent much of her early life in Spain. I have a confirmation veil belonging to her made of old lace, probably Valenciennes, and attached is an envelope on which is written 'Confirmation veil used by my mother in Spain, her 5 sisters, by me, and my two daughters Elsie and

Rowena – (signed) Ettie Jerome'. According to the family, Ettie was sent to live with relatives in England when she was about twenty years old, as her mother feared that her daughter would be immured in a convent if she did not marry.

By the time Ettie had met Jerome she was married, and with a little daughter (Elsie), then two years old. That she was still married when she met Jerome, though apparently unhappily so, must have been rather a blow for him. Eventually, Ettie decided to petition for divorce and was successful. Jerome was then able to pursue his courtship and propose marriage. The wedding took place on 21 June 1888 at St. Luke's church in Chelsea, 'according to the rites and ceremonies of the Established Church'. The marriage might well have provoked comment by Jerome's strictly Nonconformist parents had they been alive, but they, and Ettie's father too, were dead by this time, and though we do not know what views her mother may have had, it seems probable that she would have put Ettie's happiness first. There were no longer any remaining close links with the Nesza family, and it seems Ettie had decided that she wanted to be thought of as an Englishwoman. She was very proud of her adopted country and regarded her Spanish connections as a private matter.

Ettie's daughter Elsie adopted Jerome's name, and she and her stepfather became great friends – he inscribed a book for her 'to my little girl'. Elsie was pretty and petite, with luxurious dark hair, and the Spanish looks of her mother, and as she grew older, her mother seemed not to age, so that they were often mistaken for sisters. When she was twenty-two, Elsie married a man named Riggs Miller. Soon after her marriage, however, her health broke down and for the rest of her life she was to suffer increasing bouts of illness. A few years before the publication of *My Life and Times* she died. She was just thirty-eight.

Elsie would have been about eight years old when Rowena was born. This could have affected the family relationships badly, but the fair-haired Rowena, resembling Jerome more than her mother, was beloved by them all, and the family ties were strengthened by this new addition. Unlike Elsie, who preferred a quiet life, Rowena was not content to stay at home, and wanted more than anything to be an actress. To her great joy, she was accepted by the Royal Academy of Dramatic Art. She admired her father tremendously, and he, in turn, was very proud of her acting ability, and particularly of her performance as Stasia in his play *The Passing of the Third Floor Back*, as he mentions in his memoirs. Rowena inherited many of Jerome's quixotic ways, as well as her mother's natural vivacity, and I would listen spell-bound to her accounts of her life on the stage.

When Jerome was writing *My Life and Times*, life for the family revolved around their homes in London and Buckinghamshire, with summer visits to their Suffolk cottage. Wherever they were, Ettie expected to be kept informed, by those around her, of anyone in any kind of distress.

She was always ready to help in a practical way, preferring to help at a personal level rather than at the head of a committee. Like Jerome a devout and regular church-goer, she felt deeply for those less privileged than themselves.

In London there were always luncheon and dinner parties to attend, with a guest list that was a literary roll of honour. I am told that Ettie looked wonderful on these occasions. She liked jewellery, though nothing too ostentatious – I have a brooch of hers, given to me by Rowena, which is a simple square of garnets and pearls set in gold. In *My Life and Times* Jerome recalls how, at parties, Ettie would stand on the bottom stair to receive the guests 'to make herself seem taller'. She was well aware of the manners and foibles of her guests, once warning Rowena, when H G Wells was to be a guest at luncheon, that it would not be wise to be alone in the room with him as he was not always discreet in his attentions to young ladies!

Life in London provided the family with the entertainment they enjoyed most of all – the theatre. Family birthdays were celebrated by a dinner at Frascati's on the birthday night, followed by a visit to the theatre on another night – Jerome felt it was impossible to enjoy the dinner properly if it had to be rushed, and that this way they could get the best out of both treats.

Much of Jerome's later writing seems to have been done in Buckinghamshire. He worked to a strict routine, favouring a simple breakfast – often a lightly boiled egg in a silver egg-cup – working through till the early afternoon when he would break for a light luncheon (which often consisted of a very large rice pudding!). Later, after further work, there would be tea, served in the garden when the weather was warm and fine. The family would be joined by friends and neighbours and they would play tennis, or Jerome would go for a walk with the dogs. Dinner was seldom elaborate, being often a satisfying three-course meal accompanied by a glass of wine.

Jerome was greatly blessed in his peaceful home life, a fact of which he was well aware. Ettie was always at his side to provide support, even when he found himself in danger of being lynched at Chattanooga in the United States after having been outspoken on the lynching of two Negroes. On another occasion, when he was lecturing there, she responded instantly to an 'SOS' when the tour was proving too heavy for him. His 'gallant little lady', as he described her, travelled immediately to the States where, with her usual diplomacy and tact, she eased the situation. It is no wonder that, in the family papers I possess, she is addressed by him in the most endearing manner: 'dearest; sweetheart; and Queen of my sweetest thoughts'. The copy of *My Life and Times* that he gave to her he inscribed, 'to my dearest wife with 50 years' love, Jerome K Jerome, Sept '26' – a fond tribute to emphasise the 'golden' nature of his love, as by that time they had been married only thirty-eight years. Alas, they would never celebrate a golden anniversary – Jerome died the following year, in 1927.

FAMILY JOTTINGS

by Celia Lamont-Jones, OBE

In the 1950s I was taken as a bride to be introduced to Miss Rowena Jerome (JKJ's daughter) and to her life-long friend – my husband's cousin, Miss Maisie Frith. At that time they lived in what they described as a cottage near to the south-eastern beach of Selsey in Sussex. The cottage was in fact a small Victorian style house specially designed for Jerome's wife, Henrietta (Ettie) Jerome. She had come here with Rowena and Maisie after Jerome's death, preferring it to the London house in Belsize Park with all its memories of life with her husband.

It had high ceilings for a cottage yet it was rather dark. I found the furnishings comfortable but not ostentatious. The sitting room was dominated by two portraits: one of Jerome K Jerome by De Lazlo, which went to the National Portrait Gallery when Rowena died and the other, Jerome's father, which now hangs in my dining room. Jerome's father looks the complete aristocrat. It is difficult to imagine him having to accept a life of poverty and retrenchment.

The ladies had a great affection for my husband and gave me a warm welcome. Rowena was small, eager and vivacious; Maisie plump, quiet and serene. Both enjoyed the sea and went swimming every day. Maisie ran the house and garden with some village help while Rowena liked to potter. Ettie Jerome came from an aristocratic Spanish family, born a Catholic although she never practised her religion after her marriage to Jerome. Rowena converted to Catholicism after her father's death; I keep her crucifix on my study table. It is said that the Catholic Church in Selsey was built from her generous gifts of money. She was well known in the village and at Christmas, particularly, she would give presents of money, sweets and tobacco to many of the less fortunate inhabitants.

Rowena was an avid reader and a great lover of the stage: she had trained at the Royal Academy of Dramatic Art. In fact both ladies were keen theatre-goers whenever they got the chance. In later years Maisie became a Friend of the Chichester Festival Theatre. I remember Maisie telling me that their birthdays were celebrated by a dinner at Frascati's on the birthday night and a visit to the theatre another night. She explained that it was not possible to combine both as JKJ felt it was impossible to enjoy a dinner if it had to be rushed. He seemed to enjoy taking his three ladies out for the evening. Maisie always called Rowena 'Bill' which I understood was a family nickname.

Rowena talked a great deal about her father and his travels to Europe and America. I believe she went with him to Russia. Rowena was very thrilled when *Three Men in a Boat* was filmed with Jimmy Edwards in the star role. She had entertained him to luncheon and had been interviewed for television. She told me that the little house, on that day, suddenly seemed full of cable. She was glad when it was all quiet again.

I remember Rowena asking me how familiar I was with her father's work. I blushingly confessed that I had read only *Three Men in a Boat*. After that visit I left with copies of *Three Men on the Bummel* and *Diary of a Pilgrimage*.

Later, the ladies moved to Chichester to 'Chestnut Cottage'. Then Rowena died and shortly afterwards our grief was deepened by my husband's sudden death. Maisie then decided to build a one-storey residence in the style of the Selsey house on some adjoining land. She called it 'Klapka'. Maisie missed her beloved Jerome family. I visited her as often as possible and spent happy hours with her playing Scrabble and reading more and more of Jerome. I was thrilled to handle so many autographed books. Little did I think that one day all these books would be mine – a most precious heritage.

I heard many stories about life with the Jeromes – his travels, the visits of the famous literary men of his day, the family movements between the country home in Buckinghamshire to the flat in London or the cottage in Suffolk. I was told that Jerome would write all morning, indeed to early afternoon. Then he would relax and, in the summer, play tennis. He seemed to rule his household with benevolent discipline – even the dog. He constantly thought of those in difficulty through hard times; he himself had suffered that experience and felt deeply for the misfortune of others. He delighted in his home, and above all, his wife. He had fallen in love at first sight with the beautiful young widow [*sic*], whose late husband had been cruelly lost at sea [*sic*], and she was adored by him all his life.

CHASING THE NEWS
by Harold King

Jerome's secretary from 1919 who was to become a distinguished journalist. Born Harold George Rudolf Koenig in Berlin 13 October 1898, he was Reuters chief correspondent Paris 1944–67 and died in Paris 24 September 1990. For more than two decades he was one of the best informed and most widely quoted journalists in Paris.

This is an extract from an unpublished manuscript of 1978.

CHAPTER ONE: DEMOBBED AND NOWHERE TO GO

A one-time Prime Minister of France, Andre Tardieu, who also wrote for the newspapers, used to say: 'Journalism leads to everything provided you get out of it.'

Four months after the November 1918 armistice put an end to the first world war, fresh out of the British army and aged twenty, my problem was how to get into journalism for a start with some kind of paid job. For, in those days, you had to have a paid job or not eat. Paid unemployment still remained to be discovered.

For the moment I was charitably and temporarily employed at the Essex Street London offices of a Liberal weekly called *Common Sense*. I had to copy onto individual index cards the names of all the British farmers listed in a fat volume of reference.

I do not think this card index ever played a useful part in anybody's life, but the work was done under the guidance of a charming rubicund Mr. Brown who together with his father had for years been making a good living out of writing about poultry.

One day Mr. Brown telephoned me at the office: 'I am on my way to lunch, King, and I have forgotten to write my weekly article for *The Smallholder* (a then successful weekly). In the left-hand drawer of my desk you will find the manuscript of an article entitled 'How to Keep Hens'. Copy it and run it round to *The Smallholder* before 4 p.m. Don't forget every time you see the word hen to type the word duck'.

Common Sense had fought a brave but hopeless battle during the war for peace and reason between the Allies and the Central Powers. It was edited by a distinguished economist and scholar, Francis W Hirst. Because of his views about the war, he had been forced to resign from the editorship of *The Economist*, which famous periodical he had brought to heights of distinction in thought and brilliance in style never quite attained since.

Francis Hirst was a close friend of leading members of the Liberal Party, including Mr. H H Asquith, who for most of 1916 was still Britain's war-time leader, and Lord Lansdowne, who much earlier had been a member of one of Gladstone's cabinets. Both these men hoped to bring the war to an honourable end before too much damage had been done to the basic fabric of Western civilization.

The first issue of *Common Sense* appeared on 7 October, 1916, with myself as its first office boy. In November of that year Mr. Asquith asked Lord Lansdowne to prepare a confidential report for the War Cabinet on his views and proposals for 'a peace of accommodation'. Lord Lansdowne had already declared that if the war were fought to a finish, the exhaustion of all the nations of Europe, in men and money, would no longer be worth the price of victory.

When the Lansdowne Report had been communicated to all the members of the Cabinet, Mr. Asquith expressed his complete agreement with it. None of the other members of the government, as far as is known, signified any open opposition. But it enhanced the chances for the great Liberal demagogue, Mr. David Lloyd George, to unhorse Asquith.

By the end of 1916, Lloyd George was the new British war leader with unconditional surrender of the enemy as his principal policy and 'Hang the Kaiser' as his war cry. He was strongly backed by most of the newspapers, and especially by the popular daily press, always referred to in the offices of *Common Sense* as 'the gutter press'.

With the war over, the main purpose of *Common Sense* had come to an end. But there was still the faint hope of injecting some common sense into the allied peacemakers in Versailles. In fact, it turned out to be a vain hope, and only fourteen years later the world was consequently gratified with the coming to power in Germany of Hitler and his Nazi bully-boys.

Unlike their wiser predecessors at the Vienna Congress 105 years earlier, the Castlereaghs, Talleyrands and Metternichs, the political leaders of Britain and France in 1919 were sowing dragons' teeth at Versailles. The editor of *Common Sense* was looking around for powerful pens to attempt to inject some elementary statesmanship into the coming peace treaty. Among others, he invited one of England's most famous men of letters, Jerome K Jerome, to write a weekly article on the peace negotiations. Jerome told Francis Hirst: 'Yes, but in that case you must find me a secretary, preferably a young man who wants to learn how to become a journalist.' JKJ suffered from writer's cramp, frequent among professional writers before the typewriter came into general usage.

'I think I have a chap here in my office who might suit you,' Hirst replied at once, perhaps seeing a chance to cut down on his salary bill. 'Young King upstairs is not doing anything much for us at present.' I was called down to the Editor's sanctum, of which of course I had never before seen the inside, duly introduced and inspected, and then told to wait downstairs.

Half an hour later I was on the doorstep of our office talking to the great man in person. Jerome had a sweeping high forehead, partly balding, covered in a flock of flaxen and white hair. The shape of his head, reminiscent of the well-known bust of Shakespeare, shows up well in a magnificent portrait of him painted by the famous portraitist Philip de Lazlo and now hanging in the National Portrait Gallery in London.

JKJ also had the well-controlled, melodious voice of the trained actor. He started off by saying: 'I hope you can come soon.' 'Will next Monday be all right, Sir?' I inquired, just to give me time to explain to my mother, still working as a typist in the Ministry of Munitions, why I was already about to leave home again.

JKJ then said: 'I can't pay you much', and he kept his word: one pound a week and lunch with the family, except on Sundays. He then inquired whether I knew shorthand, could use a typewriter properly, and also whether I played tennis and bridge. I said 'yes' to the first three questions. With the best will in the world I dared not say 'yes' where bridge was concerned, although I murmured that 'my grand-mother before the war taught me how to play whist'. 'Never mind,' said the great man laughingly. 'We'll teach you at home.'

The big deal was fixed, and a few days later I found myself on Marlow Common at the beautiful and unpretentious home (an enlarged farmhouse) of the Jeromes, up on the Chilterns between the Thames townships of Marlow and Henley.

As soon as I arrived, I was welcomed by Mrs. Jerome K Jerome, reminiscent of a tiny Queen Victoria, and her daughter Rowena as if I had been a long-lost and well-loved relation. They took me into the drawing-room (I noticed it contained a mechanical piano) and Mrs. J said: 'Now, Harold, there is one thing we must explain to you right away. Dad and we play three-handed bridge at home every Tuesday and Friday evening, and you will now make the fourth. But please remember — Dad must always win.'

Life in the Jerome household was a permanent delight. JKJ was a man of genius but he never pushed it at you, was never condescending, supercilious or crushing. He was greatly liked by all our neighbours around

Marlow Common, usually people of substance and standing but otherwise not comparable with the Grand Old Man.

Like all authentic writers, Jerome knew what moved the human heart and mind. Herr Doktor Freud was still very much à la mode in AD 1919. Mention of the good doctor's name used to make Jerome smile, especially when some well-intentioned but not over-penetrating visitor would wax enthusiastic about the Vienna quack's 'discoveries' about human nature. 'I wonder what these people think we novelists have been doing for generations, if not reading the human heart,' he would remark, and go on to something more entertaining.

Jerome was perhaps the last of the Puritans in England, but he was puritan by fastidiousness and taste. There was no fanaticism in him unless it were about vivisection and cruelty generally. When one day his favourite cat ate one of his favourite songbirds in the garden, he found himself in a moral dilemma. The tragedy was never mentioned in his presence.

His Puritanism produced one queer quirk: he would never go near Paris. He considered it a 'City of Sin', and whenever he and his family were due to travel to Switzerland, to which the shortest way from the British Isles runs of course through Paris, he would plan the most elaborate rail and boat connections via Belgium to avoid passing through 'La Ville Lumière', even protected by an international train.

Some similar strain in his upbringing, no doubt, was responsible for an irrational aversion to the Roman Catholic Church. 'I want to become a Catholic, I need some colour in my religion,' his daughter Rowena used to confide in me, 'but I don't want to hurt the Dear Old Dad, so I shall wait until he is no longer with us.' And so she did. Of course, that was long before Vatican II.

Lunch in the Jerome home was always a festival of high-class cooking in a setting of perfect taste. It was often enlivened by some amusing story from the current book he was writing, the telling of which JKJ, the actor, had carefully rehearsed to himself in the large study over the garage before lunch.

Every item of furniture in the low-ceilinged dining room was a carefully selected master-piece. The cutlery and china on the table were a joy to the eye and to the hand. JKJ supervised all this with a watchful eye.

He was always worried about one item on the table: the bottle of tomato sauce with its gaudy commercial label, the contents of which Mrs. J and Rowena were partial to. 'Have you finished with this, my dears?' JKJ would say anxiously after his ladies had helped themselves, and would then get the maid quickly to remove the offending bottle out of sight. After coffee, JKJ, but only he, would have a glass of French brandy. 'It's for my indigestion, my boy,' he explained to me.

Jerome had a splendid new Studebaker, the latest thing in those days, and he decided to teach me to drive. One day, coming out of Henley, he passed me the wheel, and said: 'At the end of the street, turn to the right.' I turned the wheel, and the car nearly ran into a wall on the left. JKJ grabbed the wheel in time, and that was the end of his driving lessons. Obviously no talent for driving a car, he must have thought. And in fact, I went through sixty years of active journalistic life without ever knowing how to drive a car. The late Philip Jordan, of the then *Daily Chronicle*, who did not hide his light under a bushel, once wrote that one of the essential qualifications for a foreign correspondent was to be able to drive a car, but he over-generalised.

Novelist, playwright, humorist, actor and orator, Jerome K Jerome conquered the reading world all over the globe in 1889 and the subsequent decades with his famous *Three Men in a Boat*. Translated into most of the languages of the world, this masterpiece, with its profound humanity, its complete understanding of ordinary people and its keen but ever kindly sense of humour brought (and still brings) spontaneous and happy laughter to millions of all races and creeds, not only in the English-speaking and Western world, but in Russia, China, Central Africa and South America.

The literary critics greeted its appearance with condescension and supercilious sneers. 'It must have been bad,' JKJ used to tell us thirty years later; 'it sold many millions. Still, I'm not in such bad company. Other respectable writers have been widely welcomed from their first publication. Just think of Tolstoy, Balzac and Sir Walter Scott, for a start.'

The superior attitude of the sterile highbrows, the 'remote and ineffectual dons' of Hilaire Belloc, still seems to persist. All the *Oxford Companion to English Literature* in its 1978 reprinting has to say about JKJ is that *Three Men in a Boat* and *Idle Thoughts of an Idle Fellow* (published in the same year) 'by their blending of humour and sentiment proved very popular.' Talent marred by a kindly heart, don't you know.

In 1908, nineteen years after the appearance of *Three Men in a Boat*, the genial JKJ touch had another big triumph, this time with a play, *The Passing of the Third Floor Back*. It tells the story of the silent influence of a somewhat mysterious saintly man moving into the cheapest room of a cheap London boarding house, and of the effect of his presence on the querulous and dispirited boarders. Rowena Jerome, in her first stage appearance, played the female star role of a cocky Cockney slavey, and she carried London by storm that night. The play has been staged all over the globe many times since.

Seventy years after its first London production, it was produced on French television, in French, but there it didn't, perhaps for the first time, quite come off. The French are still Catholic in mentality even when not in faith, and the faint puritan aura about the play did not seem to suit either the French producer or the actors.

Early in the century, JKJ also produced a newspaper, a weekly called *The Idler*. No long sentences, no university words, it was written for the new masses who had been learning to read and write since 1870 when the First Education Act obliged every child to go to school up to the well-selected age of 13.

JKJ claimed thus, he told me, to be the real founder of popular journalism, before Lord Northcliffe came along with his *Daily Mail*. Unfortunately, *The Idler* also had a financial column, written for more astute people than its average reader. There one day JKJ attacked a notorious share-pusher. His criticisms, JKJ always stoutly maintained, were fully justified, but 'The Law is A Hass'. Jerome lost his case and a small fortune. The paper had to close down, and the Jerome family moved to Dresden where, at that time, living was much cheaper. There he wrote a follow-up to his first success, called *Three Men on the Bummel*. There, too, his daughter Rowena received her essential education by not going to school, but by reading and learning Shakespeare by heart and listening over and over again to the operas of Wagner.

In the Dresden of the first decade of this century, life was comfortable, cultured and *gemütlich*, and Jerome made many friends there. The family had returned to England before the outbreak of the war in August 1914. When it started, the great English writer was torn between his fierce patriotism and his sentiments of sympathy and affection for his numerous German friends.

During the first months of the hostilities, JKJ wrote articles for the liberal newspaper *The Daily News* in which he made a distinction between the German people and their militarists, but soon the paper refused to publish his contributions. Determined to get into the war somehow (fifty-seven years of age), Jerome bought himself a Red Cross Ambulance, got himself attached to the French Army, and drove his ambulance under constant fire throughout the battles of Verdun.

In 1919, there I was, all set to pick up the rudiments of journalism under the guidance of a literary man of genius, of undaunted bravery and of a rich heart. Things looked good, I thought. But the little earthly paradise I lived in while with the Jerome family was not to last. Eighteen months later, I found it necessary to get a full time job in order to help keep the home fires burning in London.

When I told the Master I would have to leave, I asked his advice about what to do next: should I go in for journalism or 'go into business' (a polite way of describing any old office job for a start). 'Oh, my boy,' he said, 'there is no doubt at all about what you would do. You have no talent for journalism at all.'

MAY WALKER – LIFE WITH JEROME
by Christine Stockwell

This article appeared in Idle Thoughts *in 1990. Mrs. Walker passed away on 16 October 2003, just five months before her 100th birthday*

Although Jerome K Jerome's autobiography, *My Life and Times*, is crammed with friends and acquaintances and begins with a good description of his parents, particularly his saintly Mamma, there is very little in it about his wife or daughter. Mrs. Georgina Jerome scarcely gets a mention and their only child, Rowena, appears just briefly, half-way through the book, as a young woman, when Jerome recalls members of the cast in a couple of his plays. His reference to someone called Elsie, whom he described as 'my eldest girl', only serves to baffle us. In fact this 'eldest girl' was Mrs. Jerome's daughter by her first husband, from whom she was divorced only nine days before marrying Jerome. Too busy with his literary reminiscences, Jerome leaves us to discover these small domestic details for ourselves. It is not surprising, then, that his wife's surrogate daughter, May, is omitted altogether – even though for five years she was very much part of his household.

May Walker, now eighty-six, was two when she went to live at Gould's Grove, the Jeromes' house near Wallingford. Her parents were Gertrude and Edward Hammond, newly-hired housekeeper and gardener but, from the start, it was Mrs. Jerome who played the parental role. May remembers her as 'a dear little person, gorgeous, almost like a Chinese'. Actually Mrs. Jerome, far from oriental, was half Spanish, half Irish, but it is true she was tiny – even Jerome remarked on this: 'When friends came', he wrote, 'my wife like to receive them in the hall… standing on the bottom stair – to make herself seem taller.'

It was not so very unusual, when May was a child, for the better off to contribute something towards the education of their servants' children or to, at least, behave benevolently towards them. But Mrs. Jerome went way beyond this by showing May all the little motherly attentions which she was no longer able to enjoy giving her own daughters, who were by then grown-up. She decided May's bedtime, bathed her, brushed her hair – only washed with egg-yolks – and dressed her each morning. May wore frocks from Harrods or ones specially made for her, and showed them off at dancing classes. Music lessons were arranged for her too. For being good, she was regularly rewarded with toys, which she could choose herself from a big wooden box, kept well-stocked by her indulgent 'second mother'. Mrs. Jerome clearly doted on May who, in turn, adored all the fuss. On reflection, May now thinks that she must have been 'spoilt terribly', but still remembers this as one of the happiest times of her life.

Jerome himself must have been well aware of May's presence – it was probably he who took the now half-crumbled snap of her with his dog, Bully – but she always had the impression that he hardly noticed her. In the circumstances, it seems likely that his wife's unnecessary preoccupation with the housekeeper's child made him feel slightly uncomfortable and so he deliberately acted detached. On the other hand, perhaps he was simply preoccupied himself. It was at Gould's Grove that Jerome wrote the play *The Passing of the Third Floor Back*, which had first appeared in a collection of his short stories. It was John Murray, the publisher, who suggested dramatising it but Jerome did not find it an easy play to write. May remembers him, deep in the process, pacing up and down the garden with his hands clasped behind his back. She knew he was working on a play because the house was strewn with costumes and on occasions visitors would come and act out scenes from it, but she could not fathom out what she considered to be very strange behaviour on the part of Jerome. Apparently he would get up early, before anyone else in his family, go downstairs to the dining-room and move all the chairs about before heading outside. Even to-day May is puzzled by this memory, still vivid for seeming so odd, but, as sets and scenes were on his mind, the likeliest explanation for this ritual is that he was simply stage planning – he should have explained. But however remote Jerome seemed to May as a child, she is certainly the only person alive to-day who can claim such a close association with the famous humorist.

May remembers the fire at Gould's Grove very clearly. The Jeromes were away and she and her parents woke to the sound of crackling and the cries of animals. Through the window they saw that the farm adjoining the house was ablaze and beneath them, in the yard, the few poor creatures which had escaped were tearing around, alight. It was a ghastly, never-to-be-forgotten scene. May was buttoned up in a red dressing-gown, hurried out of the house and, along with the Jeromes' little terrier, Needle, handed over the garden wall to the gamekeeper, who carried them both to the safety of his cottage across the fields. May's father and the other servants stayed behind to ferry out valuables from the house, for it seemed certain that Gould's Grove would be next to catch, but the wind suddenly changed and only the billiard room, which was nearest the farm, was destroyed, along with six bikes belonging to the maids.

Mrs. Jerome's daughters did not follow their mother's lead, with regard to May. Like Jerome, they were pleasant to her in passing but otherwise remote. Rowena was the dreamy one whom May describes as 'funny' – not for her humour, however, but for her habit of talking to the trees. Rowena seems to have inherited a touch of the 'brooding, melancholy disposition' which Jerome, surprisingly, claimed to have. He once said that, look where he would, there seemed always to be more sadness than joy in life. Gloomy words from so well-known a humorist. Rowena never married and in later life she entered a convent [*sic*] which, no doubt, suited her other-world temperament. Elsie, whom May knew as Mrs. Riggs-Miller, was apparently a semi-invalid. She lived with the Jeromes all the years May knew the family and if she ever left home it must have been around 1905, when she was married to Thomas Riggs-Miller, for by 1906, when May joined the household, Elsie was back again. Her husband rarely called but May remembers the occasions when he did and how the laughing red-faced Irishman would swing her up onto his shoulders. Practically nothing is known about Thomas, except that he was a farmer and May has the impression that he was quite a bit older than Elsie, but just from the brief visits he made, he left a far more vivid image than his spectral wife.

It is a pity that May is unable to identify any of the many visitors who called or stayed at Gould's Grove. She remembers weekend parties and croquet being played on the lawn and many comings and goings but no names. Yet H G Wells was among the guests; W W Jacobs; Conan Doyle; Eden Phillpotts and Zangwill were others. They liked to take themselves off to a corner of the garden surrounded by a thick yew hedge, known as the Nook. It made a pleasant place to work, according to Jerome, and should have had a commemorative plaque placed above it for all those who at one time or another wrote there. Apparently, in this privileged position, Zangwill wrote some of his Ghetto stories, occasionally digging up worms with his pen-nib to feed to the young birds, nesting in the yews.

When – May thinks it was about 1908 – the Jeromes moved from Gould's Grove to Monks Corner, at Marlow, the Hammonds moved with them. This unusual, low-set building, now appropriately named Jerome Cottage, is the place May calls, 'my lovely old house in the middle of a wood'. It was less grand than Gould's Grove, but cosier, more snug. May's parents had a large bed-sitting room over the kitchen; May's was a little room just to the side and it was in this home that May was happiest. The Jeromes bought a new dog, a slate-coloured Great Dane, which they named Monk. May loved to ride on his back but soon grew too big for this so Mrs. Jerome bought her a little bike which she learnt to ride, scoring a muddy track round a big urn on the lawn outside the kitchen. So, in these pleasant surroundings, May's childhood idyll continued, and lasted, in all, for five years.

When May was seven, her mother became pregnant and gave her notice to Mrs. Jerome, remarking that she intended bringing this one up herself! May's father continued working at Monks Corner, sometimes acting as chauffeur, although Jerome generally preferred to drive himself. May was taken to live in a small cottage on Marlow Common where her brother, Jack, was born. Although May no longer lived with her, Mrs. Jerome was reluctant to give up 'her little girl', still bought May's clothes and, presumably, without consulting May's parents, had her enrolled in a nearby private school. But May's mother had had enough. She moved again, this time to Bovingdon Green, and put May in the local village school. Mrs. Jerome took the hint this time and finally conceded to Mrs. Hammond's wish for independence. Gifts were still sent but the clothes buying and the special treatment stopped and a new kind of life began for May.

Edward Hammond continued working for Jerome until shortly before the outbreak of the First World War. When it came, both men joined up – and both as drivers serving in France. Jerome, already in his mid-fifties, was refused as a volunteer, but was finally accepted by the French Army as a member of its ambulance unit. Edward went to Whitehall and signed up as a driver for the A.S.C. May used to meet her father from the station, when he came home on leave, and would take him home by all the back ways – she was not proud of him, only ashamed at how muddy and tired he looked. Jerome finally returned to Marlow at the end of the war, tired, disillusioned and, according to his secretary, 'a broken man'.

May was 14 when the war ended and had already begun work; first as a helper in the stockroom of a department store and next as a between maid for a Lady Terrington in Marlow. To be a 'tweeny', May says, was the worst possible job to have. Up at five and too tired at night to undress for bed; a half day off on alternate Sundays and one extra every few weeks – all for a pound a month. Then, when May was about 17, Mrs. Jerome contacted her mother: Would May like to go and join them as a maid? They were no longer living at May's beloved Monks Corner, but in a far more modest house at nearby Woodend. May joined them but says, 'I just couldn't get on at all. I think that after being made such a fuss of I couldn't knuckle down to being a maid. Mrs. Riggs-Miller was very ill then and things were not at all happy'. In fact Elsie died of a kidney disease in 1921 which was about the time that May rejoined the household. The job lasted for a very short while, May cannot be more specific. She only knows how unhappy she was in the role of a servant after playing a so very different one as a child.

May still lives in Marlow, now surrounded by her own large family. She has seven children and several grandchildren, among whom there is a sister and brother, Rowena and Jerome! At 19, Jerome prefers to be known as Jes but maybe, later in his life, he will see the advantage in reassuming his original name and enjoy dining out on his grandmother's story.

In the garden at Wallingford: (l–r) George Wingrave, the gardener, JKJ and Rowena

JKJ AND DUNWICH
by Roy Farrow

Most people know – vaguely – that the tiny village of Dunwich on the Suffolk coast was once a great town, and harbour; and everyone knows that the bells of the churches that long ago fell into the sea can still be heard, tolling under the cold grey waters ...

In the nineteenth and early twentieth century Dunwich exerted a special appeal to artists, poets, writers; Henry James, Edward Fitzgerald, Samuel Coleridge, Algernon Swinburne and his companion Theodore Watts-Duncan, Charles Keene the *Punch* artist ... and our own JKJ.

Mrs. Scarlet ran a small shop in where Ship Cottage now stands, just west of the museum and the Reading Room. It was the hub of the village, where the gossips would gather and talk. One room was available for letting, and it was in this room where Edward Fitzgerald had translated the *Rubaiyat of Omar Khayyam*. He had found the endless gossiping disturbing, but he had his own way of dealing with the problem. Putting on his hat at the back of his head, he would bustle out and join them. 'Ah! Mrs. Scarlet,' he would say. 'You are talking about something interesting, I feel sure of it. Now tell me more about it.' After a little more of this the ladies would remember pressing tasks at home, and then drift away.

Forty years later in this same room Jerome was writing *My Life and Times*, published in 1926. He said of the room:

> I am writing these memoirs in a little room where, years ago, Edward Fitzgerald sat writing the *Rubaiyat of Omar Khayyam*. The window looks out across the village street, and some of those who passed by then still come and go ... A favourite working place of his was the ruined church upon the cliffs. It was still a landmark up to a few years ago, standing bravely against the sky. But now its stones lie scattered on the beach or have been carried out to sea, and not a trace remains ...

Jerome was not entirely accurate there. Although the last of the tower fell to the sea in 1922 – with one buttress being saved and placed in the church yard of St. James, at the westernmost edge of the village, where it stands to this day – the stones of the church were clearly visible at low tide, half-buried in the sand and shingle, up to the 1960s. Dunwich had been suggested to Jerome as an ideal place for peace and beauty. After spending one summer there with his family, he liked the place very much indeed, and thereafter they regularly returned for the summer. And they always lodged with Mrs. Scarlet.

The Scarlets were one of the three major Dunwich families. Mrs. Scarlet ran the village shop, which survived into the thirties. Mr. Scarlet was Head Gardener to the great Barne Estate in the village; he was also clerk to the Parish Council, the Secretary of the Reading Room for 25 years. For this service he was awarded a silver inkstand, which is now in the village museum. The Scarlets were always glad to have Jerome; he became more than a lodger; he was a friend, and they would stay with his family in London occasionally. During his stays in Dunwich he was a godsend to them; always kind, generous and thoughtful, and never giving anyone trouble if he could help it. His routine was hard and strict for one not in the best of health and on holiday. He would rise at 6.30 a.m., take one cup of tea, and then walk his dog for two hours. At 8.30 he would return for breakfast, and spend the rest of the day reading and writing, with his daughter acting as amanuensis. He found he could work much better in the peace of Dunwich than in London. He wrote *My Life and Times* there, and very likely, *The Passing of the Third Floor Back*, for his biographer, Alfred Moss, says that it was written in a lonely country place, the serenity of which was helpful.

Jerome was a regular visitor for a number of years, and was well known in the village. The villagers had sincere respect and admiration for him. Anyone who asked for his autograph or photograph always got it. On one occasion some people called very late at night for his autograph. 'Tell them,' he said, 'to come again tomorrow morning and they shall have it.' They did, and went away highly delighted.

The Vicar of Dunwich, the Rev. A Scott Thompson, with whom Jerome was very friendly, wrote of him:

> There is in Jerome one outstanding feature, viz, his love and tenderness to little children. During his annual visit he constantly gave the schoolchildren treats and prizes for essays. He was so interested in their welfare that they will miss his kind face, his bright and cheery words. They will long remember his generous actions. Mr. and Mrs. Jerome were great lovers of plants and animals. Personally, I ever found him a true and sincere friend.

He was ready to take up a worthy cause too. During one of Jerome's stays at Dunwich, King Edward VII issued a public entreaty about refuse and litter in the roads and countryside. Dunwich was quite a holiday centre at this time and was not free from litter. Jerome called a public meeting to arrange for some local action, but it fell flat; he was alone in his loyal enthusiasm. Undeterred, he had a special stick made with a sharpened length of steel protruding from one end. He took it with him on walks, piercing and picking up any pieces of paper he saw, and burying them out of sight.

His biographer, Joseph Connolly, says that Dunwich was suggested to Jerome 'towards the end of his life'. The reign of Edward VII was from 1901 to 1910, so the rubbish collecting took place in 1910 at the latest. Jerome died in 1927, so he was visiting Dunwich at least 16 years before his death.

The coast at Dunwich has been eroding at an average rate of one metre per year for centuries, so 70 metres have fallen since Jerome stayed there. 70 metres from the present coast stand the museum and Reading Room. In another 70 years they too will be gone; so hurry along to Dunwich, walk where JKJ walked, and learn more about the fascinating history of Dunwich, the lost city.

MEETING ROWENA ...

by Hubert Gregg

It was natural that this multi-talented actor, writer and director, who did more than anyone to promote Jerome in the 1950s and 1960s, should be one of the earliest celebrity speakers invited to address the annual dinner of the Society. It was immediately after this that he was invited to become a patron of the Society. Hubert Gregg died in 2004 at the age of 89.

My first letter from Rowena – or Billie as I was allowed to call her later – was in reaction to my broadcast of *Three Men* excerpts on a wireless programme called 'Saturday Night On The Light'. This was a new idea for a compilation that stretched throughout the evening and the content ranged from orchestral contributions to spoken verse and so on.

The opening programme had been a success and the producer, Norman Wright, approached me to take part in the second. He came to my flat to discuss it and I suggested Shakespeare. 'If you like' he said, adding 'Edith Evans did do some Shakespeare readings last week; if you remember.' I didn't because I hadn't heard it, which was unfortunate since I had begun by congratulating him and saying what a marvellous evening it had turned out to be. 'Ah,' I said. And 'Oh yes, of course. Stupid of me.'

At that moment my eye was looking – both of them were, really – straight at the Jerome books in my bookcase. 'Or ...' I said ... 'How about ...'

The broadcast was ecstatically received – the emotion evoked mostly by Jerome of course, despite the kind comments Billie makes about my performance of him! Actors know what splendid script material the great man provides. For those with a comic bent [if you don't misunderstand me], reading him aloud is a doddle.

It was followed by television broadcasts [the 'medical dictionary' excerpt led directly to my being cast in a film called *The Maggie*], several Henry Hall 'Guest Nights' and finally a series called 'Let's Go Jerome-ing' in which I ran his comedic gamut. Not only have I always loved the man, he did me sterling professional good.

Billie wrote many times and invited me to visit her in Selsey when, miraculously and to my delight, she discovered that, in fact, she had several books which she kindly passed on to me.

... AND THE 1956 FILM OF *THREE MEN IN A BOAT*

Perhaps as famous for his songs 'Maybe It's Because I'm A Londoner' and 'I'm Going To Get Lit Up When The Lights Go Up In London' as for his much loved radio broadcasts, Gregg wrote a musical version of Three Men in a Boat. *Though he failed to get his name removed from the credits, he also had a hand in the execrable film version with Jimmy Edwards et al. In a letter to the Hon. Sec. in 1999 he revealed that:*

I told Billie that my dream was to write a screen version of *Three Men in a Boat*. There had been a silent version at one time but this was to be an 'important' production, in colour, that might be internationally acclaimed.

Not being experienced in writing for the screen, I enlisted the help of another Jerome-lover, Vernon Harris, a friend of mine of many years who had produced a series of Jerome sketches I had presented on radio.

In '54 I played Prince John in the Walt Disney *Robin Hood* film (Richard Todd rendering) and told the director Ken Annakin about our script which we had just finished. Ken was under contract to the Rank Organisation and we had a meeting with Earl St. John. It was agreed that Rank should make the picture from our script with Ken Annakin directing. They paid us an advance fee and contracts were signed.

I was over the moon about the casting they decided on: I would play 'J', Kenneth More 'Harris' and Ian Carmichael 'George'.

There followed the usual waiting period during which Rank discontinued Ken's contract. They were fair enough to Ken. Since it was he who had brought the 'Three Men' project to them, they offered to give him thirty days to take it to another production company; failing this the script would remain their property and another director would be found. With Rank the project would have been 'safe'; now it was open to the four winds and they proceeded to blow it about.

Before the thirty days were up Ken Annakin rang me to say that John Woolfe would buy the script and make the film at Beaconsfield Studios but would have none of Rank's casting. In particular, Woolfe wanted his friend Laurence Harvey to play 'George'. I didn't think he would have quite the comedy of Ian but it was pointed out to me that he was a very close friend indeed of John Woolfe so there was nothing to be done. Jimmy Edwards – the comedian with the large moustache who played the trombone – was disastrously cast as 'Harris'. David Tomlinson took over 'J'. He wouldn't, I thought, give the impression of being a writer but he had done some good eccentric comedy playing in the theatre.

The script seemed somehow to be slipping out of our hands. Had I had more experience of screen-writing matters, I would no doubt have been advised to bring in lawyers but, having just survived an expensive law-suit ludicrously brought against me over my song 'Maybe It's Because I'm a Londoner' (Jack Hylton thought he was over-paying me for using it and wanted to change the contract), I wasn't really keen on litigation. Vernon Harris, I think, had his eye firmly fixed on the commercial side.

Finally the film was in progress. I didn't care to visit the studio but had I done so I might have been in time to have my name taken off the credits. Jerome's comedy, it seemed, was too gentle for some. Jimmy Edwards was allowed to 'bring in his writers'.

When, in panic, I asked Ken to remove my name he said it was too late.

I wish they had removed my contribution to the script altogether. Instead they changed and vulgarised it. As an example, the 'Zoo scene' when I wrote it ran like this:

Harris and Clara are chaperoned by Clara's mother (suggested casting, Athene Seyler) and are inspecting a llama.

ATHENE: What a peculiar-looking face!

CUT TO LLAMA WHO TURNS ITS HEAD TO LOOK DOWN AT ATHENE: CUT TO ATHENE WHO LOOKS JUST LIKE THE LLAMA (sorry Athene!). And so on.

They changed this. We are in the baboons' quarters. Clara is not chaperoned.

HARRIS: This is what is known as the 'blue-nosed baboon'.

THE BABOON TURNS ITS BUM TO THE CAMERA. NOT CONTENT WITH THE NATURAL COLOUR AND IN CASE THE AUDIENCE DOESN'T GET THE JOKE, THE MAKE-UP DEPARTMENT HAS SMEARED THIS WITH MAX FACTOR BLUE.

CLARA: What do you mean, the blue-nosed baboon.

This scene occurred early in the picture. I avoided the premiere and crept into a matinée at the Marble Arch Pavilion. When I saw and heard what they were doing to Jerome – and the lad with the dream – I slumped down in my seat and prayed nobody would recognise me.

That's the end of 'Three Men on Film'. As we know, there is next to nothing of Jerome – in word or spirit – left. There is, in fact, one line of mine; and there's a small moral here somewhere. The cinema audiences (sometimes the public shows an innate taste) didn't laugh at the baboons but did at my one line – uttered pompously by 'J' in the context of the morning dip: 'Always wash downstream of the men and the horses'. If the original script had been left alone, we might have had a pleasing result, who knows?

A decade later, I wrote a musical treatment of *Three Men* for radio in which I did play 'J', with Kenneth Horne as 'Harris' and Leslie Phillips as 'George'. They were splendid, we all were dammit, so all was not lost. Until the next showing on the box of that filmic excrescence. Then the letters will come in as they always do and the disclaimers have to happen all over again.

11
PERSONALIA

Random contributions on some of the forgotten names that crossed Jerome's path.

MILTON MELANCTHON (1855–1862)

Jerome Senior clearly took his religion seriously. His elder daughter, Paulina, was named for St Paula (347–404), one of the leading women of St Jerome's group in Bethlehem. She had personal charge of St Jerome's welfare. Blandina, Jerome Clapp's second daughter, was named for the martyr St Blandina (d.177). But what about his elder son Milton Melancthon? It is unclear whether he took his first name from the English poet or from the name of the house in Appledore in which the Jeromes lived.

Melanchthon [note extra 'h' – Ed.] was the name of the German Protestant reformer Philip Melanchthon (1497–1560) ('Melanchthon' is the Greek for his original surname Schwarzerd or 'black earth'). He was born at Bretten in the Palatinate, appointed professor of Greek at Wittenberg in 1516 and became Luther's fellow worker. (Members will recall that, to distinguish him from his father, the family nickname for JKJ himself was 'Luther'.)

His *Loci Communes* (1521) is the first great Protestant work on dogmatic theology. *The Augsburg Confession* (1530) was composed by him. After Luther's death he lost the confidence of some Protestants by concessions to the Catholics, while the zealous Lutherans were displeased at his approximation to the doctrine of Calvin on the Lord's Supper. His conditional consent to the introduction of the stringent Augsburg Interim (1549) in Saxony led to painful controversies.

F W ROBINSON (1830–1901)
EDITOR OF *HOME CHIMES*
by Ian Chapman

In the Three Men in a Boat *centenary edition of* Idle Thoughts, *Geoffrey Smith paid a well deserved tribute to the unsung editor of* Home Chimes, *Mr. Robinson.*

It had been JKJ's intention to write a story of the Thames, its scenery and history, with humorous relief. We have JKJ's own account how he wrote the humour first and added the slabs of history as an afterthought. As it was being serialised in *Home Chimes* the editor F W Robinson promptly threw most of the straight history out again, leaving us with the book so well known to-day. To Mr. Robinson history has not been so kind.

A Londoner, Frederick William Robinson was born in Spitalfields on the 23 of December 1830, the second son of William Robinson. He was put through a private education at Clarendon House in Kennington. At the age of twenty-one Robinson took up writing and journalism. Amongst the many journals and newspapers to which he contributed were the *Graphic*, *Black and White Magazine*, the *Gentlemen's Magazine* and the *Daily News*, where he was the assistant to the drama critic. Robinson wrote many books, though it is doubtful whether any are read today. Of his books, the most well known were those published in the sixties such as *Grandmother's Money* and *High Church*. Under the pseudonym of 'A Prison Matron' Robinson published the two volume account of *Female Life in Prison* in 1862. This may well have been based on the infamous female convict prison in Brixton, the women convicts being employed in picking oakum and sewing. For anyone convicted to hard labour there was the dreaded tread-wheel. At this time Robinson and his large family of six sons and five daughters lived in what JKJ has described as a 'pleasant old house in leafy' Acre Lane, Brixton.

Frederick Robinson founded a new monthly newspaper type magazine, *Home Chimes* in 1884. Many of JKJ's fellow contributors such as Doctor Westland Marston and his blind son, Philip, the poet Swinburne, Coulson Kernahan and J M Barrie, became close friends. The first series of *Home Chimes* featured *Idle Thoughts*. One of the features of the revamped new series was Gossips' Corner written originally by JKJ and similar in style to that later used for the Idler's Club. The first chapter of *Three Men in a Boat* appeared in issue number 32 in September 1888.

Through his editorship of *Home Chimes* Frederick Robinson brought to the public's attention many fine young writers, several of whom gained the general recognition they deserved.

JKJ's association with *Home Chimes* ended in January 1889 with the last chapters of *Three Men in a Boat*. Robinson continued as editor until 1894. He died on the 6 December 1901 just short of his 71st birthday.

W W JACOBS (1863–1943)

by Jeremy Nicholas

A review of the biography by Anthony James, published in 1999 by Able Publishing

If you dip into JKJ's *My Life and Times*, there's an affectionate and (for Jerome) lengthy portrait of W(illiam) W(ymark) Jacobs. This is how he introduces his friend: 'From shining examples of industry and steadfastness, I – being a lazy man myself – find it a comfort to turn my thoughts away to W W Jacobs. He has told me himself that often he will spend (the word is his own) an entire morning, constructing a single sentence. If he writes a four-thousand-word story in a month, he feels he has earned a holiday; and the reason that he does not always take it is that he is generally too tired.'

Jerome 'discovered' Jacobs. He had been wading through a huge pile of manuscripts and found nothing. 'Suddenly I heard a laugh and, startled, looked around. There was no one in the room but myself ... I read through [the manuscript] a second time and wrote to "W W Jacobs, Esq." to come and see me.' His first impression was of 'a quiet, shy young man, with dreamy eyes and a soft voice. He looked a mere boy.' This was in 1894 when Jacobs was in his early thirties and Jerome was the editor of *The Idler* and its sister, a recent newcomer entitled *To-Day*. With Jerome's patronage and encouragement, Jacobs, though now almost forgotten, became one of the most famous and successful humorous writers of the day, specialising in short stories. Like Jerome, his childhood had been spent in poverty (he was born in Mile End in 1863 and brought up in Wapping) and from 1883 to 1899 worked as a post office official. Like Jerome he began by writing about a subject he knew intimately and his yarns were of life on the Thames, the wharves, the bargees and sailors. Many were illustrated by Will Owen, such as *Many Cargoes* (1896), *The Skipper's Wooing* (1897) and *Deep Waters* (1919). His best known story was the macabre *The Monkey's Paw* (1902). Apart from its stage adaptation, it has so for been filmed no less than six times – 1915, 1923, 1933, 1948, 1983 and 1984. In fact, an extraordinary number of Jacobs' stories were adapted for the stage and the silent screen (twelve films were made of his tales between 1922 and 1927 alone). One, *The Boatswain's Mate* (already adapted as a stage play and film) was even transformed into an opera by Dame Ethel Smythe, one of England's leading composers. In this respect, Jacobs was far more successful than Jerome.

Despite his eminence and success (during his lifetime, at least) no one has previously written a life of his apparently shy, private man. By itself, the assiduous research alone undertaken by Anthony James deserves a cheer. Little is known of Jacobs' childhood (he was unusually reticent about these days when talking to journalists) but the author has pieced together his slow and awkward progress to success with painstaking detail. Another editor would have excised the numerous exclamations marks that litter the pages and would have tidied up some repetitious passages, but James writes perceptively and elegantly.

Of course, of greatest interest for our purposes is Jacobs' relationship with Jerome. The two men remained lifelong friends and, at one time, lived within a short distance of each other. The relationship, however, nearly came apart through Jacobs' wife. James describes 'W W's' married life as a 'sad waste'. 'Few writers,' opined one critic, 'in the whole of English literature have taken such a consistently low view of women [as Jacobs].' H G Wells thought Jacobs a tyrannical husband and based his 1914 novel *The Wife of Sir Isaac Harman* on the relationship between Jacobs and his wife. Glimpses like these make it hard to be totally captivated by Jacobs' personality. Mrs Jacobs, 'highly strung and emotional', and a militant suffragette more than able to stand up for herself, was probably part of the demonstration in February

1912 that destroyed property in central London – *plus ça change* – and led to the arrest of Mrs Pankhurst. A few weeks later, Mrs Jacobs was apprehended for smashing a post office window. She was carrying a muff in which was concealed a hammer and got one month in Holloway. Jerome, rather nauseously siding with his friend, observes of the incident, 'As Jacobs said, she always was difficult.'

This is Jerome being disingenuous for the sake of retaining the spirit of his affable memoirs. Anthony James offers a different picture of the relationship between Jerome and Nell Jacobs: '[She] found some comfort by at first sharing in the friendship between her husband and Jerome K Jerome, but that proved a perilous path, causing a serious rift between the two men. Though Nell and Jerome did not meet often, when they did they would talk and talk, animatedly and passionately, about the topics that interested her and thereby intrigued him. She admired Jerome's great love of freedom, his chivalry, and was moved by the deep disturbance to his nature that had been caused by his earlier poverty. She described him as "a vital and great personality" – which indeed he was. Jerome, for his part, fell in love with Nell, and her response was to fall in love with him. Their mutual romantic feelings certainly did not lead on to any sexual affair – both were strongly moral characters, and everything we know about Jerome makes it impossible to believe that he would have sought to seduce the wife of such a dear and close friend. However, they certainly had a non-sexual but nonetheless intense emotional "affair" that, though quickly nipped in the bud, was enough to cause an angry breach in the friendship between the two men.'

They were later reconciled and it was Jacobs whom Jerome invited to accompany him to Walsall in February 1927 to receive the freedom of the Borough. 'Jerome, too,' writes James, 'had fallen on a bleak, time in his career, and was in shaky health after some minor heart attacks. Like W W he had began to re-cycle earlier work in the absence of much in the way of new – though in his case the need to raise some cash was a factor.' Though the day was a great success 'it was all a bit too much for JKJ's health, so that the physical and emotional support given by Jacobs was invaluable'. Jacobs set the seal on the occasion with a memorable speech at the banquet – surprising that such a shy, retiring man was much regarded as a polished and witty after-dinner speaker. James thinks that 'Jerome never recovered from the exertions of that long, tiring day'. As we know, he died just four months later.

Jacobs died alone in 1943, having separated from Nell. Tragically, two years later she took her own life.

I thoroughly commend Anthony James's portrait of this once hugely popular writer, not only for its strong Jeromian connections. It is a labour of love, a lively read with many delightful passing period details, and is likely to be the standard work for some time.

MORE ON W W JACOBS

by Dr. Aubrey Wilson

Only a few years after Nicholas's review appeared, Aubrey Wilson contributed a brief extract from his forthcoming biography of Jacobs. Part of it revealed that the manuscript which initially attracted Jerome's attention was entitled A Case of Desertion. *It was about the river and coastal craft and their crews that were to become Jacobs' main story material.*

Nell Jacobs fell in love with Jerome and made no secret of it. Christopher Jacobs, W W's son, described the situation:

> Doubtless attracted by her looks as well as by her uncritical admiration: nobody minds being flattered, especially men over forty by young women anxious to be taught. He was married (to a divorced woman, which had caused a scandal in those unpermissive days) and whether or not he encouraged her (Nell's) romantic passion, the situation must in time have been recognised as a dangerous one

It cannot be known if they became lovers, Christopher did not believe so, but the consensus within the family is that is indeed what happened. The end of the relationship occurred in 1904 when contact between the two families ceased. This was either on Nell's and Jerome's own volition to end a dangerous situation or, more likely, because Jacobs, the mildest and most good-natured of men, knew or suspected the relationship. In any event as Christopher Jacobs concludes, '... leaving my Mother with eternal regret ... and she cherished his memory [of her relationship with Jerome] to the end of her life'. The cordial links between the two families may have been broken but, as events show, there was a reconciliation at least between the two men as they continued to see each other, despite what had occurred. They must have continued to hold each other in high regard since Jacobs was frequently the principle speaker at dinners given at various times to honour Jerome.

ERNEST BRAMAH (1868–1942)

Dr. Wilson also reminded us of another almost forgotten literary figure who owed his early career to Jerome K Jerome. Jeremy Nicholas had earlier noted this brief appraisal on the back of a Penguin edition copy of Bramah's most famous work, *Kai Lung's Golden Hours*:

> Ernest Bramah, of whom in his lifetime *Who's Who* had so little to say, was born in Manchester. At seventeen he chose farming as a profession, but after three years of losing money gave it up to go into journalism. He started as a correspondent on a typical provincial paper, then went to London as secretary to Jerome K Jerome, and worked himself into the editorial side of Jerome's magazine, *To-Day*, where he got the opportunity of meeting the most important literary figures of the day. But he soon left *To-Day* to join a new publishing firm, as editor of a publication called *The Minister*. Finally after two years of this, he turned to writing as his full-time occupation ... He died in 1942

Bramah journeyed to London early in the 1890s to seek his fortune. A shy man, he wished to become a journalist and enrolled in a course to learn shorthand and typing. He had no personal contacts in the literary world but as luck would have it he eventually met Jerome K Jerome, who employed him on his new magazine.

THE SEARCH FOR ERNEST BRAMAH
by Dr Aubrey Wilson

Extract from the biography published by Creighton & Read (2007)

For once Fate was on Ernest's side. The college where he was acquiring his secretarial skills also had an employment agency that sent him to see Jerome K Jerome, the author of the highly successful *Three Men in a Boat* and publisher of a very popular magazine, *The Idler*. Jerome was about to launch *To-day* magazine and 'wanted someone to do his correspondence'. Ernest would suit. He was now on his first step of the literary ladder. His lowly position did not at first give him any entry into the company of the successful authors who were both contributors and personal friends of Jerome K Jerome. Extant letters from Jerome to Bramah all appear perfunctory, indeed brusque, and show no warmth or amicability.

It is interesting that, despite their association, Bramah receives no acknowledgement in Jerome's autobiography or in the biographies of JKJ. One possible reason for omitting Bramah from his memoirs could have been that their political views were at the opposite ends of the political spectrum. Bramah's politics and economics were to the far right as he clearly sets out in his early books and articles. Jerome was a committed socialist and he would have been highly antagonistic to Bramah's political views which could be interpreted as totally reactionary, although Jerome clearly had no objection to W W Jacob's rejection of Socialism. He told Jacobs that he couldn't understand why he, Jacobs, was afraid of Socialism. He said that under Socialism all Jacobs' needs would be supplied. Jacobs retorted, 'I don't want things to assure me. I'd have a lot of clever people fussing about making me happy and doing me good. Damn their eyes.'

Jerome was certainly Bramah's role model or perhaps even mentor, possibly before he appreciated the political gap between them and, anyway, Ernest's lowly position was unlikely to have provided the opportunity for the exchange of political views. Nevertheless, he was advanced from mere correspondence clerk to deputy editor under Jerome's tutelage. There is no doubt whatsoever that Bramah learnt his editorial skills in the offices of *To-Day* and *The Idler*.

DOUGLAS SLADEN (1856–1947)
by Tony Gray

In Jerome's autobiography *My Life and Times* he introduces his friend Douglas Sladen as follows:

Douglas Sladen was the most successful At Home giver that I ever knew. Half *Who's Who* must have come to his receptions at Addison Mansions from 10.30 to the dawn. He had a wonderful way when he introduced you of summarising your career, opinions and general character in half-a-dozen sentences, giving you like information concerning the other fellow – or fellowess. You knew what crimes and follies to avoid discussing, what talents and virtues it would be kind to drag into the conversation.

Douglas Sladen, author of *Who's Who*, published his own autobiography *Twenty Years of My Life* in 1914. The book was 'Affectionately dedicated to Jerome K Jerome, one of the earliest and dearest of my literary friends'. The book has recently been re-published as part of Kessinger Publishing's Rare Reprints (www.kessinger.net).

In chapter IX – 'The Humorists at Our At-Homes', Sladen starts the chapter: 'Among the crowd of humorists who honoured Addison Mansions with their presence it is natural to mention first the famous author of *Three Men in a Boat*.' Sladen goes on to let us know that he was, at one stage, Jerome's chief and only book critic on *To-Day*.

Sladen says it was his duty to receive all the ladies who came to see Jerome about the paper. 'Of course, they mostly came in search of work or fame; those who wished to be written about were very numerous, and expected to succeed by making what is called the "Glad Eye" at him. He was terribly afraid of the "Glad Eye"; it made him turn hot and cold in swift succession. He was unable to say "no" to a siren, and equally unable to say "yes" when he meant "no". He was also an intensely domesticated man, entirely devoted to his family and without the smallest desire for a flirtation. So it fell to my lot to pick up the "Glad Eye", a very agreeable job, when you have not the power to give yourself away. I had no patronage to bestow upon them.'

As for Jerome's politics Sladen had this to say: 'He was more of a Conservative than a radical in those days; he had not despaired of the Conservatives then, though he was baggy about beastly little nationalities. Suffragism had not then begun its march of unreason, and we were all in favour of giving woman a vote.'

Sladen asked Carl Hentschel, who was one of the three men who went on the trip immortalised in *Three Men in a Boat*, to tell him about it. He said – 'It is rather interesting to look back to the days of *Three Men in a Boat*. Jerome at that time was in a solicitor's office in Cecil Street, where the Hotel Cecil now stands, George Wingrave was a junior clerk in a bank in the City, and I was working in a top studio in Windmill Street, close to where the Lyric Theatre now stands, having to look after a lot of Communists, who had had to leave Paris. Our one recreation was week-ending on the river. It was roughing it in a manner which would hardly appeal to us now. Jerome and Wingrave used to live in Tavistock Place, now pulled down, and that was our starting-point to Waterloo and thence to the river. It says much for our general harmony that, during the years we spent together in such cramped confinement, we never fell out, metaphorically or literally. It was Jerome's unique style which enabled him to bring out the many and various points in our trip. It was a spell of bad weather that broke up our parties. A steady downpour for three days would dampen even the hardiest river-enthusiast. One incident, which, I believe, was never recorded, but would have made invaluable copy in Jerome's hands, happened on one of our last trips. We were on our way up the river, and late in the afternoon, as the sky looked threatening, we agreed to pull up and have our frugal meal, which generally consisted of a leg of Welsh mutton, bought at the famous house in the Strand, now pulled down, with salad. We started preparing our meal on the bank, when the threatened storm burst. We hastily put up our canvas over the boat, and bundled all the food into it anyhow. It got pitch dark, and we were compelled to find the lamp, but it would not light; luckily we found two candle ends, and by their feeble light began our meal. We had hardly begun our meal when I said after the first mouthful of salad, "What's wrong with the salad?" George also thought it was queer, but Jerome thought there was nothing wrong. Jerome always did have a peculiar taste. Anyhow, he was the only one who continued. It was not till the next day that we discovered that owing to our carelessness of using two medicine bottles of similar shape, one containing vinegar and the other Colza oil, the lamp and the salad were both a bit off.'

The Passing of the Third Floor Back The reception given by the critics to the play was less than enthusiastic and one or two of them came down from London, and commiserated with Forbes-Robertson on his bad luck at agreeing to play The Stranger in the play.

'It was the miners of Blackpool who put heart into us; they understood the thing, and were enthusiastic. Then we produced it at St. James', and, with one or two exceptions, it was besieged with a chorus of condemnation – deplorable, contemptible, absurd, were a few of the adjectives employed, and Forbes-Robertson hastened on the rehearsals for another play. A few days later, King Edward VII, passing through London on his way to Scotland, devoted his one night in London to seeing the piece. He said it was not the sort of thing he expected from Jerome, but he liked it. And about the same time strange people began to come, who did not know what the St. James' Theatre was, and did not quite know what to do when they got there, and they liked it, too.'

TOM AND JERRY

Two of our national daily broadsheets published independently the same query from different readers, to wit: 'In *Three Men on the Bummel* (published in 1900) Jerome K Jerome refers to a practical joke as "the acme of modem Tom and Jerryism". This must predate the cartoon films by several decades. Who were Tony and Jerry?'

Tom and Jerry were characters created by Pierce Egan (1772–1849) in his book *Life in London, Or The Day And Night Scenes of Jerry Hawthorne And His Elegant Friend Corinthian Tom. Accompanied by Bob Logic* (1820–1). This was a racy account of the drunken, rowdy behaviour of young Regency bucks.

The sequel, *Finish To The Adventure Of Tom and Jerry and Logic* (1828), presented the names in now-familiar order.

Thus a 'Tom and Jerry Gang' was a group of rowdy men devoted to drinking, gaming, womanising and so on. 'Tom and Jerry days' even became slang for the Regency and the reign of George IV. The term 'Tom-and-Jerrying' appeared in 1828, and 'Tom-and-Jerryism' (for loutish drunken behaviour) in about 1852. In 1862 an American guide to alcoholic drinks gave a recipe for a spicy punch called 'Tom and Jerry'. In Britain, a low beer-house was called a 'Tom-and-Jerry' (1865) or a 'Tom-and-Jerry Shop' (1873), though there is some evidence that the term 'Jerry Shop' was already used in this sense before Egan's book appeared.

The names became inseparably linked, so when a tom-cat was made the protagonist of a cartoon series it was inevitable that his mouse antagonist would be Jerry. The famous cat and mouse cartoon characters first appeared in MGM's *Puss Gets the Boot* in 1940. Their names had been chosen in a contest for MGM studio employees.

DR DOYLE AND JKJ – THE WALSALL CONNECTION
by Tony Gray

Jerome K Jerome and Arthur Conan Doyle were literary friends in *fin de siècle* London. As all Jeromians know, JKJ was born in Walsall in what was then Staffordshire. What is less well known is that Arthur Conan Doyle found himself in Walsall at the start of the 20th century to investigate a sequence of events which made sensational headlines at the time as the Great Wyrley Outrages.

The outrages were in fact a series of horse maimings in and around the small Staffordshire village of Great Wyrley. George Edalji, a solicitor in Birmingham, was accused and convicted of these horrible crimes for which he was sentenced to seven years hard labour. He was released after three years prison with no explanation and no pardon. As a consequence he was unable to resume his practice as a solicitor. Arthur Conan Doyle took up the case and, although it was never proved, formed the opinion that the horse maimings had been carried out by a failed pupil of Queen Mary's Grammar School, Walsall.

This amazing tale is told by Julian Barnes in his book *Arthur and George* which was short-listed for the Booker Prize. Doyle obtained a pardon for Edalji who was then reinstated as a solicitor. The two men formed a bond and George Edalji was invited to the marriage of Jean Leckie to Doyle at the Hotel Metropole.

To quote Julian Barnes: 'To George's surprise and considerable relief, people come up and speak to him; they seem to know who he is, and greet him as if they are almost familiars. Alfred Wood introduces himself, and talks of visiting Wyrley Vicarage and having had the great pleasure of meeting

George's family. Mr. Jerome, the comic writer, congratulates him on his successful fight for justice, introduces him to Miss Jerome, and points out other celebrities: J M Barrie over there, and Bram Stoker, and Max Pemberton.'

One wonders whether Jerome and Doyle ever talked of Walsall in any of their meetings. Jerome might not have known Great Wyrley but he had, of course, very good reason to have heard of Norton Canes which is located a few miles away. The twists and turns of fate are fascinating: if Jerome Senior's venture into coal mining had succeeded then it is unlikely that *Three Men in a Boat* would ever have been written.

None of Doyle's fictions are stranger than this very strange case of the son of a Parsee vicar of a small village in Staffordshire.

ALFRED MOSS
by Dr Paul McDonald

Senior Lecturer and Course Leader for Creative and Professional Writing at the University of Wolverhampton

An edited extract from Dr McDonald's contribution to Idle Thoughts *which first appeared in the Autumn 2006 edition of* The Blackcountryman

Alfred Moss was born in Longwood, near Walsall in 1859. He began his education in the Black Country, but managed to win a place at Oxford where he studied classics. Later he became a serious student of music, studying composition under Swinnerton Heap, and singing with the notable 19 century tenor, Sim Reeves. He lectured extensively on music and in 1921 founded the South Staffordshire Music Festival. He was also a poet who published verse in periodicals as diverse as *The Poetry Review*, and the naval magazine, *Sea Pie*. Moss, then, was something of a polymath – a multitalented, creative man with a passion for all the arts. Given his interest in music, it's not surprising that much of his verse should take music and musicians as a theme. His poem 'To Sebastian Bach' was published in the *Poetry Review* in March 1919, for instance, while in July of the same year, his 'To the Memory of Beethoven' appeared in the same journal. He even writes about particular compositions: there is a poem inspired by Beethoven's Fifth Symphony and another on Bach's *Fugue in C Minor, No. IV*:

> All intertwined these mystic themes unite
> To transmit truth from God's harmonious mind,
> To bathe the soul in co-immortal light,
> And guide its halting steps the goal to find.
> Such art reveals the path that men have trod
> Who gained the very citadel of God.

Moss's poetry is often preoccupied with spiritual concerns. The music poems, like the one above for instance, tend to explore the ways in which music can put us in touch with God. He occasionally addresses Walsall themes. He has a poem about 'Sister Dora', but here again his writing has a marked spiritual aspect: 'Thy kind compassion did on earth reflect The Motherhood of God, so wondrous fair.'

Moss, as you might expect from a musician, had a good ear for rhyme and rhythm, but his poetry is often marred by exaggeration and, when addressing individuals he admires, he is occasionally prone to embarrassing hagiography. This is something that undermines his most important literary work – *Jerome K Jerome: His Life and Work* (1928) — the first biography of Jerome. Recent scholars have criticised it for being overly dependent on Jerome's own memoir *My Life and Times* (1926), also for being excessively adulatory and subjective. There is some truth in this – the reader is left in little doubt that Moss worshipped Jerome and he never really engages critically or objectively with his subject. The book is dedicated to Jerome's widow and daughter, and one feels that he treads carefully partly out of respect for them. But I think it has some merit: contemporary reviewers praised it, and local readers will certainly find it interesting, not least because Moss gives an excellent account of Jerome's association with Walsall. Moss was present when Jerome was given the freedom of the Borough and he describes the event in some detail.

Jerome with the French Ambulance Unit, World War I

Photograph taken at the unveiling of the Tablet on Jerome's birthplace: (l–r) Mrs Jerome K Jerome, Councillor Leckie (Mayor of Walsall), W W Jacobs and Jerome K Jerome

Alfred Moss's greatest service to local letters, however, is the anthology of Walsall poetry he compiled in 1920, *Songs from the Heart of England*. In the introduction to the book he [and his co-editor, Arthur Brockhurst] go to some lengths to defend Walsall as a place in which it is possible to write poetry. Though it might appear that 'poetry and Walsall are antonyms', they argue, 'the test of poetry is not whether the writer resides here or there; but whether his work is individual and of enduring significance'. Having anticipated the potential derision of the literary establishment they go on to state their intention to take stock of Walsall poetry and offer an 'inquest into our poetic resources'. Their endeavour was a laudable effort to collate and showcase the cream of Walsall verse. For this alone Brockhurst and Moss deserve to be remembered. But their own writing should not be overlooked either, and their decision to include examples of it in their anthology is certainly justified – it stands up well alongside the best contributions and serves to consolidate their laudable defence of Walsall poetry.

12
FINAL DAYS

THE BEST TIME OF LIFE
Thrice I Wished My Life would Stand Still

by Jerome K Jerome

Published in T. P.'s and Cassell's Weekly, 5 February 1927

The best time of life is the good time that is coming. It is just round the corner, so to speak, and very soon we shall enter upon it and live happy ever after.

To the infant mewling and puking in the nurse's arms, it is when he has succeeded in wriggling himself free of those same restraining arms, and can crawl where he will and grab all things that seem to him desirable.

To the whining schoolboy, it will be when his school-days lie behind him and the road to all the world's delights lie turnpikefree before him; and there are no more lessons to be learned and no more punishments for those that have not learned them.

To the lover, with his woeful ballad and his sighing and complaining, it shall be when the anxious days of courtship are over and done with; when the inexpressible she has at last consented, and they are married and settled down in the castle or cottage, as the case may be, or in the little semi-detached house in the long suburban street. Later, looking back upon those courting days, he may regard himself as foolish for having sighed so strenuously, and wish he had not made such haste to end them: for may not they have been the best time, had he but known?

To the soldier – to the fighter in this popular struggle of all men for existence, the best time will be when the battle is over and won; when the business is at last established, the position long striven for achieved; and he may take his ease and enjoy the fruits of victory in pleasant Wimbledon, or leafy Surrey, or Sussex-by-the-sea. Beside the camp fire, with half closed eyes, already he plans out his garden where at evening he will walk. Here he will plant his orchard, and here shall be the level lawn where the birds shall gather round the fountain, and here the winding paths between the flowers.

And then the justice – or shall we say, in modern terms, respected member of the local board of guardians, or prim churchwarden, or honorary secretary of the county cricket club, in fair round belly with good capon lined. It does not pan out altogether as he had expected. Those wise saws and modern instances that should have commanded applause – at least attention. Youth is and ever was irreverent. It finds him stodgy, and is far from being impressed. The wife of his bosom, once the lady of the marvellous eyebrow, has come to have opinions of her own: with the passing of the years has developed critical faculties. The fair round belly grows inconveniently assertive as if it, too, would play a part – becomes a serious handicap at golf, necessitates the calling in of the family doctor, who prescribes an uninteresting diet from which fat capons, and their like, are strictly excluded, together with all but one glass of weak whisky and soda per diem, the emphasis upon the 'weak'.

Unconsciously, he sinks into the slippered pantaloon. And, the circle now completed, becomes again the helpless child, sans everything but hope. For he, too, dreams of that best time to come, a little further on, when, creeping from the darkened nursery, his mewling and his puking ended, he shall reach the land of heart's desire.

For man is so constituted that his happiness depends upon anticipation. With realization comes the awakening from the dream. We do not know when we are happy until it is too late; and if we knew, we should be unhappy, fearing for the end. 'Too good to last.' It is a common saying, born of our common experience. We know our little world so well. Call no man happy until he is dead, the philosopher advises us. To the children of Israel their forty years of wandering in the wilderness was the best time they ever had. In the Promised Land there came to them little else but trouble. Age, looking back, imagines the best time came with the struggle, not with the success. But if youth were foolish enough to listen, it would cease to press on, and so lose the rapture of pursuing. There is no best time of life. And if there were, of what use would it be to us mortals, whose journey knows no halting place? There are good times here and there along the road and, passing them, our hearts are glad. We will treasure remembrance of them. It shall lighten weary stretches, perhaps, to come.

Thrice I have had the wish that my life would stand still for a while. The last time was during my late forties when, one morning, I was walking up Broadway, in New York. I felt in tune with the din and whirl around me. The vast buildings, shutting out the sky, fitted in with my mood. They spoke to me of strength and power. And suddenly, from no cause, there fell upon me the shadow of old age – the thought that soon my energy and alertness would begin to fail me. There was so much that I wanted to do – that I knew myself capable of doing, if only Time would let me linger, beckoning to me later. The shadow continued to haunt me, making me afraid, till gradually the things I had meant to do seemed to be of less importance, and new thoughts took their place ...

And before that was when I was a boy just entering manhood. I had the feeling I was being changed, as if by some malignant fairy's wand, into a strange new creature that would not know me, and that I should hate. My thoughts and dreams and vision he would not understand. He would drive them away. They would be as dear lost comrades.

And the first time was when I was a child and lived in a loved world that was warm and cosy, with familiar faces, and good things to eat and drink, and toys to play with. One way, at the end of it, you came to mighty monsters.

They never moved, but waved their arms and talked to one another. They had kind voices. And beyond them it was dark. And if you went the other way, you came to where the dead lived in a cold white city of their own; and from beyond came smoke and fearful sounds, and you ran back all the way and hid behind the curtains. There were no yesterdays, but a far-off country called To-morrow. But before you reached it, you fell asleep, and when you woke up it was gone.

There were things that hurt you; but, on the whole, I must have been happy, for I recollect how sad I was when they told me I should have to leave it and grow up. And one morning I could not find my frock, and instead there was a suit of knickerbockers on the bed, and my mother came in and showed me how to put them on; and then I knew the time had come.

I cried when I was by myself, and said good-bye to all my toys. But mingled with my grief was curiosity: what would it be like?

And now that I approach those three score years and ten that, according to the life assurance companies, is over and above the allotted span of man, I find – mingled with other sensations – curiosity: what will it be like?

I see that little vanished self of mine looking out beyond the garden to the tall dark trees; and I remember that in that moment his fears fell from him and his spirits rose. I thank him for bequeathing me his love of adventure. It may be the brave days are yet to come.

* * *

The following extracts from The Times *relating to Jerome, Carl Hentschel and George Wingrowe were kindly provided by Mr. Peter Shaw. The Jerome K Jerome Society is most grateful to Times Newspapers Ltd and* The Birmingham Post *for permission to reproduce the following letters and obituaries.*

The Times, *Monday, June 6, 1927. p. 12*

Mr. Jerome K Jerome

It was stated at Northampton General Hospital yesterday morning that Mr. Jerome K Jerome spent a good night, but that there was no material change in his condition. During the day, however, he made a slight improvement.

The Times, *Tuesday, June 7, 1927. p. 7*

Mr. Jerome K Jerome

The improvement in the condition of Mr. Jerome K Jerome reported on Sunday was maintained yesterday.

The Times, *Wednesday, June 8, 1927. p. 9*

Mr. Jerome K Jerome

Mr. Jerome K Jerome, who is lying seriously ill from cerebral hamorrage [sic], is making slight but continued progress.

JEROME'S OBITUARY IN *THE TIMES*
The Times, *Wednesday, June 15, 1927. p. 18e.*
The writer of this obituary had, let us say, a clear-eyed view of Jerome's reputation at his death. The original spelling and punctuation have been preserved, as have the details of his early life which, as will be seen elsewhere in these pages, have now been proved to be incorrect.

Mr. J K JEROME

Mr. Jerome K Jerome, the novelist and dramatist, died in Northampton General Hospital yesterday morning from cerebral hemorrhage [sic], at the age of 68. With his wife and daughter, he had been on a motor tour in Devon during the latter part of May, and he then had a slight seizure. He quickly recovered, however, and on the homeward journey drove from Cheltenham to Northampton on May 31, refusing his wife's offer to relieve him at the wheel. They went to a hotel, and during the night Mr. Jerome had a serious stroke which paralysed his right side. Next day he was removed to the hospital and had since been semi-conscious.

As the author of an extremely successful farcical story, "Three Men in a Boat," and of an equally successful play, *The Passing of the Third Floor Back*, Jerome will be long remembered, though the simple humours of the story, and the religious sentiment of the play, made tolerable by Forbes-Robertson's genius, belong essentially to their period. Jerome was an industrious writer, but he never equalled these two successes, and in his later work the sentiment which had always marked his writing tended to degenerate into sentimentality. He had not, in fact, kept pace with the changes of public taste, and remained to the end in the naïveté both of his laughter and his tears a typical humorist of the 'eighties.

Jerome Klapka Jerome was born at Walsall on May 2, 1859. His father, an Independent preacher, the Rev. Jerome Clapp Jerome – the middle name was derived from that of "Clapa," a Danish ancestor of the family – was at that time the proprietor of coalmines on Cannock Chase. Through business misfortunes he was compelled, while his son was still a small boy, to remove his family to the East End of London, where he tried to make a fresh start in wholesale ironmongery. Jerome in his reminiscences, "My Life and Times," has written of the horror with which the East End filled him. "It was these surroundings," he says, "in which I passed my childhood that gave to me, I suppose, my melancholy brooding disposition."

After attending Marylebone Grammar School, he began at 14 to earn his own living, and showed a certain versatility, not to say restlessness of disposition. He became by turns railway clerk, actor, schoolmaster, and journalist. Of these early occupations his efforts as an actor were probably the most fruitful. He did not indeed win triumphs; though, as he has set on record, he "played every part in *Hamlet* except Ophelia," and was once told that he had "the makings of a clown in him." But he gained in the theatrical world the material for his first book, "On the Stage and Off," published in 1885, and from his experiences at Astley's, the old Surrey, and the "Brit," he wrote his diverting satire on the melodrama of the period, called "Stageland," for which his friend Bernard Partridge drew the illustrations. He may have picked up there, too, some of the technique of playwriting, and, indeed, to the end both his plays and his books retained a smack of the melodramas at which he himself had poked fun.

His first considerable literary success was in 1889 with "The Idle Thoughts of an Idle Fellow," a discursive blend of anecdote and philoso-phizing, in which he found scope for his peculiar sense of humour, a view of the world compounded of friendly cynicism and rather obvious bathos. It was the philosophy of a Bohemian, well acquainted with the sore under-side of life, but saved from gloom by the gaiety of a London which was then (as he later wrote) "a cosier place to dwell in," and of a literary and theatrical society, which included Barrie, Bernard Shaw, the blind poet, Philip Bourke Marston, W.S.Penley, and many other stimulating figures. A greater, and a thoroughly deserved, success came the same year with "Three Men in a Boat," written soon after the author's marriage to the daughter of Lieutenant Nesza, of the Spanish Army. This farcical masterpiece grew, it appears, out of a serious design, a historical and descriptive work to be called "The Story of the Thames." Luckily, the writer's effervescent love of fun ran away with him; the humorous element swallowed up the serious, though some pretty descriptions of the river scenery and the historic associations of the Thames were fortunately spared by the author and the first publisher, who "slung out" the rest.

A sort of sequel to this work, "Three Men on the Bummel," describing a German tour, was published in 1900, and was also appreciated both here and in Germany.

From 1892 to 1897 Jerome edited (with Robert Barr) the *Idler*, and from 1883 to 1897 *To-Day*. Stevenson's "Ebb-Tide" came out as a serial in the lat-ter magazine, for which Aubrey Beardsley, Phil May, and Raven Hill all drew. A costly law-suit ended Jerome's connexion [sic] with the paper. In 1902 he published "Paul Kelver," an autobiographical novel, which is one of his most artistic books.

He had always been anxious to write for the stage, and an early play of his, *Barbara*, was accepted by Sir Charles Hawtrey. *Miss Hobbs* in 1900 proved a simple comedy that has held its place among the amateurs. With *The Passing of the Third Floor Back*, produced with Sir Johnston Forbes-Robertson in the name-part in 1907, Jerome scored an immense success of sentiment. This tale of the regeneration of the inmates of a sordid London boarding-house by a Christ-like stranger expressed both the energy and the weakness of the author's religious and philanthropic feelings. It was followed by several other plays, including *Fanny and the Servant Problem*, *The Master of Mrs Chilvers*, on the theme of woman suffrage, and *The Great Gamble*, which had the ill-luck to be a play of German life produced just before the war in 1914. During the war Jerome, in spite of his years, did good service as a French motor-ambulance

driver on the Western front. But his health broke down, and he returned to join the advocates of a negotiated peace. In 1919 he wrote "All Roads Lead to Calvary," a rather sermonizing novel, relieved by flashes of irrepressible wit, and in the autumn of 1926 published his reminiscences.

JEROME' S FUNERAL
The Times, *Saturday, 18 June, 1927. p. 17b*

Funeral. Mr. Jerome K Jerome.

The funeral of Mr. Jerome K Jerome took place at Golders Green Crematorium yesterday, the Rev. Herbert Trundle, vicar of St. Alban's, Golders Green, officiating. The principal mourners were Mrs. Jerome (widow), Miss Jerome (daughter), Mr. Harry Shorland, Mr. Frank Shorland, and Mr. Frank Banister (nephews), and Mrs Harry Shorland. Others present were:- Mr. George Wingrave (the original "George" of "Three Men in a Boat"), Mr. J A Leekie (Mayor of Walsall), Dr. Woodley Stocker,

Dr. W Walsh, Mr. G B Burgin [note: 'G B' is indistinct in *The Times* typeface] (representing the Whitefriars Club), Mr. Will Owen, Mr. K H Thompson, Mr. P H King, Mrs Patrick Graham, and Miss Levey [note: the 'v' of Levey is missing in *The Times* typeface, so this is a guess].

Letter, The Times, Friday, June 17, 1927. p. 10

Mr. Jerome K Jerome

While having little sympathy with the sort of "religiosity" which, in my opinion, weakened a good deal of Jerome K Jerome's work, I believe that the underlying moral of much that he wrote, and in especial of *The Passing of the Third Floor Back*, was the result of a conviction in the reality of "goodness," as such, that amounted to a passion. Such a conviction, finding expression in fine dramatic form, is worth a great deal, and I, for one, believe that a play of the character of *The Passing of the Third Floor Back* makes definite appeal to what is noble and gracious in the minds of us all.

Ennis Richmond, 6, Hurlingham Court, S.W.6

* * *

JEROME'S OBITUARY IN *THE BIRMINGHAM POST*

DEATH OF MR. JEROME K JEROME, CLERK, ACTOR, SCHOOLMASTER AND AUTHOR HIS EARLY ASSOCIATIONS WITH WALSALL

June 14 – Mr. Jerome K Jerome, who had a seizure in Northampton a fortnight ago while on a motor tour, died in Northampton General Hospital yesterday.

Mr. Jerome was a native of Walsall, being born on May 2, 1859, in a house in Bradford Street. Last February the freedom of the town – 'the knighthood of Walsall' he called it – was conferred upon him and a tablet commemorating his birth was placed on his old home.

His father, who had been a farmer in Devon and was a Congregational minister in his spare time, came to Walsall to invest his capital in a coal mine in Norton Canes, still known as Jerome's Pit. The workings were flooded and the family impoverished. They lived for a year or two at Stourbridge; then the elder Jerome, who is remembered in the district for his share in founding Wednesbury Road Congregational Church, went to London, hopeful of restoring his fortunes.

He tried his hand at an ironmongery business, and was vaguely and unsuccessfully 'something in the City'. He was joined by his family in a home he found for them in East London. This was in 1861, when the young Jerome K Jerome was four years old. 'I arrived in London,' he said recently 'with nothing in my pocket but a clockwork mouse, and that would not go as it had been accidentally trodden on at a wayside station – it may have been Birmingham.' London did not make his fortune, but it gave him the education which made him what he was.

His childhood was poverty-stricken and depressing; to the end of his life his schooldays remained a disagreeable memory, though London streets were an abundant source of interest to him. After his father's death he became, at the age of 14, a railway clerk at Euston, at a salary of £26 a year, with an annual rise of £10. The stage attracted him, however. He began to act in small companies in London in his spare time, and finally threw up his clerkship, then worth £70 a year, to go on tour.

SLEPT IN DOSSHOUSES

For three years he kept to the stage, just earning enough to live, often sleeping in open-air in summer or in the theatre in the winter. In his biography, *My Life and Times*, he recalled that he played every part in *Hamlet* except Ophelia and doubled the roles of Martin Chuzzlewit and Sairey Gamp in the same performance.

He returned to London, slept in dosshouses, and began reporting inquests at police-court cases; then, for a single term, taught in a private school.

He might have become secretary to Herbert Spencer but for his sister's certainty that the post would destroy his last chance of eternal salvation. Instead he became, in turn the secretary to a builder, buyer to a commission agent, and clerk to a parliamentary agent and a solicitor.

Meanwhile he had begun writing. He was on the point of enlisting in the cavalry when *On the Stage – and Off* found a publisher in 1888.

Next year appeared *The Idle Thoughts of an Idle Fellow* and *Three Men in a Boat*.

Jerome became known as 'the new humorist and 'the new humour' was expected to be a feature of all that he wrote. To his own chagrin, he never entirely outlived his reputation.

In the 'nineties', Jerome was distinguished as an editor. *The Idler*, which he edited with Robert Barr, was a delightful illustrated monthly magazine. He also started a weekly paper, *To-day*. He was remarkably quick in recognising new talent: and his group of contributors included R L Stevenson, H G Wells, W W Jacobs, Barry Pain, Richard Le Gallienne, Anthony Hope, Israel Zangwill, Eden Phillpotts, Phil May, Aubrey Beardsley, Dudley Hardy and Lewis Baumer. Unhappily, his city editor involved him in an inconclusive libel action, the costs of which were £9,000, so that he had to sell out his holdings in his papers.

THE STRANGER

A number of plays of his were produced, the most famous and re-markable being *The Passing of the Third Floor of the Third Floor Back*, produced by Sir Johnston Forbes-Robertson and included in his repertory until his retirement.

Jerome's conception of 'The Stranger' came from following a stooping figure, whose face he could not see passing along a foggy London street.

His novel, *Paul Kelver*, a very well written book, is also in a serious vein, and contains a considerable element of autobiography.

During the war, though fifty-five years old, Mr. Jerome became an ambulance-driver in the French Red Cross, and worked in Verdun until his health gave way.

Letter, *The Times*, Wednesday, June 22, 1927. p. 12

It might interest your readers to know the real origin of Mr. Jerome Klapka Jerome's middle name. To my knowledge there was no question of Danish ancestry. When the Fort of Komárom surrendered on October 3, 1849, during the Hungarian War of Independence the Press of the whole world glorified George Klapka, the courageous young General of Artillery, 29 years old at the time, who was able to hold the fort against the united Austrian and Russian armies and only surrendered when he secured an amnesty for his fellow combatants. After the surrender Klapka went abroad. When he arrived in London, Francis Pulszky, Kossiuth's [sic] secretary, considering the young hero's precarious position, advised him to write his memoirs for Messrs. Chapman and Hall, the publishers who immediately granted him an advance of £100. It was a question now of finding a quiet retreat, as the book had to be finished within two months. Klapka gladly accepted the invitation of the Rev. Jerome Jerome. In Walsall he found a home, and even in later years, whenever he tired of restless wandering, he always returned to his kind host. When, in 1859, a son was born to the Rev. J Jerome, in honour of his famous guest he named him Jerome Klapka.

— Professor Michal M Bálint, 1 Németvölgyi ut 42, Budapest

This appears to be the source of the oft-quoted story behind the acquisition of 'Klapka'. Interestingly, it comes from a Hungarian. It would be interesting to know how Professor Bálint came by this information which, as we have said elsewhere, is almost certainly a fabrication. We now know that Jerome was christened Jerome Clapp Jerome and seems to have only begun using Klapka when he became a published author.

'HARRIS'S' OBITUARY

Hentschel / Harris had a distinguished City career, one which, to judge by the last sentence of his obituary, was achieved without his youthful association with Jerome.

The Times, *Friday, January 10, 1930. p. 14b*

MR. CARL HENTSCHEL

Mr. Carl Hentschel, who died yesterday in London after a short illness at the age of 65, was a man of varied interests. He did much to improve process work for illustrations, and was a regular "first nighter," an active member of the City Corporation, and an old Volunteer.

Hentschel was born at Lodz, in Russian Poland, on March 27, 1864. His father, who was an American citizen of Russian origin, was a clever inventor, whose ideas benefited others more than himself. At the age of five he was brought by his parents to England, and had some education at Eastbourne, where his father then had a paper collar factory. Later, at the age of 14, he began to help his father, who was now working at photographing on wood. But soon the elder Hentschel, seeing that wood engraving would soon be superseded, turned to the mechanical reproduction of illustrations on zinc. At last success came, a company took up the invention, and Carl Hentschel became working manager. In 1887 he started on his own account, becoming chairman and managing director when the business was incorporated as Carl Hentschel Limited, in 1920. He invented the Hentschel colour type process, and made the first process block, which brought about a revolution in newspaper illustration. He married, in 1889, Bertha, daughter of Mr. David Posener, and he used to say that this was the cleverest thing he ever did, for her help and sympathy alone enabled him to come through his early struggles.

In the theatrical world Mr. Hentschel was a well-known figure. He claimed that he had attended every London first night, with few exceptions, since 1879. The old first-nighters were great champions of the rights of the pit, and long desired to have a meeting-place to discuss their grievances. In March, 1883, Hentschel and the late Heneage Mandell founded, at a coffee house in Holywell-Street, the Playgoers' Club, which struggled on in spite of much abuse. In 1899 Hentschel became treasurer, being handed 4s 2d., the available funds. It had a membership of 1,000 and over £500 in cash in 1900 when he, with some hundreds of other members, left it on a question of policy. He then founded the O.P. Club, of which he was president in 1902–3, in 1914–16, and again at the time of his death. With Heneage Mandell in 1889 he also started the *Playgoer*, but it did not live long. He was also editor of the *Half-Tone Times*, of which only one number appeared, and *Newspaper Illustrations*. For 20 years, till 1921, Mr. Hentschel was a member of the Court of Common Council, representing the ward of Farringdon Without. He carried a resolution that City Aldermen should not be elected for life, but the proposal came to nothing. Another reform which he had at heart was the limitation of public speeches. As president of the Bartholomew Club in 1904 he had the speeches at a dinner printed in little books, which were distributed to the company, and "taken as read." He served as chairman of the Central Markets, Guildhall School of Music and the General Purposes Committees, and as president of the City of London Tradesmen's Club. Among his War-time activities he was secretary of the Optimists Corps, founded by Sir Charles Higham, and afterwards, at the request of Mr. Lloyd George, renamed the London Volunteer Rifles. He was organising secretary of the Royal Horticultural Society's War Relief Fund. He was the original of the character named Harris in Jerome's "Three Men in a Boat."

GEORGE'S DEATH ANNOUNCED
The Times, *Tuesday, March 25, 1941*

Mr. George Wingrave, formerly manager of the branch of Barclay's Bank at 366, Strand, who was the original "George" of *Three Men in a Boat* by Jerome K Jerome, died at Cheshunt Cottage Hospital on Saturday at the age of 79.

13
BIBLIOGRAPHY

compiled by Jeremy Nicholas

This bibliography is a conflation of two valuable earlier ones by Robert G Logan and Joseph Connolly, to whom grateful acknowledgements are due. Frank Rodgers has kindly provided numerous additions and corrections to make this the most comprehensive record of Jerome's work yet published.

THE COMPLETE WORKS OF JEROME K JEROME IN CHRONOLOGICAL ORDER

DATE	TITLE	GENRE
1881	Jack's Wife	Short story
1885	On the Stage – and Off	Semi-fiction, dramatic sketches
1886	– On the Stage – and Off (reissue, illustrated edition)	
1886	The Idle Thoughts of an Idle Fellow	Essays
1886	Barbara	Play
1888	Sunset	Play
1888	Fennel	Play
1888	Pity Is Akin to Love	Play
1888	Woodbarrow Farm	Play
1888	Playwriting: A Handbook for Would-Be Dramatic Authors	Booklet
1889	Stage-Land	Satirical essays
1889	Three Men in a Boat	Novel
1890	New Lamps for Old	Play
1890	Ruth	Play
1890	What Women Will Do	Play
1890	Birth and Breeding (aka Honour)	Play
1890	The Prince's Quest	Short story
1891	Told After Supper	Ghost stories

1891	A Breezy Morning	Play
1891	The Diary of a Pilgrimage	Novel, semi-fiction
1892	Weeds. A Story in Seven Chapters	Short novel
1892–98	The Idler (editor / contributor)	Journalism
1893–98	To-Day (editor / contributor)	Journalism
1894	My First Book (editor / contributor)	Essays
1895	The Rise of Dick Halward	Play
1895	The Prude's Progress	Play
1896	Biarritz	Play
1897	The MacHaggis	Play
1897	Sketches in Lavender, Blue and Green	Sketches
1898	The Second Thoughts of an Idle Fellow	Essays
1899	John Ingerfield	Play
1899	Miss Hobbs	Play
1900	Three Men on the Bummel	Novel
1900	– Three Men on Wheels (American edition of the above)	
1901	The Observations of Henry	Short stories
1902	Paul Kelver	Autobiographical novel
1902	Miss Hobbs	Play
1903	Tea Table Talk	Essays, stories, thoughts
1904	Tommy and Co	Novel
1904	American Wives and Others	Essays
1905	Idle Ideas in 1905	Essays
1906	Tommy	Play
1906	Robina in Search of a Husband	Play
1907	The Passing of the Third Floor Back	Short stories
1907	Sylvia of the Letters	Play
1908	The Angel and the Author – and Others	Essays
1909	They and I	Novel

1909	Fanny and the Servant Problem	Play
1910	The Passing of the Third Floor Back	Play
1911	The Master of Mrs Chilvers	Play
1913	Esther Castways	Play
1914	The Great Gamble	Play
1914	Poor Little Thing	Play
1915	The Three Patriots	Play
1916	Malvina of Brittany	Novelette and stories
1916	– The Street of the Blank Wall (American edition of the above)	
1917	Cook (aka The Celebrity)	Play
1919	All Roads Lead to Calvary	Novel
1923	Anthony John	Novel
1923	A Miscellany of Sense and Non-sense	Extracts from Jerome's books
1926	My Life and Times	Autobiography
1927	The Soul of Nicholas Snyders	Play
	Three further plays, The Disagreeable Man, A Russian Vagabond and The Night of February 14 1899 were not produced. Dates unknown.	

NOVELS, ESSAYS, ETC.

All Roads Lead to Calvary
London: Hutchinson, 1919. 288p.
Novel with a political and religious message.
1st Edition: Red cloth, lettered black on spine only.

American Wives and Others
New York: Frederick A Stokes, 1904. vii, 364p. Illustrated by George McManus.
Issued in America only. Twenty-five essays in the *Idle Thoughts* vein.
1st Edition: Cream boards, title within white lozenge with silhouette of mother and child in blue and black.

The Angel and the Author – and Others
London: Hurst and Blackett, 1908. iv, 226p.
Twenty essays in the *Idle Thoughts* vein.
1st Edition: Rust cloth, black lettering on front, gold on spine.

Anthony Johns: A Biography
London: Cassell, 1923. iv, 260p

Novel with a strong religious message. The rags-to-riches story of the son of a poor engineer who made good and then sacrificed all his wealth to follow the teachings of Christ.

1st Edition: Tan cloth, black lettering on front and spine.

Diary of a Pilgrimage: and six essays

Bristol: Arrowsmith, 1891. 306p. With upwards of 120 illustrations by G G Fraser

Humour: semi-fiction. The account of a trip to Germany to see the Oberammergau Passion Play, based on a journey made by JKJ and Walter Helmore. The earlier editions also contain six essays, five of which are also to be found in *The Observations of Henry*.

1st Edition: Buff cloth, black lettering.

Idle Ideas in 1905

London: Hurst and Blackett, 1905. viii, 307p.

Twenty one essays.

1st Edition: Yellow cloth, red lettering on front, gold on spine.

The Idle Thoughts of an Idle Fellow: an idle book for an idle holiday

London: Field and Tuer, 1886. vii, 172p.

Fourteen essays. As in most of his later work they contain a blend of humour and seriousness.

1st Edition: Pale yellow boards.

John Ingerfield and other stories

London: McClure, 1894. vi, 220p.

6 plates. Illustrations on plate paper.

Tragic novelette and four short stories, two tragic and two humorous.

1st Edition: 6½"x4" in mid-green cloth.

Malvina of Brittany: (and other stories)

London: Cassell, 1916. vi, 304p

Fantasy novelette, and five short stories.

1st Edition: Blue cloth, blind stamped on front, gold lettering on spine.

The Street of the Blank Wall. New York: Dodds, Mead & Co., 1916, 316p

(American edition of *Malvina of Brittany*). Dull green cloth boards. Title & author in dark green capitals.

A Miscellany of Sense and Nonsense from the writings of Jerome K Jerome: selected by the author with many apologies

London: Arrowsmith, 1923.

374p. With 43 illustrations by Will Owen.

A personal anthology, with extracts from sixteen of his books.

1st Edition: Off-white cloth, titles within brown lozenges on cover and spine.

My First Book

London: Chatto & Windus, 1894. xvi. 309p. 185 illustrations with ¾ length pencil portrait of Jerome as frontispiece. Edited, and contributed to, by Jerome, the contents chronicle the experience of their first book by such luminaries as Rudyard Kipling, Conan Doyle, Rider Haggard, R M Ballantyne, Robert Louis Stevenson and others.

1st Edition: Blue cloth ruled like an exercise book with a quill and inkpot.

My Life and Times
London: Hodder and Stoughton, 1926. vi, 302p. plate (col). Autobiography. Contains some interesting comments on his own work and philosophy. Anecdotes of literary friends, including Sir James Barrie, Sir. Arthur Conan Doyle, George Bernard Shaw and H G Wells. The frontispiece is a reproduction of the portrait of Jerome by de Laszlo.
1st Edition: Royal blue cloth, gold lettering on spine.

Novel Notes
London: Leadenhall Press, 1983. xvi, 292p.
A series of twelve articles reprinted from 'The Idler'. They represent the supposed memoranda of the meetings of four authors in their abortive attempt to write a joint novel. Each article was illustrated by a different artist.
1st Edition: Mustard cloth with JKJ monogram.

The Observations of Henry – and others
Bristol: Arrowsmith, 1901. 186p.
Five short stories and five essays.
1st Edition: Pale brown, black line on borders, black lettering, 6½" x 4½".

On the stage and off: the brief career of a would-be-actor
London: Field and Tuer, 1885. viii, 160p.
Humour: semi-fiction. Some serious satire. The account of a young actor's progress, based on Jerome's own stage experiences. Later edition contains 100 illustrations by Kenneth M Skeaping.
1st Edition: 173 x 112mm in pink wrappers; later illustrated Leadenhall Press edition (1890) in brown boards.

The Passing of the Third Floor Back: and other stories
London: Hurst and Blackett, 1907. vi, 160p.
Six short stories. Jerome later wrote plays based on both 'The Passing of the Third Floor Back' and 'The Soul of Nicholas Snyders'.
1st Edition: Green cloth, lettered in lighter green.

Paul Kelver
London: Hutchinson, 1902
Novel, written in the first person and possibly autobiographical. Set in the East End of London. The story traces Paul's struggles from poor beginnings to the final attainment of success and self-respect.
1st Edition: Navy blue, cover has gold rectangular lozenge

Playwriting: a handbook for would-be dramatic authors. A Dramatist (pseudonym): The Stage Office, 1888. viii, III, vii pp.; illus. Almost certainly written by Jerome. (See Arnott, James Fullarton and Robinson, John William: *English Theatrical Literature 1559–1900, a bibliography*, incorporating Robert W Lowes 'A bibliographical account of English theatrical literature', published in 1888. Society for Theatre Research, 1970. p.85, no.815.)

The Second Thoughts of an Idle Fellow
London: Hurst and Blackett, 1898. vi, 360p.
Twelve essays.
1st Edition: Olive cloth, black lettering on front, gold on spine.

Sketches in Lavender, Blue and Green
London: Longman, Green and Co., 1897. vi, 360p.
Twenty short stories.
1st Edition: Mid-blue, with gold lettering within stamped lozenge on cover.

Stage-Land: curious habits and customs of its inhabitants
London: Chatto and Windus, 1889. iv, 80p. With illustrations by Bernard Partridge.
Satire. Humorously portrays the stock characters of the stage, including: hero, villain, heroine, comic man, lawyer, adventuress, servant girl, child, comic lovers, peasants, good old man, Irishman, detective and sailor.
1st Edition: Green cloth, red lettering.

Tea-Table Talk
London: Hutchinson, 1903. 128p. 16 plates. Illustrations on plate paper by Fred Pegram.
Volume of philosophical musings in the form of discussions between the woman of the world, the minor poet, the Girton girl, the philosopher, the old maid and the author.
1st Edition: Mid-blue cloth, cover has cup and saucer, and typography in white.

They and I
London: Hutchinson, 1909. iv, 328p.
Humorous novel.
1st Edition: Red cloth, front and spine lettered in gold.

Three Men in a Boat: to say nothing of the dog
Bristol: Arrowsmith, 1889. vi, 315p. Illustrations by A Frederics. Humour: semi-fiction. The story of a boating trip on the Thames made by J, George, Harris and the dog Montmorency. Based on similar trips made by Jerome, George Wingrave and Carl Hentschel. The dog was fictitious. Celebrated for its humour and also for the beauty of the descriptive passages which intermingle with the hilarity.
1st Edition: Blue-green cloth, front cover has silhouette and black lettering, spine is lettered in gold.

Three Men on the Bummel
Bristol: Arrowsmith, 1900. 328p. Illustrations by L Raven Hill. Humour: semi-fiction. Sequel to *Three Men in a Boat*. Based on a cycling trip through the Black Forest made by the same three men, now middle-aged.
1st Edition: Red cloth with pink decoration, gold letters on spine.

Three Men on Wheels.
New York: Dodds, Mead & Co. 1900, 299p. Illustrations by Harrison Fisher. American title of *Three Men on the Bummel*. Light green, brown/black silhouette on cover, gold lettering on spine.

Tommy and Co.
London: Hutchinson, 1904. iv, 256p. Frontispiece and title-page on plate paper.
Novel. The story of a waif, initially referred to as 'it' but later discovered to be a female, who drifts into journalism and becomes a lady sub-editor.
1st Edition: Royal blue cloth bordered in white, lettered in gold.

Told after Supper
London: Leadenhall Press, 1891. viii, 169p. Printed on blue paper.
With 96 or 97 illustrations by Kenneth M Skeaping.

Four ghost stories, with a connecting narration of how they came to be told after a hearty supper at a Christmas Eve Party. Fictional.

1st Edition: Bright-red cloth, printed on pale blue paper.

Weeds. A story in seven chapters

K McK (pseudonym). Arrowsmith, 1892. 118ff.

The authorship of this anonymous work is now attributed to Jerome. The evidence exists in a manuscript letter written by Jerome to Arrowsmith, the publisher. This letter, which was sold by Sotheby's in February 1968, leaves little doubt as to the true identity of K McK. It also suggests that the title of the novel was intended to be *Weeds*. It does not appear that the book was ever placed on general sale, but a copy is held by the British Museum. (See preview of Sotheby's sale of manuscript letters in *The Daily Telegraph*, 12 February 1968).

1st Edition: Brown cloth, 11cms x 17½cms

INDEX OF SHORT STORIES AND ESSAYS CONTAINED IN JEROME'S BOOKS

Key to abbreviations used in this section

American Wives (American Wives and Others)
Diary of a pil. (Diary of a Pilgrimage and six essays)
Idle ideas (Idle Ideas in 1905)
Idle thoughts (Idle Thoughts of an Idle Fellow)
John Ingerfield (John Ingerfield and other stories)
Malvina of Brit. (Malvina of Brittany and other stories)
Observations of H. (Observations of Henry – and others)
Passing of Third Floor (Passing of the Third Floor Back; and Other Stories)
Second idle thoughts (Second Thoughts of an Idle Fellow)
Sketches in lavender (Sketches in Lavender, Blue and Green)
Told after supper (Told After Supper)

The absent-minded man (Diary of a pil.)
The amenities of cheerful living (American Wives)
The American girl's etiquette (American Wives)
American professors and progress (American Wives)
American Wives à la mode (American Wives)
Are early marriages a mistake? (Idle ideas)
Are we as interesting as we think we are? (Idle ideas)
On the art of making up one's mind (Second idle thoughts)
On babies (Idle thoughts)
On being hard up (Idle thoughts)
On being idle (Idle thoughts)
On being in love (Idle thoughts)
On being in the blues (Idle thoughts)
On being introduced (American Wives)
On being shy (Idle thoughts)
Babies and birds (American Wives)
Beauty by the bottle (American Wives)
Blasé Billy (Sketches in lavender)

IDLE THOUGHTS ON JEROME K JEROME

On the care and management of women (Second idle thoughts)
On cats and dogs (Idle thoughts)
A charming woman (Sketches in lavender)
The Chinaman (American Wives)
The choice of Cyril Harjohn (Sketches in lavender)
The city of the sea (Sketches in lavender)
Clocks (Diary of a pil.) (Observations of H.)
The cost of kindness (Passing of Third Floor)
Creatures that one day shall be men (Idle ideas)
The degeneration of Thomas Henry (Sketches in lavender)
On the delights and benefits of slavery (Second idle thoughts)
Dawn o' day in the big cities (American Wives)
Dick Dunkerman's cat (Sketches in lavender)
On the disadvantage of not getting what one wants (Second idle thoughts)
Do we lie a-bed too late? (Idle ideas)
Do writers write too much? (Idle ideas)
Does the young man know everything worth knowing? (Idle ideas)
Dreams (Diary of a pil.) (Observations of H.)
On dress and deportment (Idle thoughts)
On drilling an army (American Wives)
Driftwood (Sketches in lavender)
On eating and drinking (Idle thoughts)
Evergreens (Diary of a pil.) (Observations of H.)
The exasperated hero (American Wives)
On the exceptional merit attaching to the things we meant to do (Second idle thoughts)
The fawn gloves (Malvina of Brit.)
On furnished apartments (Idle thoughts)
On getting on in the world (Idle thoughts)
Gold braid and its effects (American Wives)
The ghost of the blue chamber, or My uncle's story (Told after supper)
The ghost of the Marchioness of Appleford (Observations of H.)
Goodness that grates on us (American Wives)
The haunted mill; or the ruined home, or Mr. Coombes's story (Told after supper)
His evening out (Malvina of Brit.)
The hobby rider (Sketches in lavender)
How many charms hath music, would you say? (Idle ideas)
How to be happy though little (Idle ideas)
How to solve the servant problem (Idle ideas)
In remembrance of John Ingerfield, and of Anne, his wife (John Ingerfield)
On the inadvisability of following advice (Second idle thoughts)
Is the American husband made entirely of stained glass? (Idle ideas)
An item of fashionable intelligence (Sketches in lavender)
Johnson and Emily; or the faithful ghost, or Teddy Biffles' story (Told after supper)
The land of the happy Dutch (American Wives)
The lease of the 'Cross Keys' (John Ingerfield)

The uses and abuses of Joseph (Observation of H.)
On vanity and vanities (Idle thoughts)
Variety patter (John Ingerfield)
Wagneristic stage manners (American Wives)
Waiters I have known (American Wives)
On the weather (Idle thoughts)
What Mrs. Wilkins thought about it (Idle ideas)
When is the best time to be merry? (Idle ideas)
Whibley's spirit (Sketches in lavender)
The white man's burden! Need it be so heavy? (Idle ideas)
Why didn't he marry the girl? (Idle ideas)
Why we hate the foreigner (Idle ideas)
The woman of the saeter (John Ingerfield)
The wooing of Tom Sleight's wife (Observations of H.)
The yellow mask (American Wives)

Note: Many anthologies of short stories have included tales by Jerome. Very often, however, the pieces selected have been extracts from his books rather than short stories written as such. *Three Men in a Boat* has been a particularly fruitful source. But the most popular of such extracts would appear to be 'The Dancing Partner', a horror story, which is to be found in *Novel Notes*, pp.264–275. This has merited inclusion in such anthologies as:

Hitchcock, Alfred, ed.:
Stories they wouldn't let me do on T.V.
Sayers, Dorothy L. ed.:
Great short stories of detection, mystery and horror, 1st series
Sayers, Dorothy L. ed.:
Omnibus of crime

PLAYS

The extraordinary number of Jerome's plays, most of them completely unknown or forgotten, underlines just how important the theatre was to his career. Details of opening London performances are given, where known. These are not necessarily the first-ever performances of the plays concerned. All theatres are / were in London, unless otherwise stated.

TS = typescript MS = manuscript

Barbara		
1 act comic drama	Globe, 19 June 1886	Samuel French n/d
Biarritz (libretto by JKJ, lyrics by Adrian Ross, music by F Osmond Carr)		
Musical farce	Prince of Wales's, 11 April 1896	Francis, Day & Hunter
(Note: the title page of the vocal score states 'words by Jerome K Jerome' but does not include these in the score! Jerome's 113-page manuscript of the libretto is in the British Library)		

Birth and Breeding		
Later retitled **Honour**	Edinburgh, 18 September 1890 New York, 1895	unpublished
Adapted from the German of Sudermann's *Die Ehre*		

A Breezy Morning (co-authored with Eden Phillpotts)

	Grand, Leeds, 27 April 1891	Samuel French 1895
(Note: the published play credits only Phillpotts, but a handwritten copy in the possession of the JKJ Society states, underlined on the cover and in Jerome's hand-writing: 'and Jerome K Jerome')		

The Celebrity

First produced as **Cook**

3 act comedy	Kingsway, 19 August 1917	Hodder & Stoughton 1926

Esther Castways

Drama	Prince of Wales's, 21 January 1913	TS Bodleian Library

Fanny and the Servant Problem

Retitled **Lady Bantock** for the US

4 act comedy	Aldwych, 14 October 1908	Samuel French 1909

Fennel		
1 act romantic drama	Novelty, 31 March 1888	Samuel French (probably 1888)
Adapted from François Coppée's *The Violin-Makers of Cremona*		

The Great Gamble

Comedy	Haymarket, 21 May 1914	TS Bodleian Library

John Ingerfield		
4 act drama	Chicago, 23 May 1899	unpublished
Based on Jerome's short story of the same name		

The MacHaggis (co-authored with Eden Phillpotts)

3 act farce	Globe, 25 February 1897	MS & TS Bodleian Library

The Master of Mrs. Chilvers

'An improbable comedy'	Royalty, 26 April 1911	T Fisher Unwin 1911

Miss Hobbs

4 act comedy	Duke of York's, 18 December 1899	Samuel French 1902

New Lamps for Old

No details	Terry's, 8 February 1890	TS Bodleian Library

The Passing of the Third Floor Back

'An idle fancy in a prologue, a play and an epilogue'	First performed at the Grand Opera House, Harrogate, on 13 August 1908 St. James's, London, 1 September 1908; Drury Lane, 24 March 1913; Coliseum, 23 March 1917; Playhouse, 9 April 1917; Everyman, 23 December 1928; Everyman, 23 December 1929	Hurst & Blackett 1910

Adapted from Jerome's short story of the same name

Pity is Akin to Love

1 act dramatic sketch	Olympic, 8 September 1888	unpublished

Poor Little Thing

No details	New York 1914	TS Bodleian Library

Adapted from the French of Jules Lemaitre's *La Massière*

The Prude's Progress (co-authored with Eden Phillpotts)

3 act comedy	Comedy, 22 May 1895	Chatto & Windus 1895

The Rise of Dick Halward

3 act drama	Garrick, 19 October 1895	MS Bodleian Library
Earlier title **The Way to Win a Woman**	New York 1894	

Robina in Search of a Husband

Originally produced as **Susan in Search of a Husband**

4 act comedy	London, March 1906	Samuel French 1914
	New York, November 1906	

(Note: 'Eugene Presbrey' is listed as the author for the American production)

Ruth (co-authored with Addison Bright)		
Drama	Prince's Theatre, Bristol, 20 March 1890	unpublished
The Soul of Nicholas Snyders		
First produced as **Man or Devil**		
3 act mystery	New York, 1925	Hodder & Stough-ton 1927
	Everyman, 14 December 1927	
Sunset		
1 act play	Comedy, 13 February 1888	Samuel French 1888
Based on Tennyson's second and longer poem of *The Sisters*		
Sylvia of the Letters		
No details	Playhouse, 15 October 1907	unpublished
The Three Patriots		
No details	Queen's, 27 July 1915	TS Bodleian Library
Tommy		
3 act drama	The Camden, 3 December 1906	TS New York Public Library
Adapted from Jerome's novel *Tommy & Co*		
What Women Will Do		
Comic drama	Birmingham, 17 September 1890	unpublished
Woodbarrow Farm		
3 act comedy	Comedy, 18 June 1888	Samuel French 1904
The Disagreeable Man	Not produced	TS Bodleian Library
A Russian Vagabond	Not produced	TS Bodleian Library
The Night of Feb 14th 1899	Not produced	MS Bodleian Library
		TS New York Public Library

JOURNALS

Many of Jerome's contributions to journals were later published in book form. For example, the following books were originally serialised in the journals indicated: *On the Stage and Off* (The Play): *Idle Thoughts of an Idle Fellow* and *Three Men in a Boat* (Home Chimes): *Stage-Land* (The Playgoer): and *Novel Notes* (The Idler).

The Idler
London. February 1892 – October 1911. Ed. by Robert Barr and Jerome K Jerome. 1892–1898. v.1–14.

A monthly magazine founded by Barr, who invited Jerome to become joint-editor. The content was mainly literary and the contributors included many of the well-known writers of the day. Jerome was a regular contributor to the witty 'Idlers Club' column, which was a feature of each issue. His book *Novel Notes* was serialised in twelve parts from May 1892, Among his other contributions were three short stories which were later published in *John Ingerfield* and an article in the series 'My First Book'.

To-Day
London. 11 November 1893–19 July 1905. Then merged in 'London Opinion'. Ed. by Jerome K Jerome. 1893–1898.

An illustrated weekly newspaper founded by Jerome. It sold for twopence. The content was literary and humorous, and well-known authors and illustrators were among the contributors. R L Stevenson's 'Ebb-tide' was the first serial. Jerome wrote witty editorials on the affairs of the day and a series of pen-portraits called 'Characterscapes' e.g. 'The man who would manage'. Some of the articles from this column are included in Jerome's *Sketches in Lavender, Blue and Green*.

JEROME'S CONTRIBUTIONS TO *THE IDLER*, 1892–1898
collated by Frank Rodgers

Silhouettes
Idler 1, no.1 (February 1892): 47–56.
(Collected in John Ingerfield, London, McClure, 1894).

The Idler's Club
Idler 1, no. 1 (February 1892): 106–18.
[informal round table discussion among several authors: in this first issue, Robert Barr, Barry Payn, Zangwill, Kennedy and Jerome; Jerome comments on Valentines and buying them, 113–8].

Variety Patter
Idler 1, no. 2 (March 1892): 121–35.
(Collected in John Ingerfield).

The Idler's Club
Idler 1, no. 2 (March 1892): 222–36.
[Jerome on music halls and the ballet, 222–5; and prosecuting cabmen, 236].

Novel Notes.
Idler 1, no. 4 (May 1892): 362–86.
1, no. 5 (June 1892): 488–508.
1, no. 6 (July 1892): 607–23.

2, no. 1 (August 1892): 44–59.

2, no. 2 (September 1892): 128–47.

2, no. 3 (October 1892): 287–306.

2, no. 4 (November 1892): 369–83.

2, no. 5 (December 1892): 492–509.

2, no. 6 (January 1893): 651–67.

3, no. 1 (February 1893): 31–46.

3, no. 2 (March 1893): 174–92.

3, no. 3 (April 1893): 318–29.

(Published by The Leadenhall Press, August 1893).

The Idler's Club
Idler 1, no. 4 (May 1892): 474–84.
[Jerome on good men and oysters, virtues and vices, 480–81].

The Idler's Club
Idler 1, no. 5 (June 1892): 592–604.
[Jerome on the evil influence of automatic machines, 600–3].

The Idler's Club
Idler 2, no. 1 (August 1892): 99–112.
[Jerome on holidays, 99].

The Idler's Club
Idler 2, no. 3 (October 1892): 340–51.
[Jerome on a good bishop and a sinful reporter, pp. 340–43].
(Published, with alterations, as "The Lease of the 'Cross Keys'," in John Ingerfield).

The Idler's Club
"Shall we Have a Dramatic Academy?" Idler 3, no. 5 (June 1893): 568–76.
[Jerome wishes to educate the playgoer, 575–76].

The Woman of the Sæter
Idler 3, no. 6 (July 1893): 578–93.
(Collected in John Ingerfield).

The Idler's Club
"Nothing in Particular." Idler 4, no. 1 (August 1893): 101–10.
[Jerome asks why "Cockney" is a term of reproach; discusses book reviewing practices, 107–9].

The Idler's Club
"Are Honeymoons a Success?" Idler 4, no. 2 (September 1893): 210–18. [Jerome's contribution, 216–18]. The Idler's Club. "Is it Pleasant to Give Presents?" Idler 4, no. 3 (October 1893): 318–28. [Jerome's contribution, 327–28].

The Idler's Club
"Fireworks of All Sorts." Idler 4, no. 4 (November 1893): 430–38.
[Jerome's contribution, 436–38].

My First Book
"On the Stage and Off."
Idler 4, no. 5 (December 1893): 439–56.
(Collected in My First Book, London, Chatto & Windus, 1894).

IDLE THOUGHTS ON JEROME K JEROME

The Idler's Club
"Cabs and 'Cabbies'." Idler 5, no. 1 (February 1894): 110–12.
"Jerome Recalls a Ride in a Hansom Cab." (short ghost story), 100–12].

The Idler's Club
"Policemen – of All Sorts." Idler 5, no. 4 (May 1894): 435–48.
[Jerome describes his experience as a special constable, 447–48].

The Idler's Club
"The Same Story." Idler 5, no. 5 (June 1894): 549–60.
[Jerome's contribution: "Two Extracts from a Diary," 558–60].

The Mystery of Black Rock Creek
Idler 6, no. 3 (October 1894): 302–26.
Chapter I (303–7) by Jerome; remaining chapters by Eden Philpotts, E F Benson, F Frankfort Moore, Barry Pain.

The Idler's Club
"Should Christmas Be Abolished?" Idler 6, no. 5 (December 1894): 629–46. [Jerome's contribution, 641–46]

The Idler's Club
"Are Clever Women or Stupid the More Attractive to Men?" Idler 8, no. 1 (August 1895): 87–96. [Jerome's contribution, 87–88].

To the Readers of "The Idler"
Idler 8, no. 1 (August 1895): 97–100.
[Jerome's plans, having gained sole control of "The Idler."]

Letters to Clorinda
Idler 9, no. 1 (February 1896): 56–62.
9, no. 2 (March 1896): 284–88.
9, no. 3 (April 1896): 470–75.
9, no. 4 (May 1896): 610–14.
9, no. 5 (June 1896):760–63.
9, no. 6 (July 1896): 874–78.
10, no. 1 (August 1896):128–31.
10, no. 2 (September 1896): 270–73.
10, no. 3 (October 1896): 414–17.
10, no. 4 (November 1896): 554–57.
11, no. 1 (February 1897): 131–34.
11, no. 5 (June 1897): 684–87.
12, no. 2 (September 1897): 175–78.
(In 12, no. 2 (September 1897): 136, "Clorinda" is identified as Emie Avery Keddell, who participates in the Idler's Club discussions).

The Idler's Club
"Who is the Biggest Fool in the World?" Idler 9, no. 3
April 1896): 478–82. [Jerome's contribution, 478–79]

Reginald Blake, Financier and Cad
Idler 9, no. 5 (June 1896): 636–43.

(Collected in Sketches in Lavender, Blue and Green, London, Longmans, Green & Co., 1897).

The Choice of Cyril Harjohn
Idler 10, no. 1 (August 1896): 4–11.
(Collected in Sketches in Lavender, Blue and Green).

The Materialisation of Charles and Mivanway
Idler 10, no. 5 (December 1896): 573–80.
(Collected in Sketches in Lavender, Blue and Green).

An Item of Fashionable Intelligence
Idler 10, no. 6 (January 1897): 722–33.
(Collected in Sketches in Lavender, Blue and Green).

A Fragment
Idler 11, no. 2 (March 1897): 263–65.

Portrait of a Lady
Idler 11, no. 3 (April 1897): 282–90.
(Collected in Sketches in Lavender, Blue and Green).

A Woman's Logic, from The Way to Win a Woman. A Comedy in Three Acts
Idler 12, no. 3 (October 1897): 415–18.

The Idler's Club
"What Would you Like Santa Claus to Bring you?" Idler 12, no. 5 (December 1897): 697–704. [Jerome's contribution, 697–98].

The Idler's Club
"What Good Resolutions do you Want your Friends to Make for the New Year?" Idler 12, no. 6 (January 1898): 836–42.
[Jerome's contribution, 836–37].

SOME MISCELLANEOUS WRITINGS

Countries of the World. Described by the Leading Travel Writers of the Day.
Edited by Sir John Alexander Hammerton. London, Amalgamated Press, 1926. 6 volumes.
Jerome's article is in volume 3, pp. 1661–71: 'Dresden, Saxony's Fair Capital on the Elbe'.

Dickens's 'David Copperfield': my favourite novelist and his best book.
Munsey's Magazine. v.23. p.60. April 1900 (USA)

Dog Stories by Zola and Others. Edited by Sidney Trist. London, Office of the Animals' Guardian, 1904.
Jerome contributed a four page Preface.

Common Sense. 7 December 1918. p.244. Reprinted from the *Daily News*.
Jerome's thoughts on the World War I peace settlement.

Our Mutual Friend. Charles Dickens. London, Collins, 1955.
There is a three page Introduction by Jerome.

Printers Pie. A Festival Souvenir of the Printers' Pension Corporation. London,

Published at the Offices of *The Sphere*, 1904.
Jerome's article, pp. 73–74, is 'A Clearing House for Authors'.

The Press Album. Published in Aid of the Journalists' Orphan Fund. Edited by Thomas Catling. London, John Murray, 1909.
Jerome: Woman and her Purse', pp. 34–35.

Songs from the Heart of England: Anthology of Walsall Poetry. Moss, Alfred, Editor: Fisher Unwin. 1920. pp.5–7.
Jerome contributed the Foreword.

Women on wheels. In *Humours of Cycling*. James Bowden. 1897. New ed. Chatto and Windus, 1905.
A humorous article, typical of the work so often demanded from Jerome.

LETTERS TO THE EDITOR OF *THE TIMES*:

21 April 1885. p.9. Mat traps.
23 May 1885. p.10. Nude studies.
31 December 1885. p.4. Cruelty to horses.
14 October 1887. p.4. American copyright.
15 April 1896. p.10. on 'Biarritz'.
8 July 1902. p.4. Literary piracy in Russia.
17 October 1910. p.6. Drama and Censorship.
18 February 1915. p.17. Cinematograph and film drama. Early edition only.
28 October 1925. p.10. American income tax.

WORKS HELD AT THE BODLEIAN LIBRARY, OXFORD

Jerome Klapka Jerome (1859–1927)
Manuscripts and typescripts of works; photographs; publishers' agreements &c.
Bequeathed, together with printed books (catalogues separately), by Mrs. Cecilia Lamont-Jones, OBE, in 2000.

Box 1: All Roads Lead to Calvary, 1919. MS
Box 2: Anthony John, 1923. MS
Box 3: The Disagreeable Man, n.d. TS
Esther Castaways, 1913. TS
The Great Gamble, 1914. TS (and play bill)
Box 4: The Lease of the 'Cross Keys', n.d. MS
The MacHaggis, 1897. MS & TS
La Massière, n.d. TS
Box 5: New Lamps for Old, 1890. TS (prompt copy)
The Night of Feb. 14th, 1899, n.d. MS
The Passing of the Third Floor Back, 1908. TS (and printed ephemera)
Box 6: The Rise of Dick Halward, 1895. MS
A Russian Vagabond, n.d. TS
Box 7: The Soul of Nicholas Snyders, 1925. TS
Nicholas Snyders u seine Seele, 1925. TS
The Soul of Nicholas Snyders. Amended page proofs

The Three Patriots, 1915. TS

Box 8: 'War Articles and Common Sense Articles, 1919–1920'. Newspaper cuttings and (two) MSS

Box 9: 'Articles and Speeches'

Notebook, 'List of Books by Jerome K Jerome Translated ... into Foreign Languages'

Box 10: Publishers' agreements; printed ephemera (to be transferred to John Johnson Collection?); letters

Box11: Photographs.

Plus one outside photo of JKJ

Note: Box 1 contains a copy of CL-J's List of Jerome K Jerome Manuscripts

Index